SOUTHERN BIOGRAPHY SERIES
Bertram Wyatt-Brown, Editor

MOSES LEVY *of* FLORIDA

JEWISH UTOPIAN AND ANTEBELLUM REFORMER

C. S. MONACO

LOUISIANA STATE UNIVERSITY PRESS   BATON ROUGE

Designer: Barbara Neely Bourgoyne
Typeface: Trajan and Zaphino, display; Adobe Minion, text
Printer and binder: Edwards Brothers, Inc.

Library of Congress Cataloging-in-Publication Data:

Monaco, C. S., 1950–

    Moses Levy of Florida : Jewish Utopian and antebellum reformer / C.S. Monaco.

       p. cm. (Southern biography series)

    Includes bibliographical references and index.

    ISBN 0-8071-3095-8 (alk. paper)

    1. Levy, Moses E. 2. Yulee, David Levy, 1810–1886—Childhood and youth. 3. Jews—
Florida—Biography. 4. Jews—Florida—History—19th century. 5. Florida—History—
1821–1865. 6. Florida—Biography. 7. Florida—Ethnic relations. I. Title. II. Series.

F320.J5M66 2005

975.9'004924'092—dc22

                          2005004036

to Rose

CONTENTS

ACKNOWLEDGMENTS

*W*hen I first delved into the life of Moses Elias Levy about six years ago, few people had even heard of the man, and no one had yet pieced together his multifaceted career. There was a small number of historians who were vaguely aware of Levy, but—in the words of one scholar—he remained like the "mist . . . lacking in substance or definition."[1] The career of Levy's son, David L. Yulee, clearly overshadowed the father's contributions, and, for whatever reason, no one sought to remedy this situation. But among the unofficial privileges awarded any independent scholar is the option to follow a path less traveled, and so I ventured onward—mostly out of an intense curiosity rather than any precise expectations. Fortunately, while still in the beginning phase of my research, I was able to identify Levy's long-forgotten pamphlet *A Plan for the Abolition of Slavery* at the British Library. As a result, my quest seemed far less formidable, and a biography appeared an absolute necessity. In time additional records surfaced, and the previously enigmatic Mr. Levy began to present a human countenance.

Of course, this rewarding research would not have been possible without the assistance of able professionals, and I would like to extend my sincere thanks and gratitude to all. In doing so, I am reminded of Moses Levy's belief that every action we undertake in life has a corresponding effect on the lives of others. In this spirit I would like to recognize the special role of those few individuals who shared my early fascination with this underrated historical figure. I am indebted to Samuel Proctor and Neill Macaulay—both emeritus professors of history at the University of Florida—whose faith in this project proved essential for its completion. Sam Proctor not only fostered a sense of confidence for the task ahead but offered sound advice and encouragement along the way. Neill Macaulay first introduced me to Levy's colonization efforts and thereby sparked my initial interest. Neill shared his expert knowledge of Latin American history, provided numerous insights during our frequent discussions, read all the chapters as they were written, and kindly translated several key Spanish documents. This brief thanks hardly does justice to the enormous sense of gratitude that I feel toward both of these individuals. I would also like to express my sincere appreciation to Sherry Johnson at Florida International University. She opened the resources of the Archivo National in Havana, graciously shared information garnered at the Archivo General de Indias in Seville, and kept me abreast of Latin American scholarship, especially in regard to Levy's tenure in Cuba. Her astute comments and criticism are also most appreciated.

Many others generously volunteered their time and expertise. Jeffrey D. Needell of the University of Florida translated early-nineteenth-century Portuguese documents that shed considerable light on Levy's activities on Curaçao. Lorraine Federman and her colleagues in Israel made a valiant attempt at deciphering M. E. Levy's archaic Hebrew script. Fred Krome at the American Jewish Archives contributed helpful insights. Norman Stillman of the University of Oklahoma took time during his leave of absence to send copies of rare documents, which added to my knowledge of Levy's family in Morocco. St. Thomas historian David W. Knight graciously sent a copy of Johan Peter Nissen's *Reminiscences of a 46 Years Residence in the Island of St. Thomas,* a resource that proved quite useful. In another stroke of good fortune important documents relating to Pilgrimage plantation surfaced after Emmanuel Boëlle of Paris, a descendant of Levy's friend and creditor Seraphina Chauviteau, made his family papers available. I thank all for their generosity and kindness.

I am also pleased to acknowledge the archivists and librarians who responded to my frequent requests over the years. First and foremost is Joe Mosier at the Chrysler Museum Library in Norfolk, Virginia. Joe was exceptionally attentive to my litany of questions and was most accommodating in sharing his extensive knowledge of the Moses Myers family. The Chrysler Library's Myers Papers proved vital to the completion of this biography as it contains the largest single collection of Levy's correspondence.

Sincere thanks also go to Robert Singerman at the University of Florida's Price Library of Judaica, who, among other courtesies, wisely encouraged my initial trip to the British Library. In addition, the following people often went beyond the call of duty: James Cusick and Bruce Chappell at the P. K. Yonge Library of Florida History, University of Florida; Charles Tingley at the St. Augustine Historical Society Library; Dalia Tracz at the Jewish Studies Library, University College London; Katina E. Coulianos at the Hebrew Congregation of St. Thomas; Beverly Smith at the Enid M. Baa Library, St. Thomas; Michael Kemp at the Alachua County Public Library; Camille Servizzi at the American Jewish Archives; Richard Phillips at the Latin American Collection, University of Florida; and Cathy Moloney at the State Library of Florida.

Several years ago I presented a paper on Levy's activities in London at the Southern Jewish Historical Society Conference in Nashville, and this event resulted in many cogent remarks and thoughtful questions. In addition, my articles in *American Jewish History, American Jewish Archives Journal,* and *Southern Jewish History* benefited from the learned comments of editors and anonymous peer reviewers. Since this biography is an outgrowth of my earlier endeavors, I acknowledge all who contributed their expertise and insight.

I am greatly indebted to Bertram Wyatt-Brown—the editor of Louisiana State University Press's Southern Biography Series—not only for his steadfast support and interest in this present volume but for his seminal work as a historian. Recognition should also be given to the talented editors and staff of LSU Press, who have helped transform my manuscript into its present form.

Finally, the continual encouragement and editorial skill of Rose Widman proved invaluable for this biographical study. Each sentence was scrupulously reviewed and, in many cases, transformed for the better by her thoughtful insight. The life of Moses Levy became, in many ways, her own tender concern, and each milestone in the discovery process was a time of shared delight. It is with heartfelt appreciation that I dedicate this work to Rose.

MOSES LEVY *of* FLORIDA

INTRODUCTION

*A*bolitionist and slave owner, utopian colonizer and former arms dealer, religious reformer and biblical conservative—at first glance the life of Moses Elias Levy appears to be enveloped in a myriad of contradictions. Adding to the biographer's challenge is the difficulty of exploring a life that has been little studied and, until very recently, virtually unknown even within Levy's home state of Florida. His remarkable *Plan for the Abolition of Slavery* (London, 1828), newly discovered and now regarded as the earliest and most important antislavery document by an American Jew, was written anonymously, a fact that resulted in its absence from the body of Jewish abolitionist literature for over 170 years.[1] Despite the pamphlet's anonymity, Levy was well-known within British Protestant reform circles. His extraordinary interpersonal skills allowed him to transcend ethnic and national differences with ease, and his abilities as an orator and writer earned him high acclaim in London. As a United States citizen, his contributions during the height of the British antislavery crusade were unparalleled. In addition, records relating to Levy's colonization efforts in Florida reveal that a small group of Jewish families participated in his Pilgrimage colony—long thought devoid of Jewish settlers—as early as 1823.[2] This finding distinguishes Pilgrimage, located a few miles from the north Florida town of Micanopy, as the first Jewish communitarian settlement in the United States. Adding to Levy's mystique is the fact that he shunned publicity and denied posterity any likeness or portrait. Even his grave site is unknown. But enough factual material has emerged to establish this once enigmatic man as a progressive figure without equal in antebellum Florida.

Since his death in 1854, Moses Levy has been best remembered as the father of David L. Yulee, an important politician and railroad entrepreneur and the first Jew elected to the U.S. Senate. Levy has also been noted as one of territorial Florida's earliest pioneer settlers, a contemporary of such American Jewish notables as Mordecai Noah and Rebecca Gratz, as well as a "failed" Jewish colonizer. Few scholars have placed him in a utopian context, and the full extent of his work as a social activist and abolitionist in England has previously gone unacknowledged. In a rare biographical sketch historian Jacob Rader Marcus credits Moses Levy's 1821 appeal for the establishment of an innovative Hebrew boarding school in the United States as "the first attempt to rally Jewry as a body behind an institute designed to serve as a national center for Jewish culture."[3] Further, Marcus deems Levy "the most interesting and the most radical cultural and spiritual entrepreneur" of his time. On the other hand, he doubts whether anything of "lasting value" came of Levy's activities, questions his sanity, and claims that he had "all the makings of a pseudo-Messiah."[4] Such ambiguous and harsh assessments reveal a lack of in-depth understanding of Levy. Among other things, Marcus relied on a collection of Levy's later writings, taken out of context and compiled by a disgruntled David Yulee.[5]

This document, misleadingly labeled as the "Diary of Moses Levy," has been the source of much confusion. Consisting of Yulee's negative commentaries along with brief excerpts taken from his father's personal correspondence, it was assembled sometime after Levy's death. Without prior understanding of the nature and context of this material, the reader is left with the distorted impression that Levy was little more than a lone and disturbed individual. It must be noted, however, that Levy had excluded his son from a substantial inheritance, and Yulee then undertook a bitter and lengthy legal battle to overturn the will. Given this history of estrangement, it is not surprising that Senator Yulee, a skilled attorney, felt compelled to remedy a situation that he viewed as an affront to his honor, even if it meant accusing his father of temporary insanity when his will was drawn in 1838.[6] This tactic proved difficult. A deposition from Augustus Walker, a witness to the will, failed to confirm Yulee's charge. Instead, Walker insisted that "Moses E. Levy was a person of entire sanity and soundness of mind," although somewhat "eccentric . . . in his religious opinions."[7] Therefore, the "Levy Diary" appears to have been either a clever attempt to bolster Yulee's legal maneuvers or a kind of elaborate therapeutic exercise to come to terms with his father's rejection. Regardless, the disposition of the will was eventually settled out of court, ostensibly because of "filial regard for [his] father's memory," and so this material was certainly never presented as evidence.[8] It is indeed ironic that Yulee's biased and self-serving endeavor has imparted a negative influence upon modern historians who failed to question Yulee's motivations and have taken the "diary" at face value.[9]

This affair dramatizes the difficulty of placing both Levy and his well-known son into perspective. For many years litigation prevented Moses Levy from selling his substantial landholdings. After the devastation of the Second Seminole War and the bank failures caused by the Panic of 1837, he lived for many years in poverty. As one would expect, these catastrophic losses caused a heightened sense of desperation and anxiety; his correspondence to family and friends reflected this dark mood and self-preoccupation. He also adhered to his own version of religious perfectionism and shared with numerous Christians of the period an intense feeling of spiritual inadequacy—the proverbial "dark night of the soul"—as well as a host of apparently psychosomatic complaints.[10] Despite this bleak period, however, his faith allowed him to prevail: "I have to be thankful for the want and misery I suffered . . . Thus situated—my soul being saturated with the object of the call of Israel."[11] Above all else, religion was Levy's passion. Despite his rejection of orthodox Judaism, his total commitment to God and to the Hebrew Bible was both his strength and the source of most of his troubles. Fortunately, toward the end of his life a court settlement finally allowed him to sell large portions of the 100,000 acres of land he had accumulated. Thereafter, he began to pay off his debts and still left a sizable estate at his death.

Throughout their lives Moses Levy and David Yulee occupied opposing ends of the philosophical spectrum. Levy was a proto-Zionist, a social activist, and utopian theorist who questioned and rebelled against orthodoxy and the political status quo. His progressive ideas, especially in regard to slavery, were anathema in the South. In comparison, David Yulee disassociated himself from Judaism and yearned not only for acceptance by the southern elite but to become one of their stalwart leaders and defenders. While his father was attracted to the egalitarian theories of the Enlightenment, Yulee promoted the ideals of the Industrial Revolution and Manifest Destiny. On some level Moses Levy's liberal views seemed to generate opposing beliefs in his strong-willed son and certainly contributed to the unbending character of the antebellum states' rights champion known as the "Florida Fire Eater."

As head of the Democratic Party in Florida, a two-term United States senator, and the president of the state's first transpeninsular railroad, Yulee was a man who wielded significant power. Although never baptized, he became estranged from Judaism and married a devout Presbyterian. He added the Yulee surname just before his 1846 marriage to Nannie Wickliffe, the daughter of a former governor of Kentucky. The less Jewish-sounding "Yulee" had more appeal and was actually part of his father's full Moroccan name, Ha-Levi ibn Yuli.[12]

The senator's unprecedented name change focused attention on his Moroccan pedigree. Newspaper accounts frequently offered a fanciful and exotic alternative to any realistic assessment of his father's Jewish ancestry and appealed to Yulee's sense of showmanship. Moses Levy had long withheld any information about his past, and it was only indirectly that David became aware of it. Nevertheless, editorialists proclaimed that "the youngest man in the U.S. Senate" was possessed of a princely lineage and quipped that his "grandsire . . . [was] as staunch and phlegmatic an old Turk as ever sat cross-legged or whiffed the houka."[13] David Yulee's son Charles, in an often quoted article about his father, maintained the false notion that his Moroccan ancestor was "given the rank of prince" and was "racially Portuguese."[14] Hyperbole concerning Yulee's forebears is still in evidence today and manifests itself in Florida folklore. One long-standing myth is the assertion that Yulee's grandfather was the "Grand Vizier" of Morocco, maintained a large harem replete with eunuchs, and purchased his grandmother—presumably the shipwrecked daughter of an English physician—in the slave market of Fez. Such accounts are still perpetuated in newspaper articles and popular books on Florida history.[15] The dubious nature of much of this material underscores the need for a careful examination of the family history.

Unlike his son, who rarely traveled outside the country, Moses Levy was truly a man of the Atlantic world. He was, at one time or another, a resident of Morocco, Gibraltar, the Danish West Indies, Puerto Rico, Cuba, England, and, of course, the United States. As a successful merchant-shipper, his numerous journeys enabled him to rise above nationalist sentiments, and he actually held patriotic fervor in disdain. Levy was exposed to the revolutionary undercurrents that abounded in port towns and cities, and he advanced the egalitarian tenets of the biblical Jubilee, one of the fore-most models for radical social change in the Atlantic world.[16] Levy's cos-mopolitan roots can be traced to his early upbringing in Morocco. Raised in an affluent Sephardi Jewish household, the son of an influential mer-chant and courtier to the sultan of Morocco, young Levy attained an early command of Hebrew and spoke Castilian Spanish as well as Arabic. He also became fluent in English and French. Later, as a gentleman-merchant "of the first respectability," he earned the admiration of such diverse groups as the aristocratic sugar planters of Havana and the evangelical abolitionists of London, a truly remarkable achievement for a Jew of his time.[17]

Significantly, Levy's extensive travels also brought him into contact with the ideas of the European Haskalah movement, a distinct Jewish re-sponse to eighteenth-century Enlightenment philosophy. Followers of this ideology, known as *maskilim,* were often well-traveled, urbane business-men. Their close proximity to Gentile society and their familiarity with rationalist and secularist values caused them to revise long-held notions regarding religion and the Jew's place in society. Haskalah proponents—the word itself is Hebrew for "Enlightenment"—emphasized the Bible over the Talmud, placed high value on secular education, rejected ghetto life, and embraced fashionable clothing as well as the common vernacular. A sense of Romanticism found expression in a general longing for agricultural pursuits and a renewed pride in the achievements of ancient Israel. It was this group that Levy broadly defined as his "Enlightened Brethren," those free thinkers and progressives for whom departure from orthodoxy was a sine qua non. Quite distinct from most of his colleagues, however, Levy rejected the movement's implicit goal: full and equal rights of citizenship. Jewish exile or *galut,* according to Levy, would end only by the creation of a separate homeland and the promised reign of the Messiah, not through any misguided efforts toward full assimilation. In his attempt to reconcile Judaism with modernity he also had one foot, as it were, firmly planted in the biblical past. His search for an equilibrium between Enlightenment ideals and revealed religion (the premodern) became a recurrent theme throughout his life. Levy was both liberal and conservative, free-thinking progressive and biblical fundamentalist. Not surprisingly, he was never able truly to reconcile these dual aspects of his psyche.

Moses Levy also extolled the strong communal tradition that resided within Judaism, a trait made conspicuous by his desire to create a Jewish homeland in the United States. To this collective ethos Levy added various elements from the leading social theories of the day. Amid the reform movements that surfaced during the French Revolution, the advent of industrialization, and the Napoleonic Wars, the communitarian ideal offered bright promise for those who desired a panacea for societal ills. Both secular and religious proponents foresaw the noble and brotherly concerns of the community as replacing selfishly inspired individual motivations. The concept of a harmonious "brethren" was heavily imbued with spiritual meaning. By traveling from the mundane and imperfect world to a place of new beginnings, men and women would partake in a sacred, inner transformation. A number of Protestant sects left Europe to pursue their singular visions of heaven-on-earth on the American frontier. Often these experimental communities were intended to enact far-reaching reform within society and eventually the world at large; they would serve as a catalyst for radical change simply by virtue of example and not through force of arms.[18] This utopian philosophy exerted a prominent influence on Moses Levy. His trust that collectivism, coupled with egalitarian educational reforms and a return to agriculture, would transform his coreligionists into an enlightened community not only conformed to the communitarian standard but to elements within the Haskalah tradition as well.

Accordingly, Levy opposed the rising popularity of individualism, a concept he considered most destructive. The depth of his feeling can be seen in a premise that he called the "law of operating and being operated upon." By this phrase he meant that people never truly act alone but are always under the influence of Divine Providence as well as the actions of others. Similar in spirit to monastic communalism, the heart of Levy's utopian world was the establishment of a "triune" relationship among individuals, their peers, and God—a state of perfection alluded to in Genesis, before the fall of Adam and Eve. In contrast, the supposed merits of individualism were an illusion that gave people false notions of superiority and which led them down the path of "self-love, ambition, vain-glory, and the like."[19] Levy's expression concerning the unity of man and God was, in effect, a signature of his, and throughout his lifetime he managed to incorporate elements of this distinct phraseology in his writings and speeches. He even managed to correlate his "law" with Newtonian physics. The "law of operating and of being operated upon," he once wrote, "is as imperious in our constitution as the law of attraction which keeps harmony in the heavenly bodies."[20] It was Levy's professed "knowledge of this one great truth" which sustained him through his most difficult moments and influenced his entire career as a reformer.

Armed with millennial expectations as well as a fervent desire to enact the most progressive tenets of the European reform movement, in 1820 Levy arrived in the United States on a "Sacred" mission. For two years his young protégé, Samuel Myers of Norfolk, Virginia, had introduced important elements of Levy's plan for the "regeneration" of the Jews to important figures, including the leading Jewish luminary of the day, Major Mordecai M. Noah of New York. Noah, a playwright, journalist, and future sheriff of New York City, declared that Myers had "touched on a chord, capable, & always producing on my mind great sensations."[21] Noah would later become known as the proponent of his own colonization scheme, called Ararat, which he intended to found in upstate New York. For a time at least, however, the attention of the American Jewish community focused upon Levy, a man of wealth and social standing who seemingly possessed unbounded energy and enthusiasm.

In 1821, under Levy's leadership, various "Hebrew societies" were organized in New York City, Baltimore, and Norfolk—in actuality, the United States' first national, Jewish philanthropic organization. Membership consisted of prominent Jews, including Noah, whose common purpose was to establish a unique boarding school and agrarian settlement. The *Chenuch,* as Levy called it, would incorporate some of the ideas of the German reformer Israel Jacobson as well as the pedagogical innovations of the Swiss educator Johann Heinrich Pestalozzi. With its emphasis on "practical" courses in natural sciences as well as agricultural training and a curriculum that would include religious training and instruction in Hebrew for both boys and girls, nothing even remotely similar had ever been attempted in the United States. Apparently, regional rivalries and Levy's long absences on the Florida frontier led to the eventual abandonment of this remarkable venture. Nevertheless, the seriousness with which this elite group treated both Levy and his cause is but one example of his stature and influence and illustrates his success not only in the dissemination of radical schemes but as an organizer and leader.

One of Levy's great paradoxes was his sincere desire to "ameliorate" the condition of Jews while he steadfastly refused equal rights of citizenship. Yet Levy's "societies," his abolitionist work in London, even his status as an active Freemason, demonstrate his ability to work effectively within the civil realm. Whenever Levy deemed it necessary, he could easily cross over from utopian isolation into the public eye. But he limited his own publicity, generally avoided newspaper coverage, and was always vigilant against what he perceived to be the sin of vanity. Accordingly, his *Plan for the Abolition of Slavery* was written anonymously, and his Hebrew societies not only upheld a strict code of confidentiality but greatly limited membership. Levy's Sephardi background, with its cultural aversion to publicity, as well as his adherence to the secretive Masonic tradition contributed to his clandestine tendencies.

Levy revealed the full extent of his radical intentions—the communal rearing of children, the denunciation of the Talmud as well as the entire rabbinical tradition—to very few others. He concluded that full and immediate revelation of his plans would let loose a "light . . . too strong to bear" and therefore opted for "shewing it little by little."[22] In this respect Levy possessed a revolutionary character and, with a few notable exceptions, preferred to affect change not by public demonstrations but through a more subtle, behind-the-scenes strategy. In addition, his utopian predilections were often tempered by a businesslike pragmatism and an internal pendulum swung, not always predictably, between the two. Therefore, while he was committed to enacting global reform in preparation for the Messiah, Levy realized that certain entrenched institutions, such as slavery, could not be terminated without a gradual and carefully planned strategy. On the other hand, he considered any unjust aggression toward Jews as something that demanded immediate action. For instance, while in England he abandoned his usual caution and took up the mantle of public activist. Among other achievements he led an unprecedented campaign in London against a Russian *ukase,* or edict, against the Jews when he learned of Czar Nicholas I's persecutions in the Pale of Settlement. He castigated those Jews who still clung to long-held notions of being a "harmless, unmeddling people" and went so far as to compare their acquiescence to slaves. His actions were widely publicized and created quite a stir. Ironically, Levy's self-imposed outsider status freed him to pursue controversial paths that assimilationist leaders, in their quest for acceptance, would never have dared. While many resented Levy for his "sanguine interference," he nevertheless played a significant early role in the emergence of Jewish social activism.[23]

As with utopians in general, the most cynical can easily dismiss Levy's proposals as fatally flawed, impractical, and perhaps utterly naive. A closer look, however, reveals tangible accomplishments. For instance, while Levy's small Jewish colony survived just thirteen years, his impact in the Florida territory was substantial. Highly regarded by prominent officials, Levy reintroduced sugarcane as a viable crop; organized the first Florida development corporation; was instrumental in establishing the territory's earliest free public school; helped found the village of Micanopy, the first distinct United States town in Florida; and served for many years as East Florida's most vocal and influential Jewish resident. In addition, his colonization venture brought much needed settlers into the sparsely populated interior, and his great expenditures in sugar mill technology inspired similar investments throughout the territory—a veritable "sugar boom" that lasted until the Second Seminole War.

Wherever Levy traveled, he vigorously promoted the idea of free schools and universal education. From his brief tenure on the Dutch island of Curaçao to his activities in the British metropolis, Levy attempted to "rouse [people] from their lethargy" and encouraged local communities to implement formal education for their youth.[24] He considered such efforts to be an essential part of his "ministry." "The Bible and the book of nature are the patrimony of all men," he proclaimed, "be they poor or rich."[25] In England he advocated all-day and Sabbath schools, circulated biblical tracts, and partook in unprecedented public lectures between Jews and Christians.[26] He was a tireless advocate, and, appropriately enough, he placed education as the foundation for his abolitionist plans: "[Emancipation] must begin with children, let them emancipate their minds, and when they have education and virtue, they [will] become free."[27]

Despite these accomplishments, Moses Levy's utopian temperament predisposed him to a variety of misfortunes. Ultimately, Levy's devotion to the communitarian movement would cost him dearly. Like most of the hundred or so experimental enclaves that dotted the antebellum landscape, Levy's Florida settlement suffered an abrupt end, and his role as a "Paradise Planter"—to use a term coined by another nineteenth-century utopian—came to a close. Without a doubt, the destruction of Pilgrimage plantation represented a major turning point in Levy's life and signaled a serious economic decline. But to judge Levy's endeavor solely by conventional standards, such as profitability and longevity, is to disregard the philosophical reasoning that motivated his high-risk venture.[28] As historian Robert S. Fogarty has noted, some utopian settlements—such as New York's Oneida community—evolved into long-term, lucrative operations but were often oppressive in their treatment of members. Conversely, Robert Owen's much-publicized New Harmony settlement in Indiana lasted only two years, but Owen's stature and influence as a humanitarian innovator was considerable. Therefore, the intellectual concepts that formed the core of these communities as well as the effect these beliefs had on others should also be reckoned in any assessment and should be accorded major significance.[29]

While Levy may have been an ineffective colonizer, his skills as a communicator and as a disseminator of innovative and progressive ideas were exceptional. Very much like his secular contemporary Robert Owen, Levy never truly limited himself to utopian isolation, and both his publications and his success on the London lecture circuit attest to his strength as an activist. Among other achievements Levy succeeded in uniting Jews and Christians to take action on vital issues of the day, an event considered so unique that certain Protestants believed it heralded the millennium.

Despite Levy's progressive stance on social issues, he still held a "fundamentalist imagination," to use historian R. Scott Appleby's apt terminology.[30] Because Levy had rejected the status quo in order to serve a divine mission, the secular world and all its institutions inevitably came up short. As a result, his sense of alienation became, at times, quite profound. Given the biographer's ethic of remembering those that best inspired patriotism or achieved fame through military, political, artistic, or business prowess, it is not surprising that the name of Moses Elias Levy was not eulogized or memorialized in some fashion after his death, as was the case with the flamboyant Mordecai Noah.[31] After all, Noah was an American patriot and political operative who remained ensconced in the conventional framework of nineteenth-century society, as his Tammany Hall activities and proslavery opinions attest and despite the temporary diversion called "Ararat." In contrast, Levy's brand of utopia, with its radical restructuring of Judaism and its ultimate rejection of Gentile society, was hardly the stuff that garnered praise from more moderate-minded, assimilationist Jews. Nevertheless, any careful examination of Levy's motives reveals a most unusual and selfless character. He was genuinely prepared to "surrender" his property and all that he owned for what he considered the "spiritual good of my children and our society at large."[32] If one considers the magnitude of what he was willing to surrender, it was indeed a most heroic stance.

Admittedly, it is very unusual for a biography not to have the benefit of some artistic rendering of the subject. Unlike most prominent and wealthy individuals of the nineteenth-century, Levy avoided the portrait studio, apparently because of the biblical prohibition concerning graven images as well as his own stringent notions about vanity and self-love. Therefore, he left no image of himself for others to ponder and, perhaps, to gain insights by. Fortunately Levy's 1822 citizenship application revealed essential physical characteristics. For instance, at age forty Levy was five foot six and a rather plump 180 pounds. His appearance did not resemble some hard-edged iconoclast, but, rather, he emerges as someone with pleasant, rounded features and an average height for the period. He had black hair, dark eyes, a straight nose, and "brown" skin. Levy's physique was summarized as "oval," and he possessed a "round" forehead. His equally round, beardless chin revealed a mole. Personal reflections by Levy's friends confirm that he was a genial-looking fellow, with the bearing and sophistication of a fine gentleman.[33]

Given Moses Elias Levy's aversion to self-promotion, his unorthodox ideas, his exotic Moroccan origins and numerous foreign residences, and the hostility of his prominent son, obscurity was perhaps inevitable. Despite his many public lectures and his substantial press coverage in London, the anonymous nature of his antislavery treatise and his brief residence in the metropolis almost ensured nonrecognition after he passed from the scene. Despite these disadvantages, Levy's activities are well documented and many of his writings preserved. They offer intriguing insights into the life of one of antebellum America's most extraordinary and underrated personalities.

1. A PRECARIOUS YOUTH

*S*ituated between the imposing cliffs of its Atlantic shore and the formidable Atlas Mountains to the east, late-eighteenth-century Morocco retained the character of an isolated feudal kingdom. Within this
closed, xenophobic society, religious norms held non-Muslims in contempt.
Even foreign dignitaries were not secure from arbitrary acts of violence by
the country's monarch, Sultan Sidi Muhammad III. Arrayed in splendid
white garments and flanked by a retinue of servants, the rituals of subordi-
nation and protocol reinforced the sultan's position as the apex of Moroccan society. The tradition of self-glorification and absolutism rankled the
sensibilities of enlightened Europeans. The sultan's power, wrote one visitor, "tinged his character with that intolerable caprice which has ever . . .
disgraced the Moorish princes."[1] Furthermore, Sidi Muhammad's policies
appeared quite contradictory. While he may have opened foreign markets,
his corsairs still held free rein along the coast. This "jihad at sea" pleased
Islamic religious leaders, but it certainly reinforced the country's negative
image abroad.[2] Internal insurrections, led by the sultan's own son, added
to Morocco's troubles and threatened to dissolve all stability. As a matter of
course, the entire citizenry was subject to harsh and often erratic decrees.
These forceful royal displays, which were so despised by Europeans, actually served to increase the monarch's *baraka*, or "charasmatic power," within
Moroccan culture.[3] Nevertheless, human suffering was often the result, and
of all the sultan's subjects few risked greater peril than the Jews.

Expelled from Spain in 1492, Moses Levy's forebears joined other Jews
who refused to convert to Catholicism and found refuge across the Strait

of Gibraltar in Morocco. Although Spanish Jews once flourished under Muslim rule, their golden age would never resurface. In comparison to the native Berber Jews of Morocco, the Sephardim were wealthier and far more educated and disdainfully looked upon their brethren as *forasteros*, or strangers.[4] Although Sephardi scholars and the mercantile elite would soon dominate the Jewish community, most suffered under the country's rigid interpretation of the Koranic injunction to "humble the non-believer."[5] As a result, a permanent underclass developed which lacked any effective recourse.

This polarization manifested itself in many unusual and repressive forms. Custom demanded that Jews dress differently from their Muslim contemporaries. For instance, the ubiquitous hooded robes, or *djellabas*, worn by Moroccan men were rendered black or a somber blue to indicate a Jew's lowly status.[6] Thus visibly differentiated, the majority was better able to enforce a religiously based code of harassment. Outside the *mellahs*, or ghettos, of the large cities, Jews were forced to walk like slaves with heads lowered. If they approached a mosque, only bare feet were allowed, and in some towns shoes were prohibited at all times.[7] Muslim citizens, children included, could arbitrarily and without provocation strike or throw stones at any Jew. The payment of a special tax was yet another reminder of their inferior rank. Oppression even extended to the synagogues; worshipers who were "in the midst of reciting the Torah benedictions, or whose feet were still planted in prayer," were often beaten and carted off to perform corvée labor whenever the monarch desired it. Men and women were subjected to these affronts daily, prompting one eighteenth-century observer to compare their acquiescence to "domesticated sheep being led to slaughter."[8] Indeed, modern scholars have judged that the "ritualized humiliations imposed upon Jews in Morocco . . . were among the most rigorous in the Islamic world."[9]

Some Jews could be especially useful to the sultan, however, and therefore received preferential treatment. High-ranking merchants, such as the family of Moses Levy, maintained their Spanish language and customs, often spoke several other languages as well, and had important trading networks in Europe. As a result, a minority developed which served the sultans as emissaries and merchants to foreign lands. Trade with the "land of the infidels," or Christian Europe, ran counter to Islamic theology because it required close interaction with non-Muslim foreigners. Jews, therefore, were deemed acceptable for this purpose, and their success in international commerce enriched and strengthened the Moroccan government.[10] Within this circle of businessmen a few, known as the *Shāb as-Sultān,* would be selected as courtiers and advisors to the monarch. Despite their affluence, court Jews lacked a strong foundation within the Muslim hierarchy and were held in a constant state of uncertainty. Indeed, all royal merchants were kept in line by a system that ensured their financial indebtedness to the sultan. Since their positions were passed on to their children by official writs, alternate avenues of employment were not an option. In many respects these Jews were regarded as the monarch's personal property, a state of affairs which one historian has compared to the ancient European system of "serfs of the chamber."[11] The vulnerability of this small minority contributed to its usefulness; total fealty could be assured. While the status of these court Jews was problematic, their wealth and proximity to the monarch offered distinct advantages, and they were granted some deference. In fact, compared to the vast majority of Moroccans, Jewish courtiers appeared as true patricians.

To this select community Moses Elias Levy was born on 10 July 1782.[12] The son of the courtier and royal merchant Eliahu Ha-Levi ibn Yuli, Moses was first reared within the walls of the fortress-seaport of Mogador (Essaouira) on the Atlantic coast, a center for international trade. While certainly not the vizier, as is often stated, Eliahu—the Jewish name for the prophet Elijah or Elias—was clearly a man of wealth, influence, and talent. For example, he played a role in negotiating the first Barbary Treaty with the United States (1786), and his diplomatic skills were often relied upon by the monarch.[13] Nonetheless, there was also a ruthless and unsavory aspect to his character, about which more will be said later.

According to his high station, Eliahu maintained several residences among the imperial cities of the country, including a large building in Tangier which once had been the royal office for estate taxes.[14] At court he officially served as one of seven Jewish undersecretaries of the Treasury.[15] Joining him in maintaining the long courtier tradition of the ibn Yuli family was his brother Abraham. Some Moroccan Jewish historians believe that the Yuli surname was an honorific title, an anagram of a phrase from the Book of Psalms: "They [all the nations] shall come and bow down before Thee," or "Yavou Ushtahavou Lefanecha Adonai."[16] Eliahu's father, Judah, was an international merchant and financial advisor to the sultan.

He achieved special prominence in the Jewish communities of Salé and Ra-
bat, where he held the rank of *sheikh,* or Jewish elder. The most illustrious
member of the family was Judah's brother, Rabbi Samuel Ha-Levi ibn Yuli.
After rising to the position of counselor to Sultan Moulay Abdallah, by 1732
he became the political leader of the Moroccan Jews and was awarded the
princely title of *nagid.*[17]

Rather than follow the conventions of his forebears, Eliahu was far
more accepting of the customs of his Muslim contemporaries, and he actually had three wives. While this arrangement was unusual for a Jew, rabbinical law did allow for a second wife if the initial marriage proved to be
childless after ten years. Although one of ibn Yuli's wives was indeed bar-
ren, he broke his marriage contract and Jewish convention by marrying a
third time.[18] Additionally, Moses Levy's mother, Rachel, was not a captive
English slave—as Florida folklore has it—but a Sephardi Jew from Tangier
who was noted for her "beauty, wisdom and youthfulness" as well as her
command of Castilian Spanish. Unlike most Moroccan Jewish women, she
was also fluent in Hebrew prayers, an achievement considered a "marvel"
by one contemporary.[19] Unfortunately, little else is known about her aside
from the fact that all three of Eliahu's wives were in a constant state of
bickering over connubial rights and caused their husband much annoyance
in the process. Eliahu's polygamy and his flaunting of Jewish law were not
unique; many other courtiers also considered their behavior as beyond the
purview of rabbinical tribunals.

As was the custom for male children, Moses Levy's religious education
began early, and, according to his recollections in old age, he was able to
read passages from the Bible in several languages, including Hebrew, by the
age of five.[20] Since boys entered the *heder,* or religious school, at three and
typically mastered the alphabet by four years, Levy's remarkable achievement at such a young age appears plausible.[21] Endowed with a precocious
intellect and a burgeoning spiritual sensibility, the boy was often moved
by his readings of Scripture. On one such occasion, apparently the day
when his family celebrated his rite of passage from infancy to childhood
during his fifth year, young Levy underwent an epiphany of sorts.[22] He recognized that, while others marveled at his technical accomplishment, they
were far less affected by the "gorgeous imagery" of the holy words. "Whilst
my mother was entertaining the ladies on the occasion," Levy wrote, "I
walked up & down deeply operated upon by the glorious end of the sons

of man—heartily despising those who enjoyed the sweetmeats rather than the subject before me."[23] Evidently, a sense of alienation manifested itself early in life. Unstated was the fact that this ceremony, accompanied by a variety of talismans to defend the boy from the evil eye, marked the child's acceptance of individual responsibility. The boy's resentment toward his elders may have been heightened by the seriousness with which he adopted this weighty concept.

At six the perceptive young Levy would have noticed a new face among the household staff. In 1788 his father employed twenty-nine-year-old Samuel Romanelli as his personal secretary.[24] Romanelli, originally from Mantua, Italy, was a gifted Jewish scholar, writer, and linguist. During the preceding year he had become stranded in Morocco after losing his passport, and what began as a brief journey through an exotic land became a protracted and often nightmarish ordeal. After leaving the country, he went on to publish what would become a classic in Hebrew travel literature, *Massā' Ba'rāv* (Travail in an Arab Land).

Published in Berlin in 1792, *Travail in an Arab Land* became extremely popular within the Hebrew literate world, being reissued nine times. Aside from its literary merit, the narrative's popularity, especially in Europe, was due to its exotic subject matter. As Romanelli put it: "The Israelite community presently living in the Arab territories of Africa's Barbary Coast . . . is almost entirely hidden from the eyes of the peoples living here in the countries of Europe."[25] Significantly, the primary villain of Romanelli's chronicle was none other than his former employer, identified in the text simply as Eliahu Levi. References to the courtier are noteworthy for an impressive level of disdain.

> Such people, whether Gentile or Jew, are merely instruments of the King . . . They are feared, not loved. Capable only of evildoing, they know nothing of benevolence. They thrive only on the destruction of others. They would disown their fathers and mothers, seeing nothing of them. They would not recognize their brothers, nor would they even know their own children. Such a man would befriend another in word and win his heart, present him with a gift, and then return to plot his murder. They draw the mighty with false hopes and drag the young in their terror. But as they stand upon their heights of greatness, the abyss widens under their feet. One word from the King's mouth and they vanish. A nation will groan under their rule; a town will rejoice at their death.[26]

While hardly a dispassionate observer, the veracity of Romanelli's account has been vigorously defended by such scholars as Yedida K. and Norman A. Stillman, who translated and annotated the sole English edition of *Massā' Ba'rāv* in 1989.[27] Additionally, Moroccan Jewish historians, who often tend to romanticize the courtier caste, draw freely upon Romanelli and have conceded that Eliahu Levi was indeed "the black sheep of the family."[28] Unfortunately, the very few American scholars who have examined the life of Moses Levy have either overlooked this invaluable resource or in one case actually downplayed its significance, ostensibly because of the author's presumed bias.[29] As a sophisticated and highly educated European Jew, Romanelli frequently exhibits a dismissive tone, especially when discussing the arcane folkways of eighteenth-century Morocco. "Custom, divination, and the evil eye," he declares, "are the three destructive forces under which all of the Maghreb tremble."[30] Most of his substantive observations, however, have been verified by other sources. Accordingly, the Stillmans adamantly regard *Travail in an Arab Land* as "both a historical document and a literary work of the first order."[31] Certainly, Romanelli rises far beyond the stereotype of a disgruntled former employee, and his credibility as a keen and intelligent observer has been authenticated.

According to Samuel Romanelli, the most deplorable of Eliahu Levi's transgressions was his plan to eliminate a rival at court by presenting false evidence before the sultan, an act that led to the horrific execution of a fellow Jew. As the result of Levi's treachery, the unfortunate man, a member of the noted Cardozo family, was tortured, hacked to death, and burned by imperial order. Not only was Cardozo's death on his hands, but he committed a high crime within Jewish law merely by bringing charges against a fellow Jew before a Muslim authority.[32] This scathing portrait of Levi, whom Romanelli describes as "spotted with pock marks" and "craftier than any serpent or than all the beasts of the field," is unrelenting in its moral rebuke.[33]

As the Cardozo affair illustrates, a courtier's tenure in office was by no means certain and could be abruptly and tragically ended. By the time of Romanelli's arrival, Eliahu himself had only recently been restored to his position. After an arms shipment from England failed to appear as arranged, the courtier was forced to suffer the indignity of imprisonment, the payment of an exorbitant fine, as well as the humiliating loss of his beard.

Impetuously, the sultan suspected Levi of treachery but realized his error when the actual cause for the delayed arms cargo was discovered to be fear of piracy.[34] Although reinstated, Levi suffered considerable financial losses and was desperate to restore his former glory.

Despite his precarious position, Eliahu Levi retained an air of bravado and was undeterred in taking risks if they resulted in monetary reward or elevation in status. "He was king of the arrogant," Romanelli declared, "and would walk proudly erect, speaking as though his words were a mighty wind. He would even dare to pass an Arab mosque without removing his shoes in a display of his power at court so that all would come to fear him."[35] It is obvious that Eliahu operated within an archaic society vastly different from that of his European secretary. What the author condemned as arrogance could also serve men who aspired to power. A bold and fierce character was essential for those who had to validate their positions in a society in which rulers evoked fear.[36] In eighteenth-century Morocco, however, Jews were further hindered because they confronted a dual world with two divergent sets of rules. This conflict can be seen in another of Romanelli's firsthand accounts. On one occasion Eliahu Levi attempted to ride his mule—as all Jews were forbidden to mount horses—directly into a town market instead of dismounting as custom demanded. The Berber crowd immediately turned on him ready to administer swift justice and certain death. But Eliahu did not lose his composure. In spite of his predicament, he shouted a loud and haughty rebuke, invoking the sultan's name. His audacious reprimand stopped the mob, who suddenly realized their own vulnerability if they provoked the monarch by their actions. Levi's risk-taking behavior and resolute stand were perfectly in keeping with the Arab honor code. His claim to royal protection had to be reinforced by a fearless demeanor, and, as a result of his convincing performance, he was allowed to continue without harm.[37] Levi's real status was a complicated mixture of both slave and master, but forceful displays such as these allowed him the rare privilege of ignoring at least some of the humiliating rules set for Jews. By undertaking the risk and surviving, Levi actually enhanced his standing in society. Despite the potential for a deadly outcome, the courtier showed great discernment in his mode of rebellion. After all, as he rode away in victory, he still held the reins of a lowly mule and not those of a noble Arab steed.

Moroccan culture may have respected such daring, but it also held honor and family reputation as paramount. Therefore, Romanelli's public "unmasking" of Eliahu Levi would have placed a significant burden upon the son.[38] In adulthood Moses Levy's radical utopian nature, religious perfectionism, and depressive episodes may well have been influenced by this stigma—although to what degree may never be known. Within the millennialist climate of the early nineteenth century, however, Levy's expectation of the imminent reign of the Messiah would have put his father's behavior to the fore once again. The sins of all previous generations figured prominently in the minds of those who believed that the day of redemption was near, and, indeed, Levy made ample use of the concept in his *Plan for the Abolition of Slavery*.[39] Nevertheless, any sense of shame would have at least been mitigated by Levy's many residences abroad. In addition most Gentiles would not have had any facility in Hebrew or even been aware of Romanelli's narrative. Consequently, the full scope of Levy's Moroccan origins, like the Yuli surname, were details that he concealed even from his own children. Intensely sensitive to prejudice and social injustice, he turned his back on his rigid Sephardi past and envisioned a world free from defects and devoid of what he regarded as the tyranny of rabbis. Like Romanelli himself, Levy eventually became a Jew of the Enlightenment, a keen observer and social critic, and traveler extraordinaire. He considered "pride of family honor" to be a particularly pernicious trait that "infected" those who blindly adhered to false notions of superiority.[40] In his effort to refashion himself after the European rationalist model, he jettisoned all connections to his Moroccan past, especially the all-pervasive folk magic tradition of his youth. Ironically, despite Levy's attempt to contain his family history, his son David's unwitting adoption of the Yulee surname, his aspirations for high government office, and his disassociation from Judaism must all have been keenly felt and disturbingly reminiscent of the sins of Eliahu.

The sudden death of Sultan Sidi Muhammad in 1790 heralded one of the most disruptive episodes in Morocco's history and drastically altered the fortunes of the ibn Yuli family. As capricious as the former monarch may have been, the accession of his son and enemy, Mulay Yazid, brought about a two-year reign that far surpassed his father's in sheer brutality. In what has been described as a "catastrophic bloodbath," many Jews were grotesquely tortured, robbed, and killed in a nationwide rampage.[41] In addition to being a straightforward act of revenge against his father's coterie of advisors and confidants, Yazid's actions also appears to have been a religiously inspired attempt to reverse the country's previous dependence on the Jewish royal merchants. Yet this initial impulse soon turned into violence toward the entire Jewish community. Eliahu Levi, as others of the former sultan's entourage, was dragged from his house, beaten severely, jailed, and condemned to death, but, unlike most, he managed to evade execution after he repeatedly proclaimed his desire to convert to Islam. While several of his colleagues employed this same tactic in vain, Levi's success may be attributable to his previous incarceration and disgrace under Sidi Muhammad, an episode that could have placed the courtier in better favor with the new regime. Romanelli mistakenly assumed that Eliahu Levi died soon after his release. Records show, however, that he survived his ordeal intact, a fortunate fate given that most Jewish courtiers were hung by their ankles from the city gates of Meknès and died in tortuous agony.[42]

Instead of traveling to Fez for religious instruction as ordered by the new sultan, Levi abandoned not only his property and estates but at least one of his three wives as well during a successful escape to British Gibraltar.[43] Compounding the perilous venture was the fact that all women, whether Hebrew or Arab, were forbidden to leave Morocco. Nevertheless, Levi did manage to smuggle his wife Rachel, their eight-year-old son Moses, and one or more of the family servants out of the country. Upon their safe arrival the courtier's son would have noticed a vastly different culture from the Islamic kingdom in which he had been raised. A brief boat journey away from the Moroccan coast, Gibraltar was only three miles long and consisted of little more than a garrison town and harbor. It was, however, of central importance to the naval, commercial, and political ambitions of the British Empire. As one statesman claimed: "The fortress of Gibraltar was to be reckoned amongst the most valuable possessions of England. It was that which gave us respect in the eyes of nations."[44] It stood in defiance against all enemies as the ultimate British bulwark, having recently withstood the longest continuous siege in history and the combined assault of both the Spanish and French navies. The famed Rock, rising almost fourteen hundred feet above sea level, dominated both land and sea and served as a natural beacon for the Mediterranean's sole outlet to the Atlantic Ocean.

The Sephardi community of Gibraltar was substantial, and its members maintained close relations with their Moroccan brethren. Most retained traditional North African customs; men shaved their heads, kept full beards, and wore black robes and caps.[45] Some Jews had remained in Gibraltar during the Great Siege seven years earlier, and Moroccan Jews also had a long history of supplying the British garrison with vital supplies. They had become an integral part of Gibraltar society and were accepted in a way that was unusual in most of Europe. After Eliahu Levi arrived, he was not without assets, and it is likely he retained some wealth in the form of family jewels.[46] He also had a network of friends and business associates in Gibraltar. Once safe from Moroccan Islamic law, which considered his conversion irrevocable under penalty of death, he reverted to the religious traditions of his birth and once again pursued a merchant's life, traveling as far as Egypt.[47]

Although Britain's military engagements against Revolutionary France and Napoléon offered ample financial rewards for merchants in this military outpost, the quality of life was severely restricted. The end of the siege marked a steady decline in garrison discipline, a state of affairs which was aggravated by the extraordinary presence of no less than ninety taverns.[48] In striking contrast to this unruly atmosphere, young Moses Levy pursued a strict religious education under the tutelage of authoritarian rabbis. One such rabbi, the headmaster of the yeshiva, was said to be endowed with special powers, and, like the prophet Isaiah, he could "slay the wicked with the breath of his lips."[49] If Levy's subsequent disavowal of rabbinic Judaism is any indication, his early encounters with these holy men may have been less than ideal. Nevertheless, the depth of his religious education was considerable, and he eventually attained a "great proficiency in the Bible."[50] As Levy entered adolescence, his prospects in trade and commerce looked certain, while opportunities for higher education and perhaps a professional career were nonexistent. The significant hazards of the business world were also readily apparent. While the entire town may have rejoiced at the vessels captured in the wake of Admiral Horatio Nelson's naval victories, Levy also observed the ruin of small operators who lost their ships and cargoes in much less glorious circumstances.[51]

At fifteen the introspective teenager suffered a religious and emotional crisis of serious proportions. Describing the event many years later, Levy told of a distant relative who, after returning from a trip to "atheistical" France, informed him of the merits of the "doctrine of materialism" he had garnered from abroad. These ideas caused Levy to doubt his religious beliefs. "I made no reply," he wrote, "but my heart died within me." He went about his daily routine "mechanically" but felt as if he had "lost his identity." Depressed and feeling disconnected with the world, he wandered alone into a Gibraltar synagogue and was seized with excruciating pain. Feeling as if "melted lead was pouring" inside his head, the boy thought his agony surpassed "the idea entertained of hellfire." Crying out to God, the pain stopped, and a "pleasurable sensation" ran through his body. In that moment he "swore never to doubt the Bible."[52]

Essentially a tale of spiritual rebirth, this episode reveals a marked similarity to the conversion experiences of evangelical Protestants, including many of the abolitionists Levy later befriended in England. Similar cataclysmic events were actively encouraged and anticipated among evangelical youth in the early nineteenth century.[53] In this tradition biblicism and an emphasis on individual experience were of prime importance, and conversion was proof that someone had crossed over to the spirit realm to be "adopted as a child of God."[54] In like manner, Levy's episode led him to proclaim that he had "the love of man, providence, & belief of the Bible ingrafted in [his] soul."[55] Despite its similarity, this type of event was not encouraged within traditional Judaism, and it is unlikely evangelicals had much of a foothold in Gibraltar during 1797. Therefore, Levy's synagogue incident appears to have been a legitimate religious milestone, albeit one that raises questions regarding his psychological state—perhaps the legacy of childhood trauma in Morocco—and the degree to which he may have interpreted the experience many years later.

Another unanswered question exists. The German edition of Romanelli's chronicle, published in Hebrew five years earlier, may not have been readily available in Gibraltar, but it certainly attained a measure of success among the more urbane Jewish communities of Europe for whom Morocco held particular fascination. That Levy's intellectually curious relative was not aware of Romanelli's work seems unlikely, especially if he himself were kin to the infamous Eliahu. Surely it was only a matter of time before word of the scathing narrative would have reached Levy, and the possibility arises that either his unnamed relative or someone else played a part in its disclosure.

Not long after Moses Levy's reaffirmation of faith, several major events transpired. His father died in Gibraltar sometime between 1798, the year that Levy's sister Rachel was born, and 1800.[56] The circumstances of his death are unknown, although a virulent epidemic was taking a heavy toll in the surrounding areas of Morocco and Spain.[57] Left to fend for himself, at eighteen Levy began work as a ship's merchant, presumably outfitted in European attire, buying and selling merchandise and transporting the contents between Gibraltar and the West Indies. Shortly thereafter he resolved to settle permanently on the Danish island of St. Thomas and made arrangements for his mother and sister to follow.[58] An important element in Levy's decision was the fact that one of his family's former Jewish bondservants, Elias Sarquy, had already established himself as a merchant on the island. Freed by Eliahu Levi after the daring escape from Morocco, Sarquy sought better prospects in the Caribbean, and by 1793 he established himself in St. Thomas. Despite his newly acquired affluence, Sarquy always exhibited great deference and loyalty to members of his former household and undoubtedly offered a helping hand to young Levy.[59] In 1800 Levy arrived at Charlotte Amalie, the major commercial port on the island, and began employment as a clerk in a lumber export firm—permanently discarding the Yuli surname. Left behind him in Gibraltar was an impending plague, a near mutinous garrison, and the vestiges of his extraordinary Moroccan past.

2. A WEST INDIES MERCHANT

*W*ith its large protected harbor and its status as a thriving free port, the town of Charlotte Amalie held a certain prominence at the beginning of the nineteenth century. Denmark's long history of political neutrality ensured protection for French and American privateers during the conflicts of the previous century. Ships and confiscated cargoes were disposed of with impunity on St. Thomas. This tradition continued with the resurgence of privateering both during the Napoleonic Wars and Simon Bolivar's Wars of Independence in South America.[1] Only thirteen miles long and three miles wide, the relatively poor soil of St. Thomas, unlike its sister colonies of St. Croix and St. John, was ill suited for large-scale sugarcane production. Therefore, the island's prosperity depended almost exclusively on its position as an entrepôt, or trading center. In addition, its proximity to Puerto Rico--only thirty-nine miles away--enabled the Danish island to become an important provider of food and manufactured items to the Spanish colony, despite Spain's official policy of excluding foreign imports. Although a Danish possession, St. Thomas's predominant culture and language among white inhabitants was actually Dutch, with English and French also widely used. There was a substantial free black population, many of whom were of mixed race. They spoke a Dutch-based Creole dialect and came not only from the Caribbean but from North America and Africa as well.[2] "The confusion of tongues and colors is among the first things that attract the notice of a stranger," an observer noted. "You see and hear people of every color speaking in almost every language."[3] In the harbor ships of many nations converged at anchor, attesting to the island's status as a cosmopolitan commercial hub.

The appearance of St. Thomas, especially when viewed from the sea, was one of astonishing beauty. "Its high green hills and savannas," wrote one visitor, "[were] variegated with fields of Indian corn and sugar canes, [and] interspersed with the cocoa and broad leaf plantain tree. At its base stands the town upon three gentle eminences, the harbour in the form of a horse shoe; its extremities defended by a battery."[4] Within a few years of Moses Levy's arrival, there were about 160 Jews, and most of them were newcomers.[5] The favorable economy in St. Thomas resulted in a steady increase in population, and Jews soon constituted a sizable community. Levy, like most other Jews, resided in the central commercial section of Charlotte Amalie called Dronningens, or Queens Quarter, and eventually owned a house and loft there.[6] Primarily Sephardi merchants from the Dutch islands of St. Eustatius and Curaçao, new arrivals also included Europeans as well as a limited number from Morocco.[7] Most of the community, however, were composed of Spanish- and Portuguese-speaking Jews whose ancestors had their origins in Europe rather than North Africa and therefore belonged to a Marrano or crypto-Jewish tradition that was far different from that of Moses Levy. Other denominations on St. Thomas included members of the Dutch Reformed Church, Lutherans, Anglicans, Roman Catholics, and, of particular interest, Moravians, one of the first religious groups to serve the spiritual and educational needs of West Indian slaves.

The Moravian Brethren were pietist Christians who placed great emphasis on a personal faith based on the Bible rather than on church doctrine and theology. Their early efforts at founding day schools and Sunday schools for both slaves and free blacks were well known throughout the Caribbean, and the Moravians were especially strong in the Danish and English islands.[8] Most missionaries were trained in the Moravian outpost of Bethlehem, Pennsylvania, and their educational curriculum stressed practical fundamentals for both males and females.[9] By 1813 there were 2,253 "Christian negroes" at the St. Thomas missions.[10] Their agricultural settlements were communal in nature and stressed self-sufficiency. Despite the Moravians' doubts about slavery and their apparent egalitarian concerns, however, in practice all their island missions maintained slaves.[11] Apart from their Christocentric orientation, certain Moravian ideals reveal a distinct similarity to the beliefs Moses Levy would later espouse, both in his plan for Jewish settlements and his ideas concerning the abolition of slavery. In fact, everyday life in St. Thomas reflected various elements contained in Levy's 1828 treatise, including a diligent and productive free black population, a permissive attitude toward interracial unions, and a tradition of granting freedom to mixed-race children.[12] Most of these practices would not have been welcome in many parts of the world—particularly the southern United States. Yet this new and distinctive Creole culture must have resonated deeply with Moses Levy and acted as a catalyst for the work he later described as his ministry.[13]

Pervading this relatively permissive culture, however, was a strong sense of foreboding. The recently successful slave rebellion on St. Domingue was of foremost concern throughout the Caribbean, and St. Thomas's weak and demoralized military garrison was not a factor to be relied on to suppress organized revolt.[14] Vigilance toward any sign of insurrection began after 1733, when a bloody uprising on St. John was quashed only through the intervention of French forces.[15] At the turn of the century one official noted that slaves on the Danish islands were suddenly defiant and showed contempt for whites. Occasional acts of violence and even murder added to the apprehension.[16] As other abolitionists before him, Moses Levy utilized fear and paranoia concerning armed insurrection as an important element in his pragmatic plan for slavery's demise.

At age twenty and as yet only a clerk, Moses Levy considered his financial position adequate enough to allow him to marry, and in 1803 he became engaged to seventeen-year-old Hannah Abendanone.[17] A native of the once-prosperous Dutch island of St. Eustatius, Hannah was the daughter of St. Thomas merchant David Abendanone and his wife, Rachel.[18] The family moved from St. Eustatius some time after the British captured and sacked the island in 1781, a reprisal for the islanders' major role in furnishing the rebellious North American colonies with supplies during the Revolutionary War.[19] By the time Levy met Hannah, the large Abendanone clan of Charlotte Amalie were well-established, prosperous merchants. According to Zephaniah Kingsley, a St. Thomas ship's captain who later became a wealthy plantation owner in East Florida, the family was among "the most respectable in the Island."[20] It appears that Hannah's family also had Moroccan origins, *Abendanone* being a Spanish variation of *ibn-Danan,* one of the major rabbinical families of Morocco.[21] Most likely, the marriage was arranged in the "Old Antediluvian style," to use Levy's terminology, in which "parents consult[ed] the pedigree & purses [to] match their children."[22] Whatever Levy may have lacked in financial resources was undoubtedly compensated by his long-established courtier ancestry, a factor that was held in esteem by the Sephardi community and kept very much alive by Elias Sarquy's deferential behavior. Certainly no other Jewish family on St. Thomas could expect such royal treatment from a leading merchant. According to the accounts of Levy's daughter, Rahma Da Costa, Sarquy never directly approached any member of the family and would meekly stand with his head bowed, refusing to move until he was given formal permission to do so.[23] Such reverential displays could only improve Levy's matrimonial prospects.

An unsettling event on Moses Levy's wedding day strengthened both his belief in God and his notions about the "interposition of Providence." On this day—as Levy was fond of recounting—he was outfitted in his best attire, but the conscientious clerk nevertheless attended to last-minute business. A vessel fully loaded with mahogany logs was set to sail for the German port of Hamburg, and Levy was required to measure the cargo before it departed. Not long after climbing down the hatchway, the massive logs stacked on either side of the ship suddenly gave way, almost crushing him. Enough room remained, however, for him to jump toward the hatchway seven feet above. Losing one of his new boots in the process, he swung the unshod foot clear while the logs shifted once more, collapsing violently. After the heel of his other boot became jammed, he lunged backward, "extricating the foot from the boot." Remarkably unhurt and strolling on deck in his stocking feet, the five-foot-six-inch Levy regarded this achievement as something truly inexplicable. "Here we see instinct in the twinkling of the eye," he wrote, "causing a performance which all the calculation and judgement of a life could not accomplish."[24]

Taking place as it did on his wedding day, the near-fatal incident was regarded by Moses Levy as a portent for the difficult marriage that was to follow. Although his wife eventually bore four children, it is abundantly clear from their separation and divorce agreement—written after twelve years of matrimony—that their carefully arranged marriage had not taken into account the couple's vastly incompatible temperaments: "We have lived in discord for several years, led a most painfull life and even so far, that we in more than three years have found ourselves obliged to live entirely separated."[25] Levy's youngest son, David, later attributed his parents' divorce, a rare event in nineteenth-century society, solely to what he regarded as his father's peculiar religious notions. While David lacked any firsthand knowledge of his parents' relationship—they separated when he was two—Moses Levy's self-imposed isolation from his children much later in life adds some credence to the son's supposition. It should also be noted, however, that, as a successful U.S. senator, businessman, and plantation owner, David Levy Yulee declined to have his mother live with him in her old age, ostensibly because her "West India habits and education" would have made her "miserable" in the United States.[26] All things considered, it appears that both Moses and Hannah Levy may have shared somewhat demanding personalities.

A year after their marriage Hannah gave birth to their first child. Following Sephardi tradition, this firstborn male was named Elias after the infant's paternal grandfather.[27] The boy's circumcision ceremony was an important occasion and reinforced his father's standing within the Jewish community. As was the custom on St. Thomas, the infant's needs were attended to by a slave, one of several who were present in the Levy household—perhaps the legacy of a dowry.[28] In 1803 Denmark had outlawed the importation of slaves in its West Indies possessions, but the institution itself was still very much the norm. Many years later, while Levy was engaged in the abolitionist crusade in London, he used his son's example to demonstrate the adverse effects of slavery on both whites and blacks. "As [the boy] grew up, he was taught to look down upon and despise [the slave] as being an inferior order, and upon every occasion struck and abused him. Thus the worst and most malignant ideas were engendered in the mind of the white."[29] Levy considered his wife's role as especially negative, and he left little doubt about who was encouraging the bad behavior. In fact, Moses Levy would trace his disappointment in all four of his children to three causes: the "malignant" nature of slavery; his children's formal education among Christians, who made them feel "uneasy as Jews"; and the influence of Hannah Levy—an "unhappy woman" whose "character follows me in that of her children."[30]

Despite misgivings at home, Moses Levy regarded his financial duties as a father paramount and thus considered going into business on his own. Much like in Gibraltar, the tradition of seafaring and ship ownership was strong among West Indian Jews, and the acquisition of a vessel was thought essential for success.[31] Consequently, Levy's purchase of the schooner *La Henrieté*—"with all her tackles, apparel and furniture"—for the sum of 1,360 Spanish milled dollars enabled him to become an independent operator.[32] This ship would become the first of many that Levy would eventually own. Of course, any sort of sea journey was subject to substantial risks, not only from pirates and privateers but also from the forceful tactics utilized by various European naval powers in their quest for Caribbean dominance. France issued a "Proclamation of Death" intended for those who ventured too close to slave-held Haiti.[33] Britain briefly occupied St. Thomas in 1801, and for many years the royal navy often intercepted American merchant ships, impressed seamen, and then abandoned them with contemptuous disregard. British privateers harassed St. Thomas shipping from bases on Tortola, forcing many to seek the protection of convoys.[34] In the absence of accurate weather forecasts, hurricanes also posed an immediate threat throughout the region and often resulted in enormous losses of life and property, forcing the most prudent to refrain from travel during the summer and fall.[35] In 1793 one especially ruinous storm caused a St. Thomas resident to proclaim, "The most experienced navigator who had been exposed to severe storms and bad weather at sea had no idea of the violence of such a hurricane."[36] Vessels of all descriptions were either driven on shore or lost at sea, and large fragments of houses and furniture blocked the town streets. Trees were stripped of leaves, seawater fouled the fresh water cisterns, and the island presented such a desolate aspect that it appeared "quite destroyed."[37] Mindful of these risks and also of his duties as both husband and father, at twenty-two Levy made out his last will and testament.[38]

Not all hazards presented themselves at sea. In 1804 and 1806 a series of calamitous fires consumed much of Charlotte Amalie, and numerous buildings were decimated, including the first synagogue built in 1796.[39] Beginning in the early morning of 22 November 1804, according to one eyewitness, "The fire raged with such vehemence that in the course of ten hours more than twelve hundred buildings were burned down and it was only extinguished by daylight of the next morning."[40] Most public records were lost, so the full extent of Levy's damages are unknown. Judging by his later success, however, it appears that he was well able to endure a catastrophe that left many others financially ruined and the "best and richest part [of town] lying in ashes." Because many affluent merchants kept their assets in gold and silver dollars, the total loss was staggering. During the fire of 1804 alone the official estimate of this "terrible conflagration" was determined to be eleven million dollars.[41]

When a squadron of British warships blockaded St. Thomas for a second time in 1807, much of the town had been rebuilt using "fire-proof" materials of brick and masonry instead of wood. Commercial activity had resumed–a testament to the economic vitality of the island. British troops captured St. Thomas with ease and remained for eight years, a move that was intended to curb the activities of French privateers.[42] During the interregnum the new island government endowed the remainder of the Levy children with British citizenship. After Elias there were daughters Rahma and Rachel, followed by the youngest, David—named after his maternal grandfather—born in 1810.

David Yulee's remembrance of his youth is quite emphatic: "My earliest recollection of home is disconnected with any other presence than that of my mother and of a single visit there, of a few days only, of my father. I was told that my brother and sisters had been sent to London for their education so that I knew none of them until I met them at a late day . . . entire strangers at the time of our meeting."[43] Therefore, it appears that Moses Levy had not only taken up residence at a different location in Charlotte Amalie but went to great lengths to avoid contact with his estranged wife. Validation of their divorce was a lengthy and costly affair and was not granted by the Danish king until 1818, but their separation agreement allowed Hannah Levy an ample award for herself and their children as well as ownership of the family house.[44] While David was still very young, Levy arranged for his two girls to attend a boarding school in St. Croix when they each turned six. Miss Wintle's Seminary for the Education of Young Ladies specialized in English grammar, arithmetic, history, geography, and French as well as reading, writing, and needlework and "solicited the patronage of the most respectable" families. Later Elias, Rahma, and, eventually, Rachel were escorted by an aunt to further their education in England—a location much favored by the planter and merchant elite.[45] After David reached school age, his father had already resolved to establish a Jewish colony in the United States, and it was there, rather than Britain, that David was sent for his education. Eventually, at seventeen, he met his brother, Elias, for the first time and formed a strong bond that lasted many years. Rahma and Rachel, however, after living abroad for most of their lives, lost all contact with their youngest brother. Consequently, the sisters must have indeed appeared as strangers when they finally met David, by then someone of national political importance, after their father's death in 1854. Despite the presence of numerous other relatives in St. Thomas, David considered his youth a lonely one–the inevitable consequence of his parents' separation and divorce, his status as the youngest child, and his father's long absences.

In Moses Levy's view family unity did not take precedence over the requirements of a classical education. Later he would eschew all secular forms of schooling in favor of a radically altered system that emphasized the practical arts and sciences, and placed the Hebrew Bible at its core.[46] At this time, however, he was determined to provide all his children with certain advantages that he felt were denied to him, especially in the realm of secular education. Of particular interest was his insistence upon sending his daughters to school at a time when female education was generally considered a radical and unwarranted innovation.

Endowed with a prodigious love of learning, Levy taught himself those subjects that his religious teachers in Morocco and Gibraltar could not. Certainly, by the time he arrived in England during the 1820s he showed a breadth of understanding and a facility for writing and oratory which was at least the equal of his Oxford- and Cambridge-educated contemporaries. Consequently, the high-minded Levy was hardly satisfied with the mundane affairs of business, deeming it "drudgery, ill-looking & disgracefull."[47] Despite this intense dissatisfaction, he was willing to compromise, and, during the beginning of his career at least, he often donned the mask of a performer. Levy once wrote: "Please them I must else they will not be interested in me. I must excite their selfish cupidities to help me to my necessities."[48] Whether entirely genuine or not, a personable manner and keen intelligence eventually won the confidence and respect of an impressive circle that included colonial governors, bishops, generals, and superintendents. An American merchant once described Levy as "a gentleman who has seen and knows much of the world, possessing a sound head and a good heart, and endearing every one to him who has the happiness to be acquainted with him."[49] Thus armed, he was prepared not only to enter the business world but also to contend with whatever obstacles antisemitism presented, including the waning specter of the Spanish Inquisition.

Ironically, despite Levy's private doubts concerning his livelihood, he was highly regarded in St. Thomas as a prosperous burgher, a Freemason, and a member of both the synagogue and the local Hebrew burial society, or *hebrah*.[50] Not long after his purchase of *La Henrieté*, Levy formed a business partnership with two of his wife's relatives, brothers Emanuel and Philip Benjamin, whose family also came from St. Eustatius.[51] Emanuel was married to Hannah Levy's sister Esther. The company, known as Levy & Benjamin, Brothers, operated until 1808, when Philip, for unknown reasons, left the concern and joined his father Judah's dry goods store in Christiansted, St. Croix.[52] Again, this business relationship did not work out, and eventually Philip rejoined Levy not as a partner but as an employee, occasionally accompanying him on trips to Puerto Rico. Of special note, Philip Benjamin became the father of U.S. senator and Confederate secretary of state, Judah P. Benjamin—born in 1811 on St. Croix. Levy continued his affiliation with Emanuel and Philip Benjamin, with the brief introduction of new partner, Salomon Robles, until 1817, when Levy liquidated the company to pursue his own short-term interests in the Caribbean in preparation for establishing a Jewish colony.[53] After moving to the United States and possibly influenced by Levy's religious views, Philip Benjamin became active in the early Jewish Reform movement in Charleston.

The Levy & Benjamin store was located at 39 Queens Street, the main commercial road in Charlotte Amalie. Levy was primarily a provisions merchant and catered to the needs of the many ships that entered the harbor. The volume of business was considerable, since there were a total of seven "back Stores" to his establishment.[54] The firm also owned and leased property, lent mortgages, operated a lottery, and maintained a private wharf for loading and unloading large quantities of goods. During a typical year 3,358 vessels arrived in St. Thomas, excluding small boats.[55] While the risks of trade were substantial, sizable profits afforded enterprising merchants such as Levy and Emanuel Benjamin with substantial incomes. The company was so renowned that the local newspaper, the *Sanct Thomas Tidende*, rather than citing a specific address, simply proclaimed that its offices were "opposite the stores of Messrs. Levy & Benjamin."[56]

As previously noted, St. Thomas had long served as a market for the sale of vessels and cargoes captured by privateers, and it also had courts that sanctioned the process.[57] Letters of marque served as the mechanism for differentiating between privateering and true piracy. But fine distinctions were often blurred when goods known to have been plundered by pirates elsewhere in the Caribbean frequently showed up for sale in St. Thomas under dubious guise.[58] Levy, like other leading merchants, was an active participant in this rather ambiguous and lucrative commercial climate. After Britain terminated its occupation of the island, some of the items that appeared at auction had actually been taken from Spanish ships by privateers, so a degree of resentment could be expected from loyalists. Regardless of the Danish policy of neutrality, Levy became staunchly allied with Spanish interests. For example, in 1816 news of a mounting force of two thousand privateers of "every language and color" began to circulate in St. Thomas; these men were gathering on the secluded islands off the coast of Haiti.[59] Levy, who by this time held lucrative contracts with the military in nearby Puerto Rico, alerted officials to the danger. He then volunteered two of his own ships to take part in a large convoy that was formed to counter this threat.[60] Levy also aided the cause by purchasing an armed brigantine that was sorely needed by the Spanish government as well as diverting twelve and a half tons of gunpowder that was originally intended for the rebel stronghold on the island of Margarita—a most impressive achievement that dealt Bolivar a substantial blow.[61] These services were highly valued, and details of Levy's efforts were brought to the attention of the secretary of state in Madrid. Incidents such as these, coupled with glowing testimonials from officials at the highest level, contradict the unsubstantiated assertion by Cuban historian José L. Franco that Levy was not only in league with pirates and privateers but supposedly controlled "all the clandestine traffic of the Caribbean."[62] If true, such charges would have merited a death sentence, not praise, from the Spanish. While authorities were clearly annoyed with Danish policy on St. Thomas, Levy's reputation was exemplary, and his services, frequently discharged by placing his own interests in jeopardy, earned him the gratitude and respect of Spanish luminaries.

One such individual was Don Alejandro Ramírez y Blanco. In 1813 Ramírez, the former secretary to the captain-general of Guatemala, became

Puerto Rico's new *intendente*. Almost immediately he began a successful strategy for revitalizing the moribund island economy. Despite hundreds of years of Spanish control, real development had hardly begun. While the island may have been a colonial outpost and lacked large urban centers, universities, and extensive plantations, its potential was vast.[63] An essential first step in Ramírez's plan was to officially legitimize and encourage what had formerly been considered illegal trade with foreign countries. As a result, Spain issued a decree, the *Real Cedula de Gracias,* in 1815. This act opened colonial ports to international trade for the first time on a regular basis, thereby setting the course for economic development and the entry of foreigners, including a substantial number of U.S. merchants.[64] According to Levy, Ramírez always maintained a high regard for the institutions of the United States and promoted American business interests on the island.[65]

Ramírez was a Spanish-born economist whose accomplishments earned him wide acclaim as well as membership in the prestigious Philosophical Society of Philadelphia—the first Latin American to be so honored.[66] As intendant, he was not only the chief financial officer of the colony, but he also possessed a wide range of judicial authority. Additionally, he was responsible for economic development, as well as the more mundane aspects of feeding, housing, and paying the army, and maintained complete control of the royal revenues.[67] The new reform policies of the Spanish Cortés created a separate intendancy, an office that was independent from the governor and captain-general, Salvador Meléndez. Therefore, Ramírez answered only to the government in Spain.[68] Because the island could hardly provide for its needs and the intendant was resolved to remedy the situation, the opportunities for a St. Thomas merchant with the proper resources, credit, and full command of the Spanish language were plain to see.

Moses Levy regarded Ramírez, who was five years his senior, in the highest terms: "His perseverance, erudition, extraordinary precocity of intellect . . . were proverbial." Moreover, the intendant was "eminently endowed" with "the rare qualities of meekness and gentleness."[69] Recalling his past association with Ramírez some twenty years later, Levy remembered his friend as a kindred spirit, a true reformer and idealist who did not seek to enrich himself by virtue of his public office—a most unusual trait given the accepted standards of the time. Ramírez's family did in fact suffer serious financial hardship after the colonial officer died of a sudden stroke on 20 May 1821.[70]

The two men met shortly after Ramírez arrived in San Juan from his former post in Guatemala, and from this first meeting a friendship soon blossomed. At first glance this relationship may not seem that extraordinary. After all, Levy had many admirable qualities. He possessed a keen intellect and a genial manner, and his appearance was that of a fine gentleman—clean shaven and fashionably dressed. Viewed by the standards of Latin American culture, however, the social standing of the two men was vastly dissimilar. Ramírez represented the apex of colonial society, while Levy, according to the laws of the Inquisition, belonged to a despised minority whose members were technically barred from the island. In an amazing scenario that was unique for the time, both men transcended these differences and became, in Levy's words, "bosom friends" as well as important business colleagues. Ramírez was equally complimentary of Levy. He noted that his friend frequently risked "all his fortune in the fulfilment of his contracts" and proclaimed that "there is no one like him." The intendant did not hesitate to send letters of recommendation attesting to Levy's "rare qualities" to such notables as General Pablo Morillo, commander-in-chief of Spain's expeditionary forces in South America.[71] Surprisingly, the details of Levy's close association with Ramírez has previously gone unrecognized, despite the appearance of two remarkable newspaper articles written by Levy in 1843 which amply revealed their past association.[72]

Levy's refined demeanor set him apart from the petty merchants—primarily Catalans—who were so disdained by the Puerto Rican gentry.[73] In contrast to St. Thomas, this colony had long been a closed society that thwarted the emergence of a powerful and educated mercantile elite.[74] With Ramírez's reforms, however, societal norms were altered, and opportunities for men such as Levy suddenly came to the forefront. Despite the disapproval of some Puerto Rican traditionalists, he soon became an intimate of the Ramírez family and maintained a particular friendship with the intendant's mother-in-law, Doña Josepha. While he was away at sea, Levy noted, she would often light candles to her patron saint for his protection and safe return. In an attempt to explain such anomalies, he likened the experience to that of a "reconciled enemy, who taking the opposite extreme, profusely tenders to his new made friend, a liberality that [he] never experienced in England or in the boasted toleration of [the United States]."[75] Fortunately for Levy, this "liberality" also extended to the bishop of Puerto Rico, Juan Alejo de Arizmendi, a progressive clergyman of noble birth who personally rebuked efforts by the secretary of the Inquisition to bring charges against Levy.[76] Consequently, he was given the unprecedented privilege of keeping his San Juan countinghouse closed on the Sabbath, and, after further intervention by Governor Meléndez, Levy was allowed to acquire a sugar plantation on the island—the first professing Jew ever to have been granted such liberties in Puerto Rico.[77] While still a Danish citizen, Levy attained the status of *hacendado,* or plantation owner. Such an action by the governor was unusual not only because Levy was a Jewish foreigner but because of his close connection to Ramírez, whose policies were causing rancor among the established political authorities. Many of the intendant's reforms were opposed by Meléndez, who, after all, was used to having almost dictatorial authority on the island. According to Levy, Meléndez's generosity toward him was exceptional because the governor "was at daggers drawn with the Intendant and his friends." Levy insisted, however, that he "never meddled in politics" and thus managed to distance himself from the animosity of the rival camps.[78]

One of Ramírez's first acts was, in Levy's words, "to rescue the Island from the incubus of the depreciated currency."[79] Before the intendant took office, the governor responded to the declining economy by issuing paper money, an act that had dire repercussions. In Levy's estimation the value of this currency depreciated "ten dollars to one."[80] Ramírez was compelled to enact quick measures, such as establishing a lottery, reducing military expenditures, and taxing the foreign goods that were now legally entering the country. He abolished both tithes and the sales tax and replaced them with an innovative system of direct taxation which doubled revenues.[81] Levy claimed to have been the intendant's "principal agent to redeem the half million of paper [currency]," but he never stated what his exact role was.[82] Nevertheless, records show that Levy provided large sums of credit to the government during its fiscal crisis, a move that was sure to elicit appreciation from both the intendant and the governor.[83] The addition of a new partner, Salomon Robles, may have been in response to the increased demands during this period. However, aside from Levy's duties as a major contractor to the army and the fact that he maintained daily transactions with the government, very little has surfaced which could define his precise role during the paper currency crisis.

The three year intendancy of Alejandro Ramírez has been credited with transforming Puerto Rico from a weak dependency of Mexico, on which it long relied for economic subsidies, into an emerging, autonomous nation.[84] Yet a strong military presence and a deep distrust of outsiders pervaded the island. Emblematic of this isolation, San Juan was entirely enclosed by a massive sandstone wall rising to sixty feet in some areas. The residents of the capital rarely ventured outside. Indeed, San Juan was "a garrison town with a siege mentality" whose citizens were afraid of all outsiders, even the residents from the surrounding countryside.[85]

While culturally dissimilar from St. Thomas, an island that has been likened to a "tropical Protestant city-state," miscegenation was also a common practice in Puerto Rico, and free people of color made up a substantial proportion of the inhabitants.[86] In fact, this segment represented just over 50 percent of the total free population—comparable to St. Thomas but twice that of Cuba and far surpassing the minuscule 3 percent in the Lower South of the United States.[87] While some historians believe that intermixture may have resulted in lessened racial tensions, it also created an extensive caste system based on color gradation.[88] A common perception was that "every grade of color, ascending from the jet-black negro to the pure white, carries with it a certain feeling of superiority."[89] Nevertheless, as Levy observed, "among the coloured population . . . there are many nearly white, who possess a competent and even affluent independence."[90] While comparatively few in number, their success convinced him that the Spanish system represented the best chance for a more egalitarian society. After all, in comparison to the "grave calculating Dutchman—the aristocratic Frenchman—or the high-minded, but haughty, Englishman," only in the Spanish colonies did he observe whites working alongside their slaves or "sitting [together] at the same table."[91]

Ramírez's "outstanding achievements" in restoring the Puerto Rican economy and in replenishing the Royal Treasury were specifically mentioned by the king when he appointed Ramírez as superintendent of Cuba and the Floridas in 1816.[92] Havana, in contrast to San Juan, was much more cosmopolitan in character and was actually one of the largest cities in the Americas. Cuba also possessed an entrenched and politically powerful planter elite, a closely aligned network of aristocratic families who, together with affluent merchants and slave traders, have often been dubbed the "sugarocracy."[93] Despite the growing economic vitality of the island and its ascendance as one of the principal sugar producers in the world, Cuban interests were seriously damaged by marauding privateers. Additionally,

Ramírez had to deal with the undeveloped frontier provinces of East and West Florida—also under his jurisdiction—regions that had previously experienced hostile incursions by United States troops and Georgia militia as well as Indian unrest.[94] The political and economic importance of Cuba to the Spanish monarchy was considerable, especially in light of Bolivar's Wars of Independence. These "years of horrors and misfortunes," as General Pablo Morillo phrased it, threatened the empire with the humiliating loss of its New World colonies, and this strife was not likely to be ameliorated by grand appeals to monarchy and patriotism, as Morillo once imagined.[95] On 1 July 1816 Ramírez sailed into Havana harbor surrounded by a large fleet of warships and accompanied by the newly appointed captain-general, José Cienfuegos. Notably, two vessels in the armada actually belonged to Moses Levy and were temporarily leased to the Spanish government. The comments of the U.S. consul in Havana reflected the hopes of an emerging American merchant presence: "Ramirez is well known by his Liberality in Porto Rico, and many of his acts already meet the general approbation of the mercantile interest; we have therefore much to expect from him."[96] Cuba, however, would prove to be much more problematic for Ramírez than either he or his supporters could foresee.

While Moses Levy continued to travel extensively in the West Indies, he established a residence and business in Havana and a sugar mill, or *ingenio*, in the country—an enterprise that required a large financial outlay for slaves, land, buildings, and mechanical equipment as well as the services of an experienced manager.[97] With Ramírez's support and protection, Cuba became "Don" Moses Levy's new base of operations, and his *hacendado* status defined him as a privileged member of society. Havana rapidly became a "staging area for royal troops" destined to combat Bolivar's insurrections.[98] Consequently, Levy's transactions with Spanish authorities reached new heights, and he became a major supplier to Morillo's ill-fated expedition to South America, at that time the most powerful military force ever to have crossed the Atlantic. The value of one of Levy's convoys laden with food and munitions for troops in Venezuela totaled 82,637 pesos, a sum equivalent to well over one million dollars in today's currency.[99]

3. "AN ASYLUM . . . FOR OUR FELLOW CREATURES"

*W*hile Moses Levy pursued his vocation with diligence and ample skill, he felt uneasy toward his newly acquired wealth. His success became a moral burden, a potential source of sin that had to be dealt with in a righteous manner. Toward the end of his West Indian merchant career, he feared that he was in danger of becoming what he most despised: a "mere money-making animal."[1] The obligation to hold oneself to the highest moral standard was not unique. The devout rabbis of his youth, together with the public failings of his father, may have provided a foundation for moral perfectionism as well as a reverential regard for the Bible. In addition, apart from the Catholic colonies of Spain, the transatlantic growth of evangelical religious values was much in evidence in the West Indies. Piety, temperance, and good works as well as condemnation of any lifestyle that could be interpreted as vain and luxurious were not abstract truths to be casually acknowledged but were essential values that had to be enacted by living a "godly life."[2] Thoroughly in keeping with evangelical standards, Levy denounced what he perceived as individual avarice and looked to asceticism as his ideal.[3] Protestant fervor also extended to free blacks and slaves, particularly through the efforts of itinerant Methodist preachers who stirred many listeners by their focus "upon sin, and the devil, and hellfire."[4] Often in complete isolation from orthodox Jewish communities, Levy nevertheless sought inspiration from the Hebrew Bible and rigorously kept the Sabbath. Independent and inquisitive by nature, he included the New Testament in his religious studies and, on occasion, attended church services. Still, he declared that the doctrines of Jesus were "not new," and on close examination he found that the main Christian tenets were all to "be found in the law of Moses."[5]

"When I acquired money," Levy recalled, "I might have collected my children, perhaps [re]married & have followed in the same footsteps of my fellow debased people—eat fat turkies, drink good wines, keep a carriage, be lofty & arrogant, get husbands for my daughters who will do the same &c." To follow such a direction would have been "most wretched, debased & wicked."[6] Determined to do something genuinely "elevated" and disconnected from monetary gain, he set in motion his plan to found a colony of Jews. While he had long been preoccupied with the concept of the "regeneration of [his] people," Levy finally made the fateful decision to enact his dream.[7] His goal was not unlike the pious philanthropy of the evangelical English gentry who not only prided themselves in their acts of "charity and human amelioration" but were in the privileged position of having the "Luxury of Doing Good."[8] His intense dissatisfaction with his life in the Caribbean became overpowering. Like the proverbial repentant sinner, he would later recall the "black spots" of shame that he had "contracted" during his days in the West Indies, although the exact nature of his regret remains unclear.[9] Spurred to resolve what he considered his spiritual shortcomings and still in his early thirties, Levy was drawn to a new calling and gradually assumed the mantle of social activist and colonizer. The implementation of his plan would take several years, but his goal was set, and, consequently, in his eyes his life assumed new meaning.

While Levy derived no special sense of pride from his mercantile trade, he nevertheless belonged to a select group of highly mobile and successful Jewish merchants who maintained an international network of associates, much in the manner of his Moroccan ancestors. As such, his activities were not restricted to either the West Indies or the Americas but included Europe as well. Additionally, Levy's status as a Freemason provided access to a global association of individuals and lodges which further benefited his business interests. Throughout 1816 Moses Levy was in London, a strenuous two-month voyage from Cuba. In March of that year he purchased a well-armed ship, the *North Cray*, and then sailed back to the Caribbean, where the Spanish military eagerly acquired the vessel for use against Bolivar's privateers.[10] In the fall Levy was in the British metropolis once again. In addition to fulfilling his military contracts, he also visited his two school-age children.

At this time Britons still relished their victory over Napoléon, and the rise in nationalist spirit was matched by a corresponding Protestant religious zeal that manifested itself not only in abolitionism but in a profusion of other reform issues. In keeping with this widespread preoccupation for social change, in London Levy conveyed his plans for founding a colony of Jews in the United States to Frederick S. Warburg, a young Jewish merchant from Liverpool.[11] The specifics of this early plan have not survived, but it is significant that Levy had already determined that the United States would be his ultimate destination and suggests that he had previously visited the country during his many trips abroad. Warburg was the twenty-year-old son of Salomon Moses Warburg, a prosperous banker from Altona, a Danish town adjacent to the international port of Hamburg.[12] As the youngest son, Frederick Warburg left Altona to pursue his own interests in England, while his eldest brother, Wolff, assumed control of the S. Warburg Bank. Both Altona and Hamburg were centers of trade with the Danish Virgin Islands; therefore, it is highly probable that Levy had business connections with the Warburg family before his meeting with Frederick. The Warburgs not only had a long tradition as moneylenders and financiers but were also active in philanthropic and religious activities. A relative, Simon Elias Warburg, founded the first Jewish settlement in Sweden, and Frederick's brother Wolff, eighteen years his senior, became president of the Altona Jewish community and encouraged his wife "to do charity to her heart's content."[13]

Levy's ideas appealed to Frederick Warburg, who had a natural affinity toward experimentation and innovation. Apart from his activities as a merchant, Warburg would later acquire a patent for a new process he developed for the manufacture of lamps and candles.[14] He was attracted to Levy's proposition, and in a few years he became Levy's agent for enlisting potential Jewish settlers as well as becoming a colonist himself. Their encounter coincided with a period of radical reverses for European Jewry. In 1814 Napoléon's troops withdrew from Hamburg, ending what had been progressive rule for Jews. Full rights of citizenship were revoked, and French defeat sparked a resurgence of German nationalism and an accompanying rise in antisemitism. The year 1816 was one of economic downturn, famine, and deep unemployment, and, while most Jews suffered

equally under these conditions, the "upstart" Jewish bankers and financiers—epitomized by such families as the Rothschilds—were singled out
by some German intellectuals as well as the public at large as the root cause
of their misfortunes.[15] Earlier the respected philosopher Johann Gottlieb
Fichte had succumbed to the prevalent irrationality by asserting that Jesus
never was in fact Jewish. Further, he considered Jews as foreign and base
and certainly not worthy of assimilation into any German state. "Give them
civil rights?" he declared, "I see no other way of doing this except to cut off
all their heads one night and substitute other heads without a single Jewish
thought in them. . . . I see no alternative but to conquer their promised land
for them and to dispatch them all there."[16] Jews, then, like former slaves
in the United States, were fit only for transportation back to their "native"
land. Ironically, such threats would only have served to vindicate Levy's
ambitions for a Jewish refuge.

Aside from antisemitic ranting, Jews continued to be subject to humiliating and petty taxes, were excluded from guilds, and could not engage in
agriculture. This climate of bitter social repression peaked in 1819 with the
so-called *Hep! Hep!* riots—a derogatory term possibly derived from the
cries of German goatherds—when rioters chanted this insult while attacking Jewish businesses and homes. Dangerous riots erupted in numerous
towns and eventually included cities in other countries, including Prague,
Cracow, Riga, and Copenhagen.[17] According to one contemporary report,
Jews were "murdered, their temples profaned and overthrown, their homes
violated without exciting a single sympathetic glance."[18] Most Hamburg
Jews were fortunate to find protection in nearby Altona. News of these
disturbing events was suppressed, but Warburg would have had firsthand
knowledge of European oppression and was in the position to convey his
concerns to Levy, the very person who aspired to furnish an "asylum" in
the United States.

Levy was especially outraged at the culture of "refined malice" that was
"directed at the noble faculties of the mind." He considered "torture, the
sword, or the faggot" as preferable to "the persecution of contempt."[19] In
Levy's estimation the Jews of Europe were victims in an incessant war of
psychological abuse. A decade after the *Hep! Hep!* riots, his beliefs appeared
to be verified by German laws "so degrading . . . [that] they must recoil
on the people with whom they originated, and serve to mark them as the
most mischievous of inhuman hearts." Jews, for instance, had to pay a toll

in order to pass certain town gates, and on their receipt appeared the words *Jew* and *Swine*. "And a son of Abraham is handed this card," Levy wrote in a London newspaper, "with a pen passed through the word *swine*, retaining the words, 'The Jew has paid his toll.'" Furthermore, a Frankfurt law restricted the Jewish community from having more than fifteen marriages per year, although there were over one thousand families in the city. Levy was incredulous: "Is there any parallel in history to an act so diabolical? Pharaoh's edict aimed at destroying the innocent babe, but here the dagger of the assassin is aimed at the destruction of the soul before it is conceived." "The period will arrive," Levy warned, "when the merited cup of trembling will be drank up to its dregs, and the cup of the Lord's fury will be taken from our hands, and given to those who delight in afflicting us."[20]

Since Jews were degraded by Christians, "Mahommedans," and "idolators" alike, Levy concluded that "the prostrate house of Israel loudly calls for a remedy." Without a distinct Jewish nation "the Israelite" would continually "drag the chain of servitude" and be prevented from "soaring beyond himself." Assimilation, even the total elimination of civil disabilities, was not the answer. "Barbary, Turkey, Poland, the wilds of Prussia—[the Jews] tried them all, and every where found an enemy in man."[21] Any possibility of returning to Israel appeared closed, so the United States, with its religious freedom and its separation of church and state, was "the only place that [Jews] can look for an asylum."[22] The United States also had a tradition of religious innovation, and members of formerly persecuted religious sects thrived in frontier havens.

Significantly, Levy's transatlantic journey coincided with the genesis of Reform Judaism. While abroad, he received details of the controversial activities of the German lay activist Israel Jacobson, a man whom Levy considered a kindred spirit.[23] Jacobson, regarded as the progenitor of modern Reform Judaism, established the first Reform services and implemented many changes. Both women and children were welcomed as part of the congregation; the *tallit*, or prayer shawl, was abandoned; "Confirmation" replaced the traditional bar mitzvah; and organ and choir music augmented a much more orderly and refined service. Jacobson himself approached the pulpit wearing Protestant-style clerical garb, and sermons were conducted in German. Such changes consciously evoked Christian decorum and brought participants closer to the external religious norms of the culture at large. Despite the vehement opposition of Orthodox leaders, Jacobson's reforms filled a genuine need in the spiritual lives of significant numbers of Jews, and his innovations soon extended throughout the German states.

Both Levy and Jacobson came from the ranks of self-taught and highly successful Jewish businessmen. Jacobson was a "court Jew" and a banker by profession who was inspired by Enlightenment ideals to guide his coreligionists toward a more egalitarian position in society. He was also a man of great wealth who certainly did not possess any "ghetto fear" of the Gentile and was on intimate terms with the German nobility.[24] Most important, he regarded education as the prime factor in accomplishing his goals and looked to Jewish participation in agriculture as a way to transition from the demeaning petty trades and as a method of gaining autonomy and self-respect. In these areas Levy and Jacobson were indeed kindred spirits.

The differences between these men reveal much about Levy's core beliefs. On the one hand, it is doubtful whether Levy would have seen much value in High Church–style organs or choirs, preferring instead a stark simplicity similar to "Primitive Christians."[25] Levy's vision resembled Quakerism in that it excluded formal preaching. On a deeper level Levy utterly rejected Oral Law and the authority of rabbis, whereas Jacobson's ideas were far more restrained and reflected the assimilationist ideals of the emerging Jewish bourgeoisie. After all, he attempted to curb the power of the rabbinate, to improve their training, and to set standards but never to eliminate the institution itself.[26] Primary among his concerns was to abolish all civil disabilities so that Jews could become good, patriotic citizens, an errant cause according to Levy.

Within the Haskalah tradition there was ample room for disagreement. Whereas Jacobson's primary concern was for cultural inclusion, Levy rejected the ideal of citizenship and maintained a more traditional view that Jewish nationhood was synonymous with Jewish identity and could not be separated. In refuting the claim that his coreligionists could be both fully integrated, patriotic citizens and good Jews, Levy replied: "It is against the law of nature for any human being to have two springs of action. A person cannot be a Dutchman and an Englishman at once. . . . In short, turn where he may, the nationality of Israel stares him in the face, and makes the Dutch, French or any other patriot, in all acts of devotion, a liar."[27] The theocratic kingdom of Israel became Levy's ideal model for utopian speculation. While the yearning for a true Promised Land where Jews could live together under God's authority and protection lay at the very foundation of Judaism, Zionism as a movement did not appear until much later. When most educated Jews yearned for civil liberties and acceptance as citizens, Levy's stance appeared quite reactionary, even to those who admired him and conceded that his motives were "altogether pure."[28] Undeterred, Levy asserted: "Let Israel look up to the rock from whence they are hewn. Let them look to the law and the testimony. These, and these alone, can shew to us the true road for the amelioration of our condition."[29] Levy's proto-Zionist stance was directly counter to Jacobson's assertion that the Bible forbade the existence of a "state within a state." The German reformer's deliberate suppression of all references to the restoration of Zion in the new liturgy would also have drawn Levy's ire.[30]

As dogmatic as Levy appeared when speaking of Israel and nationality, amazingly the spirit of reform was quite strong. Compared with Jacobson, Levy was much more receptive to certain positions of Enlightenment philosophers such as Immanuel Kant, who urged Jews to adopt a "pure moral religion" and to abandon all "the old legal regulations."[31] That he possessed at least a general familiarity with Kant and others appears beyond question, especially in the light of statements written after his return from Europe: "I have consulted the different characters of the several congregations we have through Europe, their Habits and Prejudices, the Religion now observed called Judaism, on one side, and on the other the true Spirit of our Holy and abused Religion together with the native Virtues of our People, and have formed a plan which will combine them hand in hand with the liberal and enlightened Principals of the well educated portion of Society in the present times."[32] Eager to discard every trace of ritual and of rabbinic influence and teaching, Levy nevertheless still clung to "revealed religion" and looked to the Hebrew Bible for guidance on all spiritual and temporal matters. In this regard he did not follow the strict Enlightenment path but was more inclined toward the biblicism of the evangelical reformers. In regard to the rampant antisemitism of philosophers such as Voltaire, however, Levy had nothing but contempt, calling the author of *Dictionnaire philosophique* (1764) "that grand harlequin of philosophy."[33]

Evidently unaware of the full extent of their differences, in 1818 Levy expressed a serious desire to meet Jacobson personally, with the hope that their two approaches could be united.[34] Unfortunately, Levy's hectic schedule in Latin America prevented him from returning to Europe until much later. Furthermore, Jacobson's health suffered a serious decline in 1818, and he withdrew from active participation in the movement that he had started.[35]

Early in 1817 Levy left England for France but was disappointed when his colonization plans drew little interest. "I found the Jews even when educated were heartless," Levy concluded. "The doctrine of inheriting a crown of glory after death, made a Jew unmindful of his brothers," a veiled criticism of the rabbinic origin of *haolam haba*, the world to come.[36] In Paris Levy observed that secular-looking Jews were often evicted from their homes after their religious identity was revealed to the landlord. On the city streets he spent time in discussions with poor Jewish peddlers. If these men acquired a trade, as many of them did after Napoléon awarded them citizenship, they were compelled to work on Saturdays and were shunned by their Christian coworkers, most of whom would never condescend to speak to them. Rather than break the Sabbath and endure social ostracism, a meager peddler's life appeared to be the only option left for them. In short, Levy's sojourn to the Continent confirmed his low regard for the so-called privileges of citizenship. Returning once more to England, he visited the Jewish schoolmaster of his son Elias, who, in passing, boasted of a former pupil who had become an affluent Jamaican merchant. Filled with his own concepts of what constituted worthy employment and annoyed at what he regarded as the schoolmaster's unenlightened priorities, Levy retorted, "Is this the aim of a Jew [?]" He immediately took his son out of the school and placed him in another. His daughter Rahma attended a non-Jewish school in Brighton. Eventually, she was joined by her sister, Rachel, but both "were obliged to take feigned names" because of religious prejudice.[37] Such deception, albeit with the higher motive of raising his daughters as educated young ladies, humiliated Levy and reinforced his bleak opinions regarding the true standing of Jews in a Gentile world.

Moses Levy considered his colonization scheme thoroughly vindicated when he set out on his return voyage to Cuba in 1817. Unlike the initial leg of his journey, the prevailing trade winds would have made the trip somewhat less demanding, although the risk of any passage was still considerable. Once in southern waters the change of climate was dramatic. The water's hue shifted to a deep blue, and during good weather travelers often marveled at the abundance of dolphin and flying fish. Levy had little time for such pleasantries, however, and remained focused on his settlement plans. For the first time in his adult life he assured himself that he could, at

long last, "live and work to some purpose."[38] Furthermore, after his return
to Cuba and despite his deep personal affinity for individuals such as Alejandro Ramírez, Spain's past injustices were not forgotten. He increasingly
viewed his employment as a means to an end: "I am engaged as it were in
the Service . . . to a nation the most inimical to Our Brethren," he confided
to a friend. "If I am in any way to Revenge Myselfe on that nation, it'll be
by making them an indirect means of repairing the wrongs they have done
us, not by doing them harm but by making them do us good."[39]

Indeed, Cuban society had many wrongs to repair. For one it maintained an especially brutal regime for slaves who toiled on the *ingenios*.
Details of how Levy treated his own slaves are sparse, but later in Florida
he did make a deliberate effort to keep slave families intact.[40] His early
proposal to certain "opulent" Cuban planters to institute marriages among
slaves, to keep their families together, and to offer Catholic religious instruction may be a good indication of Levy's own behavior on the island.[41]
His humanitarian motives appear to be beyond question. "How can we
expect that religion or civilization shall find its way among persons compelled to live as brutes?" he once asked these same planters. The measures
that Levy promoted were considered extremely humane for the time, although they merely reflected the official church-government position,
which, of course, was rarely implemented. As the antislavery bishop of Havana Juan José Díaz de Espada noted: "Any [slave] family union could be
broken by the unilateral and unappealable decision of the [slave owner] to
sell, hand over, transfer one or another member of a nuclear family"; and
"Marriage, as practiced in the society of whites, was impossible in the slave
gangs."[42] In the sugar mills especially, slave gender was highly skewed toward males, making any hope of procreation, let alone marriage, quite rare.
Levy knew of one "establishment of 1,000 negroes [that] did not have fifty
females amongst them."[43] A common belief, according to historian Franklin F. Knight, was "that it was more economical to work a slave to death as
quickly as possible and then replace him with a new purchase than to care
for the slave properly and encourage reproduction."[44] In comparison with
the southern United States, it was an exceedingly harsh system.[45]

While the practical advantages of marriages may be debated, it is noteworthy that abolitionists invoked the institution as one method of slave em-
powerment, of "righting the slave, restoring him to himself."[46] The impulse
to keep families intact, to retain the powerful bonds between husbands and

wives, parents and children, and siblings was something that Levy shared with very few slaveholders in Cuba. He sincerely believed that it was "not only necessary to abandon the system of persecution and oppression hitherto pursued against the blacks, *but to turn that very system into an instrument of blessing.*"[47] Yet the planter class had a vested interest in limiting slave rights, not in expanding them. Furthermore, the few Caribbean slave owners who were deemed too permissive or indulgent could bring censure upon themselves, especially if gossip began to erode the master's image of absolute power.[48] Nevertheless, Levy's journey to England, a place where abolitionism was elevated almost to the status of a religion, would naturally have turned his attention once more to the oppression of the "unfortunate sons of Africa." He was careful, however, to frame his opinions within acceptable limits while residing in slaveholding countries. The mood of planters approached paranoia when broaching the topic of the English abolitionists. One Jamaican sugar planter summarized the general feeling throughout the islands when he wrote in 1816: "the higher classes are all in the utmost alarm at rumours of [William] Wilberforce's intentions, to set the negroes entirely free; the next step to which would be, in all probability, a general massacre of the whites."[49]

Antislavery philosophy was hardly restricted to British Protestants. The influential works of Enlightenment authors such as Jean-Jacques Rousseau were allowed to be printed in Cuba, apparently under the auspices of the liberal Bishop Espada.[50] Clandestine editions of the Abbé Guillaume Raynal's *Histoire des deux Indes,* despite its denunciation by the Inquisition, became an important mode of propagating Enlightenment views toward slavery and was widely read among the literate classes of Latin America.[51] Raynal's observations go beyond the physical sufferings endured by slaves. His discussion of the negative behavior that constant psychological abuse created in slaves parallels Levy, as this same concern appears in both his *Plan for the Abolition of Slavery* and in his lectures and writings concerning the "degradation" of the Jews. As Raynal stated, "We have neglected nothing that might tend to degrade those unfortunate people, and we have afterwards upbraided them for their meanness."[52]

Moreover, Francisco de Arango y Parreño, one of the wealthiest mill owners in Cuba and a leader among the *hacendado* class, developed his own distinct ideas for slave emancipation. By 1816 he developed a plan—never implemented—whereby white European males would be imported to the island both for their labor and for intermarriage with black women. The resultant "whitening" process, according to Arango, would "wipe out or destroy the concern about color."[53] In his theory a new class of free workers would arise to replace slaves. This eugenics approach bares a certain similarity to Levy's own theories, but it should be noted that racial mixing schemes were not that unusual in Cuba. More than likely, Levy had firsthand knowledge of Arango's ideas. While important differences existed between the two men, both shared the common assumption that African physical characteristics presented an insurmountable obstacle in society.

Economics rather than humanitarianism, however, appears to have been the chief inspiration for Arango's scheme. As the owner of La Ninfa mill, the largest sugar estate in Cuba, Arango foresaw a serious labor problem.[54] His solution, according to the Marxist historian Manuel Moreno Fraginals, required that traditional slavery be replaced by a form of wage slavery. Arango's eugenics goal amounted to nothing less than a "cattle-farm-proletariat system" in which the resultant workforce would be less expensive than traditional slavery.[55] The supposed physical superiority of blacks, compared to persons of mixed race, apparently would be offset by a labor pool that Arango anticipated to be in the millions.[56]

In distinct contrast, Levy's utopian vision regarded communitarian values and revealed religion as paramount. Far from viewing racially mixed workers as pawns to be exploited, Levy foresaw a community of equals. Within these small, cooperative, agricultural settlements, he suggested that each family, "independent of their principle occupation or pursuit," would raise between "one to five acres of sugar cane." Neighbors would unite in harvesting the cane for processing in communal sugar mills. According to Levy, "each shall be entitled to his portion of sugar which is to be assessed by competent judges amongst themselves, not with a saccharometer in the hand, but with the spirit of neighbourly consideration." He likened this "festive season" to the spirit of cooperation that existed during the "vintage season in wine countries."[57] Such a pleasant and idealized scenario, in which profit was secondary to mutual respect and cooperation, was Levy's response to unrestrained capitalism. While Levy and Arango were both attracted to social engineering, the goal and substance of Levy's position was the antithesis of "wage slavery." Clearly influenced by evangelical economic theory, Levy envisioned an enlightened collective will that would replace individual avarice and Mammonism.[58] He also had much in common with such radical social theorists as Charles Fourier and Robert Owen, a fact that becomes even more apparent from his private correspondence.[59]

Unlike most slaveholders, Levy's progressive outlook rejected the pseudo-science and racist demagoguery of slavery defenders, who argued that blacks, while possessing superior physical strength, were by their very nature subhuman. Levy's subsequent proposal to provide free education as well as religious and agricultural training to the children of slaves would have been regarded as futile by those who maintained that Africans were hardly more than "orang-outangs." Typical of the "physical and moral proofs" propagated during the antebellum period, one American pamphleteer characterized the Negro as "a race incapable of receiving education and of comprehending the *terrors* of religion, much less of perceiving the value of our majestic system of Law."[60]

Levy may have concluded that it was beyond the capacity of even the most liberal abolitionist to accept blacks as true social equals, but the same pessimism also applied to Christian attitudes toward Jews.[61] Characteristically, he believed that "any attempt to injure or benefit any part of the family of man" would have an equal effect on the whole of mankind.[62] Human fallibility may have resulted in the unjust treatment of blacks and other minorities, but the inherent humanity of all was indisputable. Levy considered, however, that "[the Jew's] separation from the mass of mankind is by the Most High ordained." Lest anyone forget the magnitude of this distinction, he warned his coreligionists: "Every Jew who contributes knowingly to the . . . amalgamation of the house of Israel is an enemy to his nation, to his religion, and, consequently, to the world at large."[63] Furthermore, Jewish exile would end only by the creation of a separate homeland and the arrival of the Messiah and not through assimilation.

Levy continued to formulate his abolitionist views, but his colonization scheme took immediate priority. In 1817 he divested himself of his long-term partnership with Emanuel Benjamin and sold his company holdings in Charlotte Amalie. Although trade continued to flourish on St. Thomas, a yellow fever epidemic resulted in the death of hundreds, "especially amongst the mariners."[64] That same year former partner Philip Benjamin left the island bound for the United States. Both Levy's mother and sister still resided on St. Thomas, and he made financial arrangements so that if he failed in his "Sacred Cause . . . none shall suffer with [him]."[65] Levy's belief in the divine nature of his mission overruled caution. Not only were righteous and risk-filled ventures widely esteemed by evangelicals, but within Judaism the concept of *tikkun olam* (repairing or perfecting the world) necessitated a call to action.[66] In fact, it was essential before the reign of the Messiah could take place.

Maintaining a hectic business schedule, Levy visited the United States in October 1818 with stopovers in New York, Philadelphia, Rhode Island, and Norfolk. Despite his workload, he thought of "nothing but the regeneration of [his] people." Levy drew a parallel between himself and the biblical Noah: "the first Sally of Noah's Dove . . . was forced to return seeing no diminution of that destruction which deprivd her & her species of their proper home." Now Levy awaited "the second trip of the Dove," perhaps she would return with an olive branch "denoting that she'll soon have a resting place to her feet."[67] Levy believed the United States, like Noah's Mount Ararat, would serve as the final destination for his oppressed brethren and that a new era of agrarian prosperity would emerge to fulfill God's plan.

4. TOWARD AMERICA

*W*hile the United States was still predominately a nation of farmers in 1818, the country witnessed the first stirring of the Industrial Revolution in New England as well as the vigorous growth of cities along the eastern seaboard. This was the so-called Era of Good Feelings: westward expansionism gained new momentum, and the religious fervor of the Second Great Awakening was transforming American culture and institutions. Despite the upsurge in spiritual revival, the nation was plagued by violence. Vigilantism, riots, lynch mobs, as well as individual acts of drunkenness and murder were quite common and threatened the young democracy with anarchy and tumult.

Thus, Moses Levy's visit brought him into intimate contact with a newly established republic in transition. Jews totaled only several thousand at most. Although the majority of Jewish newcomers were of poor Ashkenazi or German background, the original Sephardi inhabitants, many of whom claimed noble descent from their Spanish or Portuguese Jewish forebears, enjoyed the highest status, and their influence predominated in the relatively few established communities.[1] In marked contrast with Europe, ghettoization had not surfaced, and the number of Jews was so low that most Americans had no firsthand knowledge of them. While the nocuous image of the "mythical Jew" persisted, postrevolutionary ideals stressed tolerance and egalitarianism.[2] Amid this overwhelmingly Protestant society, certain acceptance was granted to affluent Jews who, consciously or not, defied negative stereotypes.[3] Such was the case with Moses Levy.

Levy's scrupulous reputation, wealth, and social connections defined him, in the words of one member of the New England gentry, as a "Gentleman of the first respectability."[4] His prominent merchant friends included both northerners and southerners, Jews and Gentiles—all with strong ties to the West Indies: William and James Savage of Boston, James De Wolf of Rhode Island, Peter and Colin Mitchel of Savannah, Rudolph Dietz of Philadelphia, and the Myers family of Norfolk, Virginia, the first stop on Levy's journey.[5]

"Situated almost on the shores of the Atlantic; with a safe and commodious harbour," the town and port of Norfolk also had the prerequisite banking and insurance institutions that secured its position as one of the leading commercial destinations on the eastern seaboard.[6] Norfolk's merchant-shippers had long supplied the Caribbean with such staples as grain, meal, flour, lard, and tobacco, while the island trade brought in large quantities of sugar, molasses, fruit, and rum.[7] One of the town's highest-ranking merchants was sixty-five-year-old Moses Myers. His firm of Moses Myers & Sons, like Levy & Benjamin, operated a fleet of ships and maintained wharves in the town harbor. While the company suffered a decline during the various Embargo Acts and many vessels were lost during the War of 1812, the subsequent peace "restored commerce to its usual energy," and prospects improved for Myers & Sons.[8] Regardless of the economic climate, Myers's social standing and reputation was solidly fixed in the community. Previously, he had served as city councilman, was appointed superintendent of the local branch of the Bank of Richmond, held the rank of major in the Virginia militia, and was a member of the Norfolk Masonic lodge. His impressive political connections included such men as Thomas Jefferson.[9] Myers's ownership of one of Norfolk's most exquisite homes, a substantial Federal style mansion, further enhanced his status. Levy was on close terms with Myers and visited for social as well as commercial concerns; Myers's company supplied Levy with crucial foodstuffs intended for the Spanish army in South America. Early in Myers's career, he had circumvented the British blockade during the American Revolution by shipping supplies to the rebellious colonies from the island of St. Eustatius.[10] Like Levy, Myers also spent much of his adult life outside the influences of formal Judaism. Norfolk had very few Jews and no synagogue. Only during times of great stress did Myers draw consolation from what his family termed the "old

forms" of Judaism. Nonobservance was the norm in the household, and at
least one of Myers's sons was known to be uncircumcised.[11]

While a guest at Myers's home, Levy spoke with enthusiasm about his
colonization scheme. His ideas met with approbation from the free-thinking Myers as well as from other members of the family, including the eldest
son and business partner, John. Both father and son had often journeyed
to Europe and were well aware of Old World repression. Myers's twenty-
eight-year-old son Samuel, a graduate of the College of William and Mary,
had recently embarked on a legal career. He was especially stirred by the
righteousness of Levy's cause. "I can hardly believe My Senses," Levy wrote
to Samuel after he departed for New York. "Your first remark to my Observations on the General Condition of our poor degraded people shewd me
that yr. Soul caught the Spark."[12] Well before Levy's arrival the entire family
were distressed by what they regarded as the "dreadful" state of European
Jews. Moses Myers and, to an even greater degree, his children fully realized that the "most respectable" class had to maintain some distance from
synagogues.[13] The social stigma of orthodoxy, especially the Old World
variant, was far too great a burden for the sophisticated and well-to-do
Myerses. As a result, Levy's innovative ideas held great promise, both for
their own identity as Jews and for the temporal and spiritual advancement
of their less fortunate brethren. Furthermore, Levy had good reason to believe that Samuel Myers would join Frederick Warburg, another idealistic
son of wealth and privilege, and become an active participant in his lofty
enterprise. In a gesture of his commitment Samuel, recently married with
children of his own, would eventually accept the guardianship of Levy's
nine-year-old son David.[14]

Before his departure the Myers family provided Moses Levy with letters
of introduction, one addressed to Miss Rebecca Gratz of Philadelphia.[15] A
member of a socially prominent Jewish family, Gratz distinguished herself
by her leadership in a variety of philanthropic causes. Her physical beauty,
social standing, and "selfless" image have endured to this day, and Gratz
has assumed something of an iconic stature as the ideal nineteenth-century
Jewish woman. Indeed, it is often claimed that she served as Sir Walter
Scott's inspiration for the character of Rebecca in *Ivanhoe*, a Jewish hero-
ine who refused to marry outside her faith and was therefore destined to
remain single. While there is little evidence to support this assertion, Gratz
never married and possessed a large circle of influential Gentile admirers,

including the writer Washington Irving.[16] Her sterling reputation certainly preceded Levy's first encounter with her. Their initial meeting proved to be awkward. Shortly afterward Levy confided to Samuel: "I must be in no favr with her I am afraid—for you must know that I miss'd a day in my reckoning—& having but two hours to stay in Philadelphia—I never dressed my face & hurried to her House in a Coach & did not know that it was a Holiday [Succot] until I left her."[17] Levy's apparent ignorance of the Jewish holiday reflected his hurried schedule as well as his highly independent lifestyle, a life that was spent in almost perpetual travel and was well removed from the controlling influences of stable Jewish communities. Embarrassed by his lapse of proper etiquette, Levy quickly sent his apologies to Gratz via one of her relatives who resided in New York City. Despite the brevity of their first encounter, Rebecca Gratz made a resounding impression on him.[18] Later, in a moment of romantic tenderness, he claimed to have seen "her pure and tranquil heart through her sweet eyes."[19] Indeed, a long friendship did eventually ensue between them, and they corresponded for many years.[20] Levy harbored the most loving sentiments toward Gratz, but it appears that he relayed these feelings only to his closest male confidants. While their relationship remained platonic, it is obvious that Rebecca Gratz exemplified those personal attributes that Levy found utterly lacking in his former wife. Dignified, virtuous, and "elevated," Gratz also impressed Levy with her "meekness." Similarly, she showed "confidence in God" while "doubting in herselfe." Such virtues struck Levy as "more than charming." Here was a Jewess, he concluded, who was worthy of emulation by all women.[21] Levy believed that traditional Judaism had unfairly excluded women from full participation in Jewish affairs. So, Gratz's independent nature and charitable activities—she helped found Philadelphia's Female Hebrew Benevolent Society in 1819—merited his wholehearted praise.

In a few weeks Moses Levy had established important contacts among the highest echelon of American Jewry. In addition, he was elated to discover a willing advocate in Samuel Myers. As this young man was now "engaged Solemnly in The Sacred Cause," Levy felt that his plan could proceed immediately. Myers accepted the challenge and proclaimed that he would "not pause or tremble at the task." Both pledged their unwavering support for their idealistic crusade, "without reward—glory—or any consideration but the good of Our people." They regarded themselves as the initiators of a grand and solemn enterprise. While in New York, Levy took decisive action and instructed his Norfolk protégé to purchase former military lands in the Illinois frontier. Levy had just been informed that not only was there abundant acreage available at good prices but these parcels held valid titles and were selling rapidly.[22] Therefore, Illinois, rather than Florida—still a Spanish possession—became the initial focus of Levy's desired settlement. In time Myers would perform another crucial role by contacting other influential Jews on Levy's behalf, including the leading Jewish luminary of the day, Mordecai Noah.

While attending to business concerns in the United States, mere "sordid" commerce in Levy's estimation, he never lost sight of his high-minded goal. After all, he was now committed to a mission whose purpose was nothing less than the survival and spiritual fulfillment of the Jewish people. Levy reasoned that such a task would be impossible without an educational component. He wrote to Myers about his desire to found a national society or "Brotherhood" whose sole purpose was to provide "for the education of Jewish Children." This fundamental idea had never been seriously addressed in the United States. Therefore, the establishment of a formal center for Jewish youth—a school that would incorporate nonreligious courses into the curriculum as well as attract students from the various states—was an objective that Levy felt others would eagerly support. Encouraged by Israel Jacobson's previous educational experiments, Levy directed Myers to proceed with their own scholastic undertaking and to raise a fund of fifty thousand dollars for this purpose. Levy immediately donated a thousand dollars toward the cause, an ample sum equivalent to the cost of a substantial middle-class home.[23] Concerned that their radical preferences toward the curriculum might dissuade potential supporters, he advised Samuel to "propose a plan of education as near to our plan as you think they'll admit." As far as Levy was concerned, education and colonization were inseparable, and he wanted the two enterprises united together in the same locale. He pictured these dual concepts as "2 machines" working toward the "essence and spirit of our religion."[24]

Pressed for time, Levy was only able to send Myers a "bare-bones" outline regarding the "regeneration" of the Jewish people. He prefaced his remarks by reiterating his low regard for orthodox Judaism, "which by ignorance and superstition is erecting barriers and fences [,] . . . disfigured the Temple itselfe and rendered it so inconspicuous that it makes no figure at all among all the tawdry stuff they surrounded it with."[25] Such fiery criticism was by no means unique, as the sentiments of the European *maskilim* attest. In his brief dispatch Levy revealed a revolutionary stratagem. He envisioned that Jews would forsake the cities in order to participate in a communal, agrarian lifestyle. Accordingly, he felt that only cooperative communities allowed men and women fulfillment in life, communities whose allegiance was to God and not to political regimes. The "Master Key" of Levy's plan rejected the Talmud and emphasized the Hebrew Bible instead. If anything arose from their Bible study that they could not fully comprehend, Levy proffered: "we must be Humble & Say rather we don't understand it—All we Know is that we can't err by following its spirit—Indeed the very Bible recommends Simplicity by the verse—'Simple thou shall be with the Lord thy God.'" In a fundamental departure from accepted Jewish belief and practice, he proposed that all prayers and rituals be replaced by a more contemplative worship. This would include a portion devoted to a "discourse on morality blended with some branch of natural philosophy adapted to raise the greatfull Soul to its benefactor." Furthermore, Levy was convinced that full responsibility for children rested with the community and not with the parents. In the educational realm both Hebrew and English would be taught to children of both sexes. His proposed curriculum for boys included "Mathematics, Geography, Astronomy, Botany, & Chemistry—the exercise of the field Tillage, the use of arms only for defence, never offencive." Girls would engage in similar instruction—excluding farming and arms training—as well as "indispensably to know how to cook, sew, spin & wash. Music and "the other fine arts" would complete the girls' course of study. All books, other than the Bible and instructional texts, would be prohibited. Each man would own "5 acres of land from which he can't depart," and the total number in each community would be limited to five hundred families. Levy's reductionist theology regarded sin as "injouring God in His fellow creatures." The only acceptable penance was to engage in reform. While committed to theocratic principles, Levy rejected monarchy and declared: "None but republicanism must be our gov[ernment]." Cognizant of the opposition his scheme could face from traditional Jewish quarters, Levy warned Myers to adopt a Masonic-like secrecy when approaching others about the more radical aspects of his plan.[26]

However extreme Levy's proposals may appear, he still desired to preserve a distinct Jewish identity and language and regarded the Hebrew Bible as the revealed word of God. While he omitted any mention of the

Sabbath or the Mosaic dietary laws in this particular document, in his personal life he went to great effort not to perform any work on the Sabbath and, if his subsequent instructions regarding his young son David are any indication, abstained from eating pork.[27] While his exact views toward *kashrut,* or the dietary laws, have not surfaced, it appears that he held a nonliteral interpretation of the biblical injunctions, similar in spirit to current Reform practice. Since the Bible does not emphasize pork any more than the other forbidden foods, his selective abstinence apparently reflected broader cultural imperatives, as swine traditionally took on the specter of the unclean. Avoidance of pork became, as one scholar has noted, the very "symbol of Jewish dietary distinctiveness."[28] In a more conservative vain Levy opposed intermarriage; maintained conventional views toward ritual circumcision, or *brit milah;* and believed in the restoration of the Jews as God's chosen people. By becoming cultivators of the soil, his coreligionists would once again follow in the path of Abraham, Isaac, Jacob, and Moses. While his rejection of the Talmud shares a superficial resemblance to the Karaite movement in Judaism, Levy never belonged to this rather conservative sect.[29] As one later critic of radical reform made manifestly clear: "They [the reformers] rejected the oral law, and all rabbinical authority, and desiring to take the Bible alone as the rule and guide of their faith and actions, were diametrical[l]y opposed to the views of the 'Caraites,' who construe it literally, and conform rigidly to all its requisitions."[30] Clearly, Levy's reform sensibilities derived from the rationalist tenets of the Enlightenment and not from medieval Karaitism. Yet his mission to amend Judaism went farther than most of his later contemporaries. His unadorned form of Judaism fell somewhere between the Deism of the Canadian Moses Hart—who attempted to create an entirely new, universal religion in his 1818 publication, *Modern Religion*—and the more moderate efforts of Israel Jacobson.[31] Despite his profound opposition to orthodox Judaism, Levy refused to discard his Jewish identity. Quite the contrary, he believed the full implementation of his plan would hasten the coming of the Messiah. In essence his idealized agricultural settlements became Covenant communities of the simplest form.

Moses Levy's ideology reveals distinct similarities to other social movements of the early nineteenth century. For instance the French social theorist Charles Fourier, an early forerunner to Karl Marx, envisioned a society that would be reduced to small cooperative agricultural settlements, or "phalanxes," which would assume full responsibility for the needs of the individual. According to Fourier, this arrangement would result in an equitable distribution of wealth and create a new era of idealistic harmony.[32] Additionally, while in England, Levy would certainly have been aware of the highly publicized activities of Robert Owen in Scotland. Owen, a successful textile mill owner and a secular rather than a religious reformer, reacted to the social turmoil and brutal work conditions spawned by the Industrial Revolution by enacting a series of radical and humane policies in the workplace. By 1818 his New Lanark mill was the world's leading model of industrial, social, and educational reform and was a commercial success as well. Owen envisioned a drastically reordered, egalitarian society composed of small cooperative villages based on agriculture. Participants, according to Owen, would be "trained from earliest infancy to acquire only kind and benevolent dispositions."[33] He believed in the communal rearing of children, and his educational endeavors implemented the progressive methods of the Swiss reformer Johann Heinrich Pestalozzi. Formal education had long been restricted to upper-class males, maintained a curriculum that stressed the Greek and Roman classics, and excluded natural science. Pestalozzi, whose theories were well-known in progressive circles, reversed these priorities and stressed hands-on experimentation and practical learning for all classes and for both sexes.[34] Owen successfully implemented many of these innovations among his New Lanark workforce; this accomplishment proved to be a powerful lure for those who sought practical justification for their own idealistic schemes. In time Owen looked to the United States, according to one contemporary observer, "[as] the theater of . . . future experiments on the facility of rendering the human species happy."[35]

Aside from the influence of such reformers as Owen and Pestalozzi, Levy was fascinated by the appearance of new Pietist sects in the United States. On at least one occasion in New York, he actually attended the services of an unnamed "New Religion," possibly the Disciples of Christ, which included the British consul as one of the congregants.[36] In their simple meetinghouse worshipers merely read from chapters of the Bible and "pray'd extempore." Such austerity impressed Levy, and he regarded their service as retaining the simplicity of the early Christian conventicles. Numerous communally based sects embodied these principles and appeared to prosper in backwoods outposts. Radical Pietist communes, such as the

Rappites in Harmony, Indiana, were not dissimilar to Levy's planned settlements, and, appropriately enough, they also shunned the "classics" in favor of providing only practical, technical skills for children.[37]

Levy was irresistibly drawn to these innovative, alternative communities and saw in them a way to "regenerate" the Jewish people. In his mind he found ample precedent in a pre-rabbinical past and interpreted the history of ancient Israel in light of the new egalitarian models: "The poor and the rich, the master and the slave, and even the stranger, sympathizing in the same feelings and banishing all distinctions, regarded each other as members of the same family." Levy often looked to Scripture and, like numerous social reformers and radicals, found the institution of the Jubilee as a way to further justify his views. Every seven years, according to ancient biblical law, required the remission of debts as well as permitting the poor to gather food from the fields. During the close of seven of these so-called sabbatical cycles was the Jubilee year, which commanded the manumission of all slaves as well as the return of land that had been previously sold. These cycles resulted in a continual leveling process, with debt cancellation, land redistribution, and the emancipation of slaves being the principal features. Ordained by God, the Jubilee was directed at both rich and poor, but the underlying impulse came from the struggles of the oppressed. Levy believed this process was a Divine method of assuring social equality and fraternity among men.[38]

Moses Levy's religious reforms should also be examined in relationship to the American Jewish standards of the early nineteenth century. Rabbis, those who had been ordained to serve as Talmudic experts as well as spiritual heads of congregations, did not arrive in the United States until the 1840s. In their place were *hazzanim,* respected laymen with some knowledge of the Hebrew language and *halakha,* or Jewish law, who were elected to serve as readers and chanters and performed ministerial duties as well. Services often lasted four to five hours, sermons were nonexistent, and, since many members were not well versed in Hebrew, boredom was inevitable. During such an extended period of time a heightened sense of disorder ruled, and the auctioning of honors and privileges further eroded any possible resemblance to Protestant-style propriety. Generally, attendance was poor, and those few who did participate often engaged in conversation or wandered throughout the service. While women sat separately in balconies, the men occupied the more prominent sections and wore large, fringed *tallits,* or prayer shawls. Children often roamed at will; even heated arguments among the congregants were not uncommon. Such Old World decorum was certainly at odds with contemporary American culture. Lack of a proper reverential attitude shocked Gentile visitors and embarrassed many Jewish leading citizens. Years would pass, however, before increasing numbers of educated and assimilated Jews would abandon such "foreign" behavior and adopt a more ordered and "Protestantized" service.[39] Viewed in this context, Levy's vision of reform, with its Protestant-inspired notions of a simplified and coherent religious practice, certainly becomes more understandable.

Like others in early-nineteenth-century society, Levy was influenced by a polar shift in Protestant religious outlook often described as postmillennialist. A new sense of optimism replaced visions of the apocalypse. The success of the American Revolution was interpreted by many to be a harbinger of a new messianic age, and, prior to Christ's Second Coming, believers expected that all people would gradually improve their lives. Individual acts of piety and good works, as well as activism in the form of proselytizing, went hand in hand with this new eschatology.[40] Jews also had a role to play, for the restoration of Israel had yet to take place. Beginning in England and soon to be followed by the United States, conversionists set about their anointed task. The temporal and spiritual welfare of Jews as well as the study of Hebrew were suddenly topics of polite society, but others viewed these efforts as complete folly. One frustrated conversionist proclaimed: "fetching home these out-casts to the flock of Christ, [has] become a bye-word and an object of scorn and ridicule amongst [Europeans], being scoffed at as '*the English madness.*'"[41] Conversionist strategies, aimed primarily at Jews of the lowest economic strata, would eventually provoke deep indignation from Jewish leaders. The full brunt of their actions had yet to be felt, however, in the United States. During his subsequent journeys to England, Moses Levy would come face-to-face with representatives of this movement, many of whom were also leading exponents of the antislavery crusade.

Levy's messianic expectations and his desire to establish agricultural communes in a de facto Jewish state certainly hinders any facile definition of his beliefs. His communal-utopian impulses contradict traditional assumptions about Jews of the early nineteenth century. On this subject historian Jacob R. Marcus is especially adamant: "Jews were quite content to remain loyal to their own collective ethnos and tradition. Gentile communitarianism, with its centrifugality, left them untouched. All Jewry constituted a 'community.'"[42] In Marcus's view Jews enacted their differences, even in the most extreme cases, merely by the formation of splinter congregations. He never imagined they would share in the same notions that compelled many Christians to join backwoods enclaves, at least not during this early period. Marcus may have ignored the liberality of some Jews as well as underestimated the influence of Protestant culture. Certainly, Levy was not the only Jew who harbored utopian ambitions. In any case his plan was intended for European Jews and was imagined as a safe haven and refuge for the oppressed. In time he hoped that others would join these settlements and a distinct Jewish "nation" would emerge. Levy did not anticipate, however, that American Jews would immediately abandon their trades and businesses and join him en masse for the rigors of frontier life.

Levy's rationalist dismissal of all Jewish ritual and traditions establishes him as a precursor to the radical Jewish Reform movement. His scheme even exceeds the intentions of the forty-seven members of Charleston's Beth Elohim Synagogue—among whose members was Philip Benjamin, Levy's former business partner—who petitioned for German-style reform in 1824.[43] Yet this group's audacious demand for the end of "bigotry and priestcraft" is certainly on a par with Levy and also strongly parallels Protestant concerns.[44] Additionally, Moses Levy's later insistence that his son David's education be supervised by a "liberal Unitarian clergyman" predates by many years the strong relationship that developed between Reform Judaism and the Unitarian Church during the turn of the twentieth century.[45] In fact, according to one view, "it would not have been farfetched for a historian of ideas to predict a merger between Reform Judaism and liberal Christianity [during this period]."[46] Despite the animosity generated by centuries of oppression, Levy still admired certain characteristics of Christian society, especially women's rights. In religious affairs, Levy noted, Christian women were considered equals of men, and within the household the woman took on the mantle of spiritual custodian. "[This] gives a dignity and a determined c[h]aracter to all she does," he concluded. "No wonder that such mothers will surpass Ours in the bring[ing] up of Children & making better men & women of them than our own degenerated people." In Levy's mind the "degenerated interpreters," or rabbis, had corrupted Judaism by exempting women from many "commandments" and by placing "the man as sole agent & director" of the family. The subsequent loss of dignity and status relegated women to being "merely machines & conveniences."[47]

With a few important exceptions, such as his very public demonstrations in London, Moses Levy promulgated many of his progressive social and religious views in a very cautious manner. Discreet societies, brotherhoods, and, in the case of his abolitionism, anonymous publication—these were his primary tools for implementing ideas that, had they been fully attributed, could have excluded him from the Jewish community or, in the case of his antislavery views, may have caused personal injury or financial loss. Convinced that full and immediate revelation of his plans would let loose a "light . . . too strong to bear," he opted for "shewing it little by little as they do to the blind man when first they remove the cataract from the Eyes."[48] Less controversial topics, such as his amended educational plans, could be broached more openly. For this reason any assessment of the full range of his activities remains quite challenging. Nevertheless, Levy's efforts in the United States would prompt important figures in the Jewish community to examine their positions on a wide array of reform issues. The support of the Myers family was vital in gaining the notice of the "native Hebrew." The Myerses, as characterized by one contemporary, were "well informed, genteel, and uncommonly handsome in the younger part of the family."[49] Moses Myers and his sons proved to be excellent emissaries and maintained substantial social connections as well as bonds of kinship with other high-ranking Jews. This allowed Levy—still an outsider—entrée into a small and elite circle.

Moses and John Myers responded enthusiastically to Levy's call for a national school and figured prominently in eliciting support for it. It is therefore likely that they understood and approved of their guest's entire agenda. What is incontrovertible, however, is Samuel Myers's key role as Levy's intimate friend and trusted protégé. The reasons behind Myers's willingness to challenge convention and to follow a contrary path are not readily apparent. Seven years earlier a tragic event, which initially centered on Moses Myers, altered Samuel's life and may have predisposed both him and his family toward the acceptance of utopian alternatives.

During the evening of 24 May 1811 a heated business dispute developed between Moses Myers and his former partner Richard Bowden. The following morning, while Myers was walking in Norfolk's Market Square, Bowden suddenly struck him with either a cane, a stick, or a butcher's knife, depending on the various accounts of the incident. Unconscious and covered in blood, Myers was carried to his house. Samuel, who assumed that his father had either been killed or was near death, loaded his pistol, entered Bowden's office, and delivered a fatal shot to the man's chest. Samuel fled town but was soon arrested, jailed, and tried for manslaughter. Fortunately, Moses Myers fully recovered from his injuries and made certain that his son had the finest legal representation. Samuel's attorneys included such notables as William Wirt, the future U.S. attorney general. Largely through the efforts of this superior legal team, Samuel Myers was found innocent and by December 1811 was a free man. Because public sentiment in Norfolk staunchly opposed Myer's full exoneration, he was forced to leave town. He lived in Portugal, England, and Scotland and visited family and friends in the United States. Samuel Myers had only recently relocated in Norfolk and undertaken a legal apprenticeship by the time of Moses Levy's arrival.[50] Despite Myers's long absence, some people still disapproved of him, as the following characterization from one of his wife's relatives amply illustrates: "I could say nothing happier for S. Myers than that I never hear his name mentioned, a proof that the propriety of his conduct silences malignity itself. Probably time will erase from the minds of men his past error—but from his own heart can time ever wash the stain away? Alas, I fear it will nestle there until it breaks--amiable, unfortunate young man!"[51]

Consequently, Samuel Myers's earnest zeal could be interpreted as the heartfelt desire of someone who had been alienated and shunned from his hometown and wished to remake his life according to some "enlightened" design. His activist convictions may also have been a way further to please his father, who had obviously approved of Levy. Regardless of whether he was spurred by a sense of atonement, familial obligation, impulsiveness, or the reclamation of lost honor, Samuel Myers signed on as a spokesman for a quest he considered to be far greater than himself, and he certainly felt some recompense in doing so. Myers was also taken with Levy as a man of great substance and integrity. Despite the brevity of their meeting, he reserved high praise for Levy and considered him to be "one of the most respectable [men] whose acquaintance it has been my fortune to contract."[52] Similarly, Levy was immediately taken with his new protégé and valued his "capacity, talents, & youth."[53] Nonetheless, as a visitor who spent limited time in Norfolk, it is entirely probable that Levy was unaware of Samuel Myers's past misfortunes.

Before embarking once more for the Caribbean, Moses Levy reaffirmed his commitment to the "Sacred Cause" when he applied for United States citizenship while on a stay in Rhode Island.[54] This was less an act of allegiance and patriotism and more of a purely pragmatic gesture, for Levy was under the impression that U.S. citizenship would help in his land acquisition plans. The naturalization process would take five years, and Levy was anxious to expedite the procedure.[55] His exact itinerary in New England is not known, but it is possible that his presence was related in some way to another business associate, James De Wolf.[56] De Wolf, a native Rhode Islander and veteran of the Revolutionary War, organized privateering expeditions against the British during the War of 1812, became a pioneer in the textile industry, served in the Rhode Island legislature, and, eventually, became a U.S. senator. He also maintained extensive investments in Cuba and participated in the slave trade. While details are scarce, Levy's association with De Wolf, a man of considerable wealth, appears both amicable and extensive. De Wolf's involvement in the slave trade suggests that Levy may also have been embroiled in this commerce. Moses Levy's intended purchase of "40 or 50 negroes" in Havana late in 1820, presumably for quick sale elsewhere, confirms at least a marginal participation in the "inhuman traffic" that he later so adamantly condemned.[57] Certainly, any involvement would have contributed to the intense regret that Levy exhibited when recalling his days in the West Indies. When he finally abandoned his career and headed for the United States on his colonization mission, he also deliberately avoided the Caribbean, the location of his greatest financial success and, apparently, his greatest remorse.

By mid-November Moses Levy was back in New York City prepared to board a ship bound for the Danish West Indies.[58] Rather than return to Cuba, he devoted the next year in the fulfillment of his most pressing contracts with the Spanish military, sending supplies, mostly foodstuffs, to the hard-pressed "gov[ernment] of Caracas."[59] From the port of La Guaira on the Venezuelan coast and from the Dutch island of Curaçao, an important distribution center to the South American mainland, Levy attended to business and also maintained a steady correspondence with Samuel Myers. Fearing that their letters would be scrutinized by inquisitive officials,

Levy cautioned his colleague "to write with circumspection to Spanish places."[60] Tensions in Venezuela were high, and it was a dangerous destination, even for heavily armed vessels. Incredibly, Levy managed to evade the numerous privateers on the Spanish Main whose sole objective was to prevent supplies from reaching royalist forces. In characteristic manner he accepted these risks as a matter of course. He also viewed the conflict in South America with a mixture of detachment and skepticism. Bolivar's apparent lust for power caused Levy to doubt his intentions. Similarly, he was untouched by Spain's motivations. Surrounded by the heightened passions and uncertainties of war, Levy retained an air of cool pragmatism. "I hope to extract meat from the eater and sweets from the strong," he confided to Myers.[61] Spain's payment for his services would go directly to serving the interests of his less fortunate brethren. In this manner an act of atonement could be made—albeit indirectly—for past degradations.

While on a brief stopover in Puerto Rico, Levy conjured romantic metaphors of his intended refuge: "We have only need to plant fields of simple flowers & sweet herbs. They [persecuted Jews] will soon flock to them." Furthermore, he warned Samuel Myers to be prepared for a drastically altered lifestyle, a spartan existence with few amenities. Levy hoped to meet with Israel Jacobson the following year in order to consolidate their efforts, but he doubted that his schedule would allow him the option of traveling to Germany.[62]

According to plan, Samuel Myers used the utmost tact and discretion when approaching influential members of the Jewish community on Levy's behalf. On 12 February 1819 Myers wrote to Mordecai Noah, former U.S. consul to Tunis and a rising star among the New York Jewish leadership, and revealed enough substance to captivate the astute and ambitious Noah. "You have touched on a chord," Noah replied, "capable, & always producing on my mind great sensations." Such a resounding response must have astounded Myers. Noah continued: "Are we, educated with just views, capable of appreciating the blessings of civil liberty & religious toleration, to do nothing for the less fortunate & less tolerated portion of our brethren? These are questions that we are bound to put to ourselves." Noah admitted that he was more than prepared to "put my shoulders to the wheel" for such a cause and enjoined Myers to communicate more fully on the subject. Without knowing the precise details of the colonization plan, Noah claimed that Myers's "insinuations" were "well understood" and that he had been "engrossed . . . daily & nightly" with similar intentions. "Your Communications will ever be considered confidential by me," he ended, "and I solicit their continuance."[63]

After such an emphatic and amicable reply, it can be assumed that Myers did satisfy Noah's request and revealed even more precise information to the multitalented journalist, playwright, and aspiring public servant. The first appearance of Noah's own colonization scheme, some six months later, could not have been mere coincidence. In addition, other settlement plans were beginning to emerge, most notably the publication of William D. Robinson's pamphlet *Memoir Addressed to Persons of the Jewish Religion in Europe on the subject of emigration to, and settlement in, one of the most eligible parts of the United States of North America* (London, 1819). Robinson, U.S. businessman, former Latin American adventurer, and Gentile, claimed support from England's influential Rothschild family as well as the affluent Cardoza family of Gibraltar. He visited the United States in April 1819 to advance his scheme. On the surface his actions appear to have been a humanitarian response to the antisemitic riots that were erupting in Europe, and it is certain that he did not subscribe to any conversionist ideology. According to Robinson, the spread of violence "will certainly be viewed not only as a disgrace to the present age, but also as a proof that society is still extremely unhinged in the Old World."[64] Not content to restrain himself to purely philanthropic appeals, Robinson also added a strong economic incentive and suggested that "large fortunes" could be made if the settlement were located in the fertile lands of the Mississippi Valley.

Noah, never hesitant to capture the limelight, reap financial rewards, as well as serve a noble quest, may have felt the time was right to preempt his rival colonizers. Noah's early efforts would result, however, in unexpected delays and altered plans. His 1820 proposal to acquire Grand Island in the Niagara River as a Jewish "asylum" caused some controversy, especially since Britain also laid claim to this 17,381-acre tract on the Canadian border. Noah waited an additional six years before he tried to resurrect his Grand Island scheme in his much publicized "Ararat" proclamation. For a time Noah put his own colonization plans on hiatus and endorsed Levy's proposal for a settlement and school. Nothing came of Robinson's venture, since he died before any of his ideas were realized.

In comparison to Noah's intense interest, the response from Samuel Myers's father-in-law, Joseph Marx, exemplified the characteristic caution and pragmatism of an eminent banker and businessman. In Marx's thoughtful reply to his son-in-law, dated within days of Noah's letter, the Richmond financier repudiated the very concept of "forming an extensive Jewish settlement." While admitting that such a plan "might probably attract & collect a number of Jewish Families," Marx foresaw two main problems. First, assimilation into the mainstream would be denied, and therefore "mostly uneducated" European arrivals would not be able to acquire the social skills and "improvements of the mind" which he deemed necessary for success. Second, if "the Settlement were to grow into importance . . . [it would] hasten the very intolerance you dread." "The Zealot would not be idle," he warned, "the moment we are forming into a body politic." A German emigrant himself, Marx had firsthand knowledge of the acculturation process. In his view the seclusion of new arrivals in frontier enclaves would deny newcomers the very opportunities that he took advantage of in his legitimate quest for "Honor & Fame." Clearly, colonization would be another form of ghettoization, and any success would only generate hatred and suppression by Gentiles.[65]

Marx's assimilationist stance as well as his circumspection certainly typified the views of many of his contemporaries. He trusted entirely in the character of his newfound country and had no trouble anticipating that others would benefit as he did, if they were left to their own devices. Real opportunity awaited in the cities, not in some secluded agrarian enclave. His conservative nature overruled utopian solutions, and he also evoked the new standard of individualism. But men such as Levy, Noah, and Myers believed they were on the cutting edge of enlightened thinking as well as philanthropy. In their view the occupation of farming served as a perfect antidote to centuries of physical and psychological oppression in urban ghettoes. A romanticized vision of country life predominated. Levy and his colleagues would certainly have been in agreement with Robinson's plea: "Convey them . . . to a rich soil, a smiling country, and congenial climate, where every thing breathes content and plenty, and where they can eat of the fruit of the trees planted with their own hands."[66] A farmer's physical labor and his pride in providing sustenance both for his family and others seemed an innovative and honorable occupation for the "poorer classes of Jews," the despised peddlers of Europe. A nobility of character, it was thought, would certainly follow if an industrious and pristine environment were provided. As historian Arthur Bestor has posited: "The advocates of experimental communities did not think they were stepping aside from the path of progress into an arcadian retreat. They presented themselves in all earnestness as guides and pathfinders to the future."[67] Joseph Marx may also have been cognizant of the increasing popularity of the communitarian-agrarian ideal, hence his prophetic warning about future success.

While Marx rejected Myers's appeal for frontier communities, he wholeheartedly embraced the educational component of his scheme. He attached much importance to this aspect of the proposal and volunteered to promote the project. But the older man entirely misconstrued Myers's allusion to Jewish "essentials" and interpreted the word in a traditional sense—that is, the retention of "forms & ceremonies." In a friendly demonstration of his own capacity for innovation, however, Marx proposed that Jews could easily substitute Sundays as their day of rest, drastically reducing "time & labour lost" by having to take both Saturdays and Sundays off.[68]

While much of Samuel Myers's idealistic vision may have been lost on Joseph Marx, his persistence would eventually attract the interest of other influential men. In addition, Myers proceeded with Levy's land acquisition plan, using a portion of the forty-five hundred dollars that Levy provided for such a purpose.[69] Acting both for himself and as Levy's proxy, Samuel Myers entered into a convoluted arrangement with another purchaser, Israel Baer Kursheedt of Richmond, whereby all three men owned a total of 5,440 acres of former government land in Illinois.[70] It is unknown whether Kursheedt was fully aware of the purpose of this venture. He may have been merely an investor, since speculation in western lands was rampant.

Also in 1819 Samuel Myers wrote to Moses Levy of his involvement in the legal defense of Lieutenant Uriah P. Levy, a young Jewish naval officer. Myers used his newly acquired judicial skills to confront the antisemitism that pervaded the ranks of the United States Navy. Myers, not yet admitted to the Virginia bar, took part in one of many inequitable courts-martial that Lieutenant Levy had to endure before his belated rise to the rank of commodore. Uriah P. Levy simply would not accept the stream of petty and spiteful insults that were inflicted on him by fellow junior officers and he paid a price for his stubbornness. Unfortunately, Myers did not dissuade the military court from its intentions to cashier the determined officer out of the service, a verdict that was later reversed by President James Monroe.[71]

Despite the negative ruling, Moses Levy reassured Myers of the justness of his struggle. The experience gained "by defending the oppressed [and] protecting the innocent" would enable Myers to be of even more service to their mutual cause. All too often, Levy counseled, "your profession is disgraced in many hands by making the exercise of the Law the hatchet to hew down justice." By using his talents in such an exceptional fashion Myers was living up to the highest ideals of his profession and thereby far exceeded the mere "drudgery" of commerce.[72] Unstated, however, was the fact that the naval affair merely confirmed Levy's pessimism regarding the position of Jews in Gentile society. The "persecution of contempt" which Levy objected to in Europe was still present to some degree in the United States. Jews, like other members of stigmatized minorities, had to deal with the social and psychological restraints imposed upon them. Individuals proceeded at their own peril if they, like the lieutenant, did not demean themselves and reassure members of the dominant group of their superior status.[73] This cultural oppression did not go unrecognized, for it rankled the egalitarian sensibilities of such men as Thomas Jefferson, who viewed antisemitism with great enmity. "More remains to be done," Jefferson once confided to Mordecai Noah. "For altho' we are free by the law, we are not so in practice; public opinion erects itself into an Inquisition and exercises its office with as much fanaticism as fans the flames of an Auto da fé."[74]

During the spring and summer Moses Levy divided his affairs between La Guaira, an embattled fortress and military depot that had already fallen twice to the rebel forces, and the island of Curaçao.[75] While on Curaçao, he tried to persuade the large and fractious Jewish population to set aside its internal squabbles and institute a school for Jewish youth. Levy's attention also turned to the educational welfare of his two remaining children, who were still on the Danish islands. He considered sending both Rachel and David to join their older siblings in England, but after "mature delibera-tion" he thought that his nine-year-old boy would "do better in America," but only if Samuel Myers would assume his guardianship. Knowing very little of the youngster's disposition, Levy nevertheless selected him to be the recipient of a more unconventional schooling. "I want him to be educated in such a manner," Levy wrote to Myers, "as to give him a Chance of his being some use to our undertaking." This meant a general education under the guidance of a liberal Unitarian minister who, undoubtedly, would con-vey a progressive outlook and would not interfere with the child's Jewish identity. Religious observance would consist of nothing more than to rest on Saturdays and to abstain from pork. Levy expected that, after being endowed with "simple ideas" and unencumbered by religious orthodoxy, his son David, when fully grown, would become an asset to their mission. "As a Son I give him up to Our Cause," he proclaimed. "I hope that he may prove worthy of it."[76]

Myers agreed to assume guardianship, and in June 1819 Levy arranged for David to leave St. Thomas in the company of his longtime partner, Emanuel Benjamin.[77] Levy knew that Philip Benjamin, then residing in Wilmington, North Carolina, had recently consented to take in his brother's four children and to place them in a local school. The trip would offer safe passage for David, who would then be met by Samuel Myers and escorted to Norfolk.[78] Levy regarded Philip Benjamin's situation in Wilmington as far from ideal, and he was adamant that David not stay long. David was promptly taken to Norfolk, but, rather than follow Levy's unique ground rules for the boy's education, Myers enrolled him in the reputable Norfolk Academy, the same institution that Samuel and his brothers attended as youngsters. The boy would also enjoy the comforts of the Myers's Norfolk home rather than stay at a boarding school, as Levy expected. David's enrollment in the Norfolk Academy, much under the influence of unenlightened "Christian enthusiasts," in Levy's estimation, would later cause great anguish and concern over the boy's welfare.[79]

By the end of summer it became very clear to Levy that Moses Myers's long-established company was heading into great difficulty. The family's Baltimore branch was forced to close, and in Curaçao Levy waited in vain for the provisions that he had paid for six months earlier. Levy was "duty bound" to deliver a large shipment of rice and beans to the hard-pressed loyalist government in Venezuela, and the delay caused "great injury indeed." Regardless of the hurricane season, Levy dispatched his schooner *Noah Brown* to his agents Bailey & Russell in New York City to ascertain the problem and to facilitate delivery.[80]

5. INCIDENT AT CURAÇAO

*T*he uncertainties of the business world did not prevent Levy from continuing what he regarded as his ministry. He remained keenly interested in the status of Jews wherever he traveled and was anxious to relay his impressions to Samuel Myers. Curaçaon Jews were undergoing a tragic upheaval during Levy's stay on the island, a situation that troubled him deeply. The divisiveness and enmity, centering on the employment of a newly arrived and much reviled hazzan, eventually resulted in excommunications and even formal renunciations of faith. In fact, the episode ranks as one of the most troublesome in the entire history of the island and threatened the largest Jewish community in the Western Hemisphere with ruin.[1] Regardless of Levy's unease toward traditional Judaism, he strongly upheld the notion that the "union" of all Jews superseded national identity and was "the fundamental point of our religion."[2] While a substantial part of his character certainly leaned toward the quixotic, Levy nevertheless demonstrated his ability to devise practical solutions. During his several months stay on Curaçao he assumed an active leadership role in the synagogue, Mikvé Israel, and promoted a method of reconciliation which was successfully adopted, with minor variations, two years later. In the process he exhibited a remarkable capacity for compromise and diplomacy, traits that would also serve him well during his future endeavors in both the United States and England.

At first glance Curaçao presented a welcome aspect. On 4 April 1819 Moses Levy entered the Dutch colony's superb natural harbor and shortly encountered an extraordinary sight. The main commercial section of the capital town of Willemstad was completely closed not for any Christian holiday but because it was the first day of Passover. "In no part of the world have I seen the Jews appear to have as much weight in a com[m]unity," Levy wrote to Samuel Myers.[3] For someone who had seen much of the Atlantic world and had just committed himself to forming a Jewish colony, the island's cultural and religious freedoms fascinated Levy and ran counter to his rather pessimistic expectations. Indeed, while Curaçaon Jews numbered about a thousand, ghettoization and repression were nonexistent.[4] Unlike any other location Levy had visited, he found that Jews were often planters, despite the island's poor soil and dry climate. Fascinated, Levy presented Myers with a detailed sketch of the town and harbor as well as a lengthy description of the inhabitants.[5]

The common vernacular was a creole language called Papiamento—"a medly of corrupted Spanish, Portuguese & Dutch"—but many also spoke proper French, Portuguese, English, and Dutch. Levy estimated that, while Jews composed one-third of the entire population, they held half of the wealth of the island and constituted the majority of positions in commercial management. Despite their reputation as the most "polished" segment of the population, Levy reckoned that the older generation of Jews lagged behind "a century or two to any European congregation."[6] The irony, of course, was that, although their lives were free from ghetto oppression, Haskalah values did not hold much sway with the Jews on this island located forty-three miles from the Venezuelan coast. One result of their isolation was a scarcity of formal education for Jewish youth, a fact that Levy tried to rectify without success.

The obvious cause of Mikvé Israel's troubles was its new hazzan, Jeosuah M. Piza. Selected by the "mother community" in Amsterdam, Piza was an immediate disappointment to most congregants. Dour and hard of hearing, he nevertheless began to institute some unnamed "innovations" in the liturgy and was immediately reprimanded. Despite orders from Amsterdam to conform to the wishes of the local congregation, Piza's defiance surfaced again, this time in the form of a particular word pronunciation. During the traditional blessing of the wine, *Bore P'ri Hagefen* (creator of the fruit of the vine), the hazzan substituted the unfamiliar *Hagafen,* a variation of the Hebrew preferred by Dutch Jews. This minute departure from the norm caused immediate and forceful objections from the most conservative element, and Piza's recalcitrant attitude caused the affair to escalate out of control. This sort of liturgical quibbling was antithetical to Levy's progressive nature. In his letters to Myers, Levy could not restrain his sarcasm. "This poor devil [Piza]," Levy exclaimed, "[was] cringing, malicious, spitefull & mean—none of these disqualifications are alleged against this man, no, the charge is in[n]ovation, as they call it." In a satirical mood he referred to the two warring factions simply as "Gafens" and "Gefens."[7]

In Levy's version of events Hazzan Piza relished the opportunity to deliver the offending word in his readings. Spitefully, the hazzan paused and then exaggerated his pronunciation while looking upward at the powerful few who supported him. Infuriated, the "Gefens" demanded Piza's removal, and, when the Mahamad, or synagogue leadership, backed the miscreant hazzan over the wishes of a sizable portion of the congregation, a host of painful repercussions followed. Ninety-nine members officially resigned from Mikvé Israel, and, Levy observed, "the major part of the Congregation" avoided the synagogue entirely. Marriages and circumcisions were performed separately, regular services were held in members' homes, and the renegade faction even started their own cemetery. Among other retaliations the Mahamad stationed a police officer inside the synagogue and also callously ejected persons from the community poorhouse if they dared to show any support for the separatists. In this combative environment Levy valiantly tried to interest leaders of both factions to erect schools "for the education of Jewish youth," and his "fine speeches" actually managed to make an impression. While some agreed with Levy's arguments, the general mood was hardly conducive to such an enterprise. Finally, at the request of certain influential members, Levy agreed to attempt a formal reconciliation.[8]

On 25 May 1819 Moses Levy composed a rather remarkable document, and copies were presented to both sides. Written in English with the inclusion of appropriate Hebrew phrases, his appeal was crafted with utmost care and masterful diplomacy. Unity, forgiveness, and the common suffering of all Jews were the key themes, and no mention was made of the disputed Hebrew. He attributed the real origin of the "unhappy division" to "misunderstanding." Any proposed remedy could not involve "stern and harsh Justice" but, rather, required "the soft, tender, flexible, & rich emollients of Charity and brotherly love." Levy's address was both passionate and persuasive: "Our only stay my brethren is union, to keep and hold this precious gift of heaven ought to be our first[,] our last duty; to it we must sacrifice all other considerations. . . . pause! pause, before you go further, if in this difference there is any point in religion (as some will have it) we cannot, we must not sacrifice the fundamental, the corner stone, the pillar of it, to one of its smallest points. It will be like endangering the f[o]undation of a house, for the preservation of one of its shingles."[9]

Levy's heartfelt appeal for unity revealed his true priorities. Vicious feuding and hatred were more repellent to him than the needless hairsplitting over *Hagefen*. After all, Jews had weathered persecution from others but had always remained intact as God's chosen. At the conclusion of his address Levy presented a simple proposal. The first step toward the desired reconciliation would be for each party to nominate three representatives, "in order that they may meet & agree upon the best & nearest mode of making every individual happy by a perfect union." Formal arbitration, with each faction on equal footing with the other, offered the best hope of peace. In presenting this plan, Levy followed the Danish model of mediation, an innovative practice that bypassed the traditional court system. While this approach was much favored on the Danish islands, particularly as it related to civil disputes, it was a rarity elsewhere in the Caribbean and was certainly not part of the synagogue tradition. On Curaçao all previous conflicts among Jewish congregants—and there were numerous incidents through the years—were settled by the unilateral rulings of the Mahamad, the Amsterdam synagogue leadership, or the governor and Island Council.[10]

On the surface Levy's recommendation may appear well outside the norm, but there was ample precedent for mediation within the Jewish tradition. Maimonides, for instance, strongly urged this technique to settle disputes, and the same striving for compromise and for peaceful reconciliation can be seen throughout the Bible and the Talmud. Furthermore, Levy's suggestion of appointing three representatives loosely followed Jewish civil law (*dinei mamonot*), which allowed litigants to select three laymen to sit in judgment and to seek compromise solutions. This type of arrangement, however, was never intended to be used for intra-congregational disputes. Traditionally, the responsibility for limiting communal strife and for fashioning remedies was the purview of the synagogue elite. In this instance that select group was incapable of fulfilling its role, and it was fortunate indeed that someone of Levy's stature could play the part of peacemaker.[11]

Contrary to the Curaçaon norm that typically placed all strangers at the margins of society, Levy's Sephardic credentials, his reputation as a high-ranking merchant, and his well-intentioned manner allowed him to transcend his outsider status, and he was actually accorded much deference.

Replies (in Portuguese) came in from the leaders of the two factions. Eighty-four-year-old Abraham de Mordechay Senior and the equally venerable Isaac de Abraham de Marchena wrote on behalf of the "discontented party," and Moise Cardoze, president of Mikvé Israel, responded on the side of the Mahamad.[12] Senior and Marchena presented a litany of past grievances, but their praise for Levy's intentions was profound. In their eyes Levy was a "benevolent Stranger, a compassionate Being from overseas" who came "to preside like an angel of peace, as a mediator between the majority of a community and its Regents!" Ultimately, however, they deemed the Mahamad's behavior so offensive that they declined Levy's kind-hearted intervention. In their minds Jeosuah Piza was an "imposter with Ecclesiastic decoration" who was maliciously appointed "with the sole aim of irritating us." The Mahamad's arrogant decisions had defamed their "Holy House" and could not be overlooked. "[Any] mediation between us and that group is useless and inadequate," the separatists retorted, "and it would not be fitting to cover it with the mantle of honor." Cardoze, informed of this refusal, accepted Levy's invitation in an effort to gain the higher moral ground and, apparently, to win favor with the Curaçaon government. Levy addressed the Gefen faction once more and persuaded its members to reverse their decision. Yet an amicable resolution was not immediately forthcoming. Disappointed that they had not truly adopted a spirit of accommodation and brotherly love, Levy considered each side's acquiescence as a mere tactical ploy, an opportunity to "outwit" the other by the selection of superior representatives. Unknown to most of those involved was Levy's prior meeting with the governor's secretary, Willem Prince, a fellow Freemason, who, despite his disagreement with many of Levy's conclusions, promised to promote acceptance of his plan. Levy described Prince as the "real president" of the synagogue and "the spring of all their actions." Significantly, the day after Levy delivered his address, he found the secretary in a "tête à tête" with Cardoze.[13]

The role that Levy played in the Piza incident as well as his collaboration with Willem Prince have gone unacknowledged in subsequent historical accounts, most notably Isaac S. and Suzanne A. Emmanuel's *History of the Jews of the Netherlands Antilles* (1970)—still the most definitive study of Curaçaoan Jews. Given Levy's relatively brief residence in the colony and the informal nature of his activities, it is not surprising that he escaped notice by island historians. Until very recently, the bulk of Levy's correspondence to Samuel Myers—which included his address to the Curaçao congregation—remained largely unnoted in a Norfolk, Virginia, archive.[14]

As one may suspect, the bitter feuding between the two factions was certainly a manifestation of a deeper social rift within the Curaçaon Jewish community. Indeed, there is strong evidence to conclude that class conflict was an important component in the controversy. In the "discontented party's" reply to Levy, the group addressed the synagogue leaders' propensity to "raise themselves above their equals . . . forgetting that the greatest grandeur in wealth is humility."[15] Personal riches did play an important role in the selection of the Mahamad, but these individuals did not have a monopoly on wealth. Social rank, rather than affluence alone, should also be considered in any assessment. As synagogue leaders, these men were not only endowed with elite status, but they were also expected to act as true custodians of the congregation. In this capacity Moise Cordoze and his associates failed—rather dramatically—to rise to the occasion. In fact, Levy's correspondence presents a complex portrait of island life, an environment in which social position, jealousy, and excessive feelings of family honor were paramount. These tensions certainly set the tone for the divisiveness and ill will that followed.

As Levy surmised, the whole affair could be reduced to a "formidable . . . point of honor." The Mahamad's support of Piza had so affronted the "discontented" that these men, together with their wives and children, were fully prepared to forsake their lives and property rather than compromise. One can also conclude that the Mahamad held similar sensitivities and that these leaders viewed the actions of the renegade faction as an assault on both their authority and honor. Long-established family alliances were another factor. Indeed, the influence of extended families—called *famiya* in the local dialect—permeated the Jewish community and was analogous to clan organizations.[16] "All," Levy declared, "are infected with the pernicious pride of family honor." As an example of the prevalence of this "empty pride," Levy found it impossible for a visitor such as himself to find a Jewish boardinghouse: "because it looks too much like tavern keeping which is degrading to these nobles."[17] This heightened concern over outward appearances, the high value placed on the opinions of others, and their veneration of ancestors further defined the Curaçaon Jews as participants in an ancient honor code that had little in common with Enlightenment ideals or, in Levy's view, true Judaism.[18]

Regardless of the community's faults, Levy presumed that in time "policy will oblige them" to reach an accord. Although negotiations were initiated, matters rapidly disintegrated after Levy's departure, and feuding reached new heights. Bodies were exhumed from the old cemetery to be reburied in the new one, and, because the colonial government would not recognize any other congregation than Mikvé Israel, eighty-two separatists officially renounced their faith rather than yield to the despotic Mahamad. Notably, their renunciation included an oath to "recognize the existence of one God," a legal loophole that allowed all of them to nullify their statement at a later date.[19] Finally, on 1 September 1820 the separatists petitioned the Dutch king—through their governor—for redress. Rather than alert the government in the Netherlands to the embarrassing situation, the island administration retained the petition until a resolution could be fashioned. Significantly, the method ultimately relied upon was a variation of Moses Levy's earlier proposal, with the addition of arbitrators from the Curaçaon government—all things considered, a most unusual experiment in conflict resolution. Willem Prince was chosen as one of the Mahamad's representatives. On 18 December 1821 prayers were offered in thanks, Jeosuah Piza agreed to resign his post, and Mikvé Israel returned as one congregation. The agreed-upon scapegoats for Piza's dismissal were the government arbitrators. In accordance with the community's stringent code of honor, neither side declared itself victor, and all documents in the proceedings were ordered to be burned.[20]

One may be tempted to view this entire episode as an isolated island squabble that escalated out of control, but some scholars have actually linked this affair with the genesis of Reform Judaism. Most notably, historian Jonathan Sarna has placed the difficulties on Curaçao within a larger reform impulse that spanned both sides of the Atlantic and eventually led to the well-known events at Charleston's Beth Elohim congregation.[21] Because the Charleston schism and the emergence of the Reformed Society of Israelites had such a major impact within American Judaism, the implications of any such connection are most serious.

As this event has demonstrated, however, the mere act of dissent did not qualify the separatists as religious reformers. Indeed, the incident at Curaçao was antithetical to Jacobsonian ideals and more closely resembled the intracommunal conflicts of the seventeenth and eighteenth centuries. These earlier European disputes—complete with direct appeals to the monarchy—were indicative of a growing discontent with authoritarianism and sometimes erupted in response to the arbitrary acts of Jewish oligarchs.[22] Internal power struggles rather than challenges to religious orthodoxy usually defined these imbroglios. In addition, the actions of the Curaçaoan Jews should be viewed within the context of their own exceptionally conservative, isolated, and honor-bound culture. Surely, if the progressive ideas of Israel Jacobson had any presence at all on Curaçao at this time, it resided in the transient form of Moses Elias Levy. It was Levy—rather than any of the elderly, traditionalist leaders of Curaçao—who actually had the most in common with Charleston's future "Israelite" firebrands.

While finding the time to relay numerous details about the affair to Samuel Myers, Levy also grew increasingly worried about the absence of his provisions. This state of affairs corresponded with several other misfortunes in Moses Levy's life. "Everything seems to be gloomy in the Commercial world," he complained. The failure of a London establishment in which he had extensive dealings, coupled with the collapse of a new Havana "House of Commission," due to the unexpected death of Levy's copartner in the venture, had already strained his resources. Money was tight, and Levy was determined not to rely on credit from his various American friends. "I don't know what will be the Consequences," he declared impatiently, "if I don't receive the supplies I wrote for."[23] To compound Levy's difficulties further, on 7 August 1819 Bolivar achieved a remarkable victory over General Morillo's forces at the Battle of Boyacá. While Venezuela was still under royalist rule, this triumph was a strong indicator that Spain's days were numbered in South America.

The source of Myers & Sons's difficulties in fulfilling Levy's order was nothing less than the Panic of 1819, the United States' first major economic depression. The flurry of commercial activity and land speculation which erupted after the conclusion of the War of 1812 came to a resounding end. In Norfolk the depression was intensified by the liberal borrowing terms previously established by the local branch of the Bank of the United States.

"Very large sums were borrowed," according to one contemporary, "and a heavy business was done." Accordingly, many of the principal merchants, including Myers & Sons, found themselves in great debt, and the "consequences were ruinous." The community had already suffered through the war with Great Britain. Now, after several years of bountiful growth, companies failed, and many individuals were reduced to poverty.[24] Nationally, thousands of persons were sent to debtors' prisons. On 28 October 1819, several months after the closing of its Norfolk establishment, Myers's firm declared bankruptcy. In the process many assets were lost, including Moses Levy's portion of the Illinois land. Creditors allowed Moses Myers his "household and kitchen furniture," and he continued to reside in his mansion, although he now paid a yearly rental.[25] Samuel Myers and his brother John were also caught in the downward spiral. In 1820 John endured a brief prison term, and the following year Samuel too was forced into bankruptcy.[26] In the end Moses and Samuel Myers were in debt to Levy for ten thousand dollars.[27] Young David Levy, only recently separated from his mother in St. Thomas, dwelled as a newcomer in an unfamiliar household that had narrowly averted complete disaster and managed to stay intact only by the benevolence of creditors.

Before learning of the collapse of Myers & Sons and unaware of Samuel's own misfortunes, Levy could not resist sharing his views regarding the causes of the economic downturn in the United States. In doing so, he revealed his acceptance of a biblical economic standard in which morality superseded individual self-interest.[28] "As for the difficulties of the American commercial world with its stimulant—*The Banks*—it more than deserve[s] them," he asserted to Myers. "Your countrymen are intoxicated with their advantages & instead of making use of them where their strength & real utility points to they turn them to acquire the tran[s]cient glories of other nations."[29] Americans were "gifted by their indulgent creator" with abundant resources. Therefore, unlike most other nations, U.S. citizens could share in a more equitable lifestyle, a self-sufficient, agrarian existence that did not require support from or involvement in the banking and financial sector. Economic collapse, according to Levy, was apt punishment from God because Americans had strayed from the plain and virtuous path. Ultimately, vanity, greed, and selfish commercial exploitation had to be vanquished. Influenced by evangelical asceticism, Levy declared that the "considerate man" should discard "imaginary wants" and "be content with simplicity & competence." "The vacant house," Levy judged, would inevitably lead to "the cultivation of the mind."[30] Once avarice could be restrained, a financial equilibrium would take hold. Despite the country's immediate misfortunes, Levy was still optimistic. He viewed the United States of America as unique among nations—a true land of promise where, through proper example, the mistaken notions of the past could be avoided.

6. NEW BEGINNINGS

*B*y the fall of 1819 Moses Levy eagerly awaited the arrival of the *Noah Brown* to take him from Curaçao to Havana. He viewed the royalist position as increasingly desperate and judged that the popular mood in South America had shifted to Bolivar.[1] For the first time tensions arose between Levy and Samuel Myers, apparently brought on by Myers's financial losses as well as the forfeiture of the Illinois land. Levy assumed that he could freely "indulge in ideas" without offending Myers. Furthermore, Levy claimed that he "would have never touched upon the subject" of the land purchase in his letters had he been aware of his protégé's true situation. Given the magnitude of Levy's losses, he exhibited uncommon restraint: "I pray that you may not have the least consideration for me & dispose of things in their regular course. We'll not want for lands in better times." Despite Myers & Sons's bankruptcy, some business managed to continue under the supervision of appointed trustees. Moses Levy demonstrated his continued loyalty to the family by advancing three thousand silver dollars for the purchase of more foodstuffs required at La Guaira. He also placed nine ounces of gold in Samuel Myers's care. Additionally, he entrusted Myers with his personal items, such as his books, will, and *mohel* (circumcision) instruments—all of which were sent to Norfolk via another of Levy's ships. Levy informed Myers that he had chosen him, along with his Philadelphia friend Rudolph Dietz, as one of the executors to his will. Distressed by Myers's defensive ire, Levy pleaded for their continued friendship and brotherly demeanor. "For heavens sake," he implored, "don't write me so again."[2]

Levy's gestures placated Myers, and during the next several months Myers continued a more regular and congenial correspondence. With his sense of honor restored, he proceeded with his duties on Levy's behalf. Among various other contacts, Myers made significant overtures to the "President & Vestry" of Charleston's Beth Elohim synagogue, then one of the leading congregations in the United States. Only one document has survived which refers to Myers's hitherto unknown "Circular" as well as his "several letters on the subject of the Jews" which were sent to Charleston during this period. Written by Dr. Mordecai H. DeLeon, a self-described "Enlightened" Jew, this brief letter was addressed to Myers and dated 15 February 1820. DeLeon, the future mayor of Columbia, South Carolina, and a physician of some renown, informed his Norfolk friend of the congregation's refusal to "Co-operate with their Bretheren in Virginia." DeLeon was clearly frustrated by the negative response, both among the "lower orders" and the "more Enlightened parts of the Denomination." Because Myers was actively promoting Levy's ideas at the time, one can easily assume that DeLeon's effort was directly related to the ongoing "Sacred Cause." Unfortunately, details are very limited. Nevertheless, questions naturally arise about what effect, if any, the incident had on the subsequent actions of those congregants who rebelled and launched the Reformed Society of Israelites in 1824. The vehement disapproval that DeLeon noted suggests that Myers could have revealed far more of Levy's radical plan than was originally intended. It is difficult to imagine that philanthropic educational appeals or equally well-intentioned pleas on behalf of distressed European Jewry could have elicited such a negative response. While evidence is meager, the Myers-DeLeon affair presents an intriguing, although ill-defined, scenario of intellectual conflict during one of the seminal stages in Reform Judaism.[3] The incident also underscores the often circuitous influence that Levy had in the United States.

It has been commonly assumed that the actions of Charleston's "Israelites" constituted the "first organized attempt to reform Jewish liturgy and practice in North America."[4] Yet the efforts of Levy and Myers—a unique and potent influence that has previously gone unacknowledged—also constituted an organized challenge to American orthodoxy. Through Moses Levy's leadership, vision, and financial support, new concepts concerning Jewish religious life, colonization, and education were introduced throughout the eastern seaboard. Far from being the prototypical ideologue, Levy's pragmatic nature enabled him to modify his radical preferences in order to attain the support of as many leading Jews as possible.

As the events in Charleston unfolded, Levy, in Havana, became absorbed with his settlement plans. The financial crisis in the United States presented formidable obstacles, but a diplomatic breakthrough the previous year also offered new opportunities. On 22 February 1819 Secretary of State John Quincy Adams and Spain's minister, Luis de Onis, signed a document that ceded East and West Florida to the United States. The Adams-Onis Treaty would be subject to further modifications and delay, but the inevitability of U.S. jurisdiction was a forgone conclusion. Accordingly, during the winter of 1820 Levy made full use of his connections in Havana to pursue a most ambitious land acquisition scheme.

Anticipating the loss of Spain's Florida provinces, Ferdinand VII transferred immense tracts in these regions into private hands, the beneficiaries being three of the king's royal favorites. One of these individuals, the duke of Alagon, suddenly became the proprietor of half of peninsular Florida. The validity of all these grants became a highly contested issue in the United States. Nevertheless, the duke's eight million–acre tract was offered for sale in Havana.[5]

In Levy's opinion not only did these lands offer a tremendous value—the entire Alagon grant could be purchased for a mere one million dollars—but the timing was fortuitous.[6] News of both William Robinson's and Mordecai Noah's colonization plans had reached Levy in Cuba. These schemes presented a real concern because they could direct financial resources into what Levy believed were dubious and futile enterprises. He regarded Noah's selection of uninhabited Grand Island, New York, situated near the imposing Niagara Falls, as a particularly poor location for any "Colony of Agriculturalists." Indeed, both plans required the transportation of families, at "immense Sums," to remote regions of the interior. Levy predicted that the neophyte farmers, like "the Israelites of old," would soon flee for the comfort and opportunities of the coastal cities. Furthermore, he was particularly displeased by what he perceived to be the underlying financial motives of these rival undertakings. In fact, monetary incentives figured prominently in Robinson's proposal. Likewise, Levy implied that Noah aspired "to nothing above the character of a Broker." Both plans, according to Levy, neglected the selection of the settlers themselves and mistakenly assigned the highest priority to land acquisition. "These people want first to obtain lands," he declared to Myers, "and we want first to get people worthy of them."[7] Frederick Warburg, whom Levy had recruited several years earlier, would supervise this facet of his plan while in Europe. No further mention was made of Levy's original enthusiasm for the Illinois frontier.

The appearance of two highly publicized settlement proposals coupled with continued reports of European persecution caused Levy to reevaluate his approach to the American Jewish community. While in Cuba, he had no way of judging the depth of support for either Noah or Robinson, but, in order to tap whatever momentum existed, he felt he had to respond with his own bold initiative. Noah may have envisioned the purchase of Grand Island, but Levy believed he could deliver the entire Alagon grant, a virtual country in itself. The cost would be shared by a consortium of philanthropists.[8] Half of this land, Levy assumed, would be "fit for Cotton, Rice and Indian Corn and some spots will produce Sugar." Further, he was informed that "the Olive and the Fig as well as most of the fruits of Europe grow in perfection." Families could be transported to Florida for a fraction of the cost of traveling hundreds of miles into the interior. The mild climate would also benefit newcomers who were unaccustomed to the rigors of farming. Moreover, the peninsula afforded easy access to both sides of the Atlantic, and the progress of the settlement could be monitored more closely by its "Protectors." In conclusion, Levy expected land values to increase by a factor of twenty or thirty, a vital concern for the colony's future well-being. Once again, he was determined that Myers keep these proposals out of public notice and submit details only "to fifty persons of our most enlightened and liberal Bretheren." Their mission was of such great importance and the obstacles so immense that caution was the only appropriate course. Ironically, Levy predicted that the greatest objection would come from their fellow Jews and not from Gentiles. "The less noise we make," he reasoned, "the surer will be our success."

Levy was aware of U.S. opposition to the Spanish grants. Consequently, he recommended to Myers that agents of suitable character and credentials approach President James Monroe and attempt to "excite his benevolent heart" to look favorably upon their project. Levy admitted that he was a neophyte to Washington politics, but it was conceivable that their compassionate enterprise would "concur with the Policy of the Government of the United States." Animosity toward the grants, especially if based solely on a "Point of Honor," would likely diminish as soon as the president was informed of their altruistic intentions. After all, with the consent of the United States, a large segment of the new Florida territory would be transformed into a productive haven for the downtrodden of Europe.[9]

As a businessman, Moses Levy was certainly adept at ascertaining risks and formulating compromise solutions. Similarly, while he may have differed in his colonization approach, he still realized the benefit that could arise from a united effort. For this reason he ordered Samuel Myers to proceed immediately to New York City and to inform Mordecai Noah of their new initiative. If Myers could succeed in delaying Noah and others from entering into any definitive engagements while keeping their "minds and hearts alive for some undertaking," then Levy could personally meet with them in a few months to present his case. Levy also insisted that Myers call on the Gratz family in Philadelphia and keep them abreast of developments. "The good and excellent Miss G[ratz]," Levy assumed, "will no doubt take the part of the angel of mercy and plead in favor of the cause."

Although Levy was especially optimistic about Florida's prospects, this region did little to inspire confidence among the American Jewish leadership. Outside of the small and increasingly dilapidated garrison towns of St. Augustine and Pensacola, the Florida frontier was regarded as a dangerous location, populated by hostile Indians, bandits, and runaway slaves and prone to malaria, yellow fever, and unhealthy "miasmas."[10] Aside from the earlier writings of naturalist William Bartram during the previous century, few substantive accounts of Florida existed, a fact that certainly contributed to its mysterious and exotic reputation. Abortive incursions by the Georgia militia and the U.S. military during the so-called Patriot War, coupled with Andrew Jackson's recently concluded First Seminole War, confirmed the region's image as an unsettled and perilous destination. Thus, while Rebecca Gratz sympathized with the humanitarian impulses of colonization, she found the Levy-Myers's Florida proposal wanting. "Some gentlemen to the south have the same object in view as Noah," Gratz politely noted to a friend. "Me thinks I would place foreigners in a more interior situation, both for their own security, and that of our borders in case of war."[11] This sentiment was apparently shared by the majority of Jewish leaders.

In contrast to his American colleagues, Levy was long accustomed to both life in the tropics and to high-risk ventures and, consequently, viewed Florida with intense optimism. He was certain that the cession to the United States would transform the neglected wilderness area into a productive territory. The pristine Florida landscape became a vast tabula rasa on which Levy could implement his idealistic vision. In March 1820, without waiting for Myers's reply, he purchased 15,000 acres from Don Fernando de la Maza Arredondo, a Havana business associate with major assets in East Florida. This acreage, located on the St. Johns River just south of Lake George, was not part of the Alagon controversy, and Arredondo's land grants, awarded earlier by Alejandro Ramírez for services rendered during the Patriot War, appeared beyond reproach. That same month Levy sent an agent on an expedition to claim the Florida land and to assess its value. Based on this initial favorable report, he extended the purchase to include 52,900 acres located in two widely dispersed parcels in East Florida. At the very least, he reasoned, these tracts could be quickly sold at a large profit after the U.S. assumed jurisdiction. Indeed, with a total price of $38,875 these lands appeared to be a bargain, averaging 73 cents an acre. Levy also managed to barter $15,000 worth of copper kettles as part of the deal. Technically, however, any such purchase by foreign nationals, and most especially by Jews, was prohibited by Spanish law, so an arrangement was made by a Cuban firm to hold title and then transfer it to Levy as soon as the Florida cession was concluded. By virtue of his substantial connections in Cuba, Levy became one of the very first investors in the future United States territory.[12]

Also during this period, the political situation in Cuba changed dramatically. In March 1820 a military coup in Spain forced Ferdinand VII to accept the liberal tenets of the Constitution of 1812. Previously, Alejandro Ramírez had instituted important reforms on the island, such as the termination of the royal tobacco monopoly and the initiation of free trade with foreigners. According to Moses Levy, Ramírez's efforts resulted in a striking twofold increase in government revenue. Also through the superintendent's endeavors, a botanical garden, anatomical museum, national academy of fine arts, and numerous public schools were founded. For the most part the new reforms and institutions were welcomed by the sugar oligarchy and the emerging bourgeoisie, but they had little immediate impact on the lives of small farmers. The oppressive Spanish system of press censorship also continued unabated. After the constitution was reinstated, provincial elections and a free press became tangible signs of a new democratic regime. Unfortunately, the advent of press freedom did not, in all cases, bring about a corresponding sense of editorial accuracy and good judgment; soon partisan publications created a tyranny of their own making. José de Aguiar, a lawyer and editor of the new periodical *El Tio Bartolo,* presented rumors and libelous innuendos concerning the Ramírez administration. Aguiar's motivations appear to have stemmed from vindictiveness, as he had long been denied promotion within that very bureaucracy. In fact, there were many who had been excluded from the superintendent's patronage and therefore desired a change in the power structure. Ramírez's efforts to curtail the lucrative contraband trade also contributed to the discontent. Aguiar's broadsides escalated into direct accusations against the superintendent when the newspaper claimed that Ramírez had offered Treasury appointments for sale. This allegation brought an immediate denunciation from Ramírez, who then sought legal restitution. The superintendent, however, had voluntarily relinquished his judicial authority in Treasury matters shortly before the charge was leveled, and he consequently lost a major advantage. Events escalated, and Ramírez was forced to withdraw from office in August 1820. He died soon after his subsequent appointment as captain-general of Guatemala.[13]

Later historical accounts have stressed Ramírez's innocence and have portrayed him as a victim of an ignoble and vengeful fourth estate. Levy's comments, written in a lengthy newspaper article many years after the event, confirm this interpretation. He derided the offending publications as being the product of a "swarm of lawyers" who were themselves the epitome of corruption. "The instrumentality of the freedom of the press, let loose upon a people unaccustomed to it," presented such an obstacle that "the amiable and upright heart of Ramírez could not contend with [it]." Levy's admired and trusted friend then "fell a martyr to the very constitution he cherished and supported." The final irony, according to Levy, was that Ramírez himself had been credited as the author of the revered Constitution of 1812, a remarkable, and as yet unsubstantiated, achievement that Ramírez supposedly undertook before his appointment in Puerto Rico. Furthermore, Levy asserted, unlike numerous high-ranking Spanish officials who had routinely used their positions to enrich themselves, Ramírez's death in 1821 revealed that his modest estate could not provide for the basic needs of his own family, a fate about which Levy had constantly forewarned his confidant.[14]

Levy's impressions were certainly skewed by a potent desire to defend his associate's honor. Nevertheless, Levy's recollection of Ramírez's downfall offers valuable insight regarding the similarity of their characters and the nature of their friendship. For one, both men were highly adept at compromise and pragmatic action while simultaneously adhering to a lofty idealism. In Ramírez's case a dedication to democratic and liberal reforms did not preclude vigilance on behalf of the king's interests. Both were astute, if not brilliant, men of finance who possessed a certain ambivalence toward their own welfare and often turned a blind eye to mankind's base tendencies. Their trusting temperaments and fine humanitarian impulses could also lead them into serious pitfalls. These traits proved catastrophic for Ramirez and almost equally ruinous for Levy, as he would eventually spend years in impoverishment and isolation. Such "martyrdom," Levy mused in true romantic fashion, was the fate of all genuine reformers.

The change in the political regime as well as the dangers of the hurricane season delayed Levy's departure for America until November 1820.[15] Before leaving Cuba, he was startled to learn that Samuel Myers, who had once proclaimed that he would "not pause or tremble at the task," had withdrawn from Levy's colonization venture. The news was yet another "veil" that had descended over their recent letters. While details are scarce, Myers's decision was probably related to the pressures of his own bankruptcy, his substantial indebtedness to Levy, and the Illinois land debacle—all of which presented Myers with a humiliating scenario. No longer could he afford philanthropic gestures, and, as an honor-bound southerner, he could not accept Levy's continued generosity. Myers was also disheartened that his exertions on behalf of their "polar star" did not bring immediate success; his rejection by the Beth Elohim congregation evidently contributed to his mood.[16] It is doubtful, therefore, that the proposed meeting with President Monroe ever took place. After the cession of the Floridas, Myers planned to leave Virginia with his wife and children in order to pursue a legal career in Pensacola, West Florida. The choice of location would place Myers at an enormous distance from Levy. Not only was Pensacola four hundred miles west of St. Augustine, but the safest and most practical method of travel was to circumnavigate the entire peninsula by ship.

This news did not deter Levy from his plans, but he was, nevertheless, saddened and disappointed by Myers's decision. After all, Levy had judged him to be a man of his word, and he had even entrusted his son to Myers's care. For two years they had engaged each other in extensive correspondence and had established an intimate friendship. Now, as Levy's twenty-year career in the West Indies was drawing to a close and at the precise moment when he needed Myers the most, Levy resigned himself to continue without his colleague. He viewed any setback as an unavoidable component to his righteous and risk-filled undertaking, and he had already relinquished himself to the dictates of Divine Providence. The ancient maladies of "Ignorance & Self interest" could hardly be vanquished without the application of "labour & perseverance."[17] As Levy departed Havana Bay in November, he was filled with a sense of finality and closure. Aside from a single arms shipment that he was unable to deliver, all of his contracts with the Spanish government were satisfactorily concluded. At last he could abandon degrading commerce for the most blessed of causes.

Levy's first destination was Charleston, where, with letters of introduction in hand from Samuel Myers, he met some of the "virtuous of our people." Levy considered his one-week stay as an adequate period to form an opinion of Charleston's large congregation.[18] While his exact itinerary is unknown, he dined at the homes of some of the city's premiere Jewish families, including the residence of the affluent businessman Michael Lazarus. Coincidentally, Lazarus himself had invested heavily in Florida lands, but it is unknown what he thought of Levy's project.[19] In addition, Levy was especially impressed with Myers's friend, Dr. DeLeon. Proceeding onward, Levy introduced himself to Jewish leaders in Richmond and then stopped in at Norfolk to see both the Myers family and his son David. By this time the elderly Moses Myers had assumed responsibility for David's upbringing, an arrangement that evidently satisfied Levy. He then journeyed to Philadelphia and to New York City. While in the North, Moses Levy's proposal for a Jewish school met with particular success. On 9 May 1821 enthusiasm for his ideas resulted in the formation of the Hebrew Society of New York, a select organization that included the newly appointed sheriff of New York City, Mordecai Noah.

Interest in Noah's Grand Island scheme had subsided after it was discovered that Britain had a competing claim on the property. For unknown
reasons support for Robinson also appears to have waned. Therefore, Noah's backing of Levy during this time was highly significant, and, for a while
at least, influential American Jews looked to the new arrival from the West
Indies for leadership. Demonstrating an innate capacity for compromise,
Levy devised a greatly modified proposal in which he made his educational
plans the center of focus. In a printed, three-page "Circular," or leaflet, Levy
utilized his membership in the Hebrew Society of New York to present
twelve resolutions regarding the creation of a boarding school, or *Chenuch,*
a Hebrew word that emphasized practical or vocational training. Levy's
pedagogical concerns were interwoven throughout this document. The
Chenuch, or Probationary, as it was also called, was planned as a coeduca-
tional institution—a significant innovation by itself—and would feature an
unusual curriculum. Instead of teaching a literal and unquestioning adherence to Jewish law, "Hebrew youth" would be taught "to comprehend both
letter and spirit." In addition to instruction in the Hebrew language, boys
and girls would be introduced to the "elementary branches of education,
and such branches of the useful arts and of science." Pestalozzian ideas of
utility and hands-on learning were advocated, a radical departure from
the traditional emphasis on rote memory and dependence on the classics.
In accordance to new reform principles, particular attention was given to
the students' physical activity and health, a concern that had been virtually ignored in the upper-class academies. In accordance with the ideals of
Israel Jacobson, the acquisition of basic farming skills—for boys only—was
given special emphasis. After the completion of their course of study, male
students would be given land in the vicinity on which to start their own
farms and to raise a family.[20]

Notably, it was further resolved: "That a tract of land of suitable magnitude shall be purchased in a healthy and central part of the Union, for
the accommodation of a certain number of families, and the establishment
of this Institution." Therefore, Levy's dual concepts of Jewish settlement
and education would be implemented, albeit in a different location than
Florida. While the resolutions did not specifically mention Jewish immi-
grants, it is most unlikely that the school was intended for the children of
affluent contributors. On the contrary, the entire endeavor was conceived

as a purely philanthropic enterprise, and no mention was made of student fees. Therefore, it appears that the *Chenuch* was designed, like Jacobson's schools, to serve the needs of the Jewish poor, recent arrivals included, and to inculcate proper civil and religious values. Aside from purely humanitarian motives, interest in such an undertaking may have been a reaction to the appearance of a conversionist organization in New York City during the previous year, the American Society for Meliorating the Condition of the Jews. One of this organization's publicized goals was to form farming colonies where converts, presumably of the poorest class, would be provided with both a livelihood and a Christian education.[21] Similarly, the Hebrew Society of New York lauded Moses Levy's "plan for the education of Jewish youth" and acknowledged his laudable intentions of "ameliorating the condition of the Jews."

The circular was never intended to be distributed to the general public. Instead, it served as a method of introduction for Levy, who would then solicit the patronage of other prominent and liberal-minded Jews. It is clear that whatever the resolutions lacked in specificity would be left to Moses Levy to "explain at length," a tactic that reflected Levy's desire for confidentiality. The leaflet called for additional "societies" to be formed in other cities, and Levy soon initiated meetings with "the principal Hebrew Residents" throughout the eastern seaboard. Membership in each city was expressly limited to four "Israelites," who were then expected to forward the interests of the *Chenuch*. Aside from Noah and Levy, the New York membership included Judah Zuntz and the Reverend M. L. M. Peixotto, the hazzan of New York City's influential Shearith Israel synagogue. Additionally, there were societies formed in Norfolk and Baltimore and, most likely, other cities as well. Moses Myers joined his son John and son-in-law Philip I. Cohen in the Norfolk society, while Jacob I. Cohen, a powerful, civic-minded businessman, led the Baltimore faction.[22] Significantly, the American Society for Meliorating the Condition of the Jews also established affiliate groups throughout the union and garnered the support of prominent individuals.

The existence of a unified network of Hebrew societies in various states whose members included some of the country's most influential Jews is a fact that has either been ignored or deliberately downplayed by some American Jewish historians. For instance, Jacob R. Marcus, who drew a negative assessment of Levy after a limited reading of his more radical ideas—including those contained in the "Levy Diary"—viewed the Hebrew societies as insignificant. In his discussion of this episode in *United States Jewry, 1776–1985* Marcus failed to mention that Levy's associates, all of whom, he says, "could have been counted on the fingers of two hands," represented some of the leading characters in early American Jewry. Curiously, he also labeled the Hebrew societies as "cells," as if they consisted of shady revolutionaries instead of influential civic and religious leaders. While Marcus did cite the participation of the Myers family, he suggested that they took part out of pure obligation; they were, after all, "bankrupt and indebted to the rich Floridian [Levy]." Any interpretation, other than a positive one, seemed plausible to Marcus.[23]

The sole exception to this pessimism was Marcus's appraisal of the religious/agricultural school. In a dramatic turnaround Marcus conceded that Levy's desire to found a school represented "the first attempt to rally Jewry as a body behind an institute designed to serve as a national center for Jewish culture."[24] For Marcus it was this one goal, separate from the problematic Levy or his influential colleagues, which was of ultimate historical importance.

Marcus's ambiguous assessment notwithstanding, Levy's Hebrew societies should merit special recognition. Not only was their plan of establishing a national school significant, but the endeavor was also the first instance of American Jews rising above their own synagogue, city, and state loyalties in order to devote themselves to the interests of a benevolent "National Institution." A precursor to later service organizations, such as B'nai B'rith, Levy's organization became the first expression of a truly national Jewish philanthropic organization in the United States. The fact that Levy was able to convince high-ranking Jews to implement at least some of the reform tenets of Israel Jacobson, as well as Pestalozzian educational methods, is also noteworthy and was certainly without precedent. While scrupulously avoiding all newspaper coverage and publicity, Levy proved adept at advancing European notions of religious and educational reform in the United States.

According to Jonathan Sarna: "The 1820s formed a remarkable decade in American Jewish history, paralleling the Second Great Awakening and the beginning of the Jacksonian age." Sarna believes, with good reason, that the decade "transformed American Judaism" and was nothing less than "a religious revolution that overthrew the synagogue community."[25] In its place a far more diverse and less authoritarian structure gained ascendance.

As a man of social standing and great wealth, Moses Levy entered the United States at the dawn of this uncommon decade. Far from being a marginal presence, as some historians have portrayed him, Levy made significant progress in implementing his ideas among the Jewish leadership. When viewed within the framework of a true "religious revolution," Levy's actions become even more central to any full understanding of this exceptionally formative period.

Interior view of a typical West Indian sugar mill. From the *Illustrated London News* (1849).

Seraphina and Jean Joseph ("Salabert") Chauviteau and children. Havana, Cuba (c. 1817).
Courtesy of Emmanuel Boelle, Paris.

Moses Myers (c. 1808) by Gilbert Stuart.
Courtesy of the Chrysler Museum of Art, Norfolk, Va.;
Moses Myers House (M51.1.269)

Portrait of Rebecca Gratz by Thomas Sully (1831).
Courtesy of the Rosenbach Museum and Library, Philadelphia.

Mordecai M. Noah of New York.
Courtesy of the Jacob Rader Marcus Center of the
American Jewish Archives, Cincinnati.

A modern rendering—based on Levy's written instructions
to his carpenter—of the main plantation house at Pilgrimage.
Drawing by the author.

Prewar portrait of Micanopy, chief of the Seminoles.
*Courtesy of the Florida Photographic Collection,
Florida State Archives.*

Having narrowly escaped a lynch mob, Massachusetts abolitionist Jonathan Walker
endured several punishments—including the pillory and branding—while imprisoned in
territorial Florida. From Jonathan Walker, *Trial and Imprisonment of Jonathan Walker,
at Pensacola, Florida, for Aiding Slaves to Escape from Bondage* (Boston, 1845).

David L. Yulee, antebellum U.S. senator, railroad entrepreneur,
sugar planter, and leader of the Florida Democratic Party.
Library of Congress.

Dr. Jacob Mendes Da Costa (Moses Levy's grandson),
a distinguished nineteenth-century physician, teacher, and author.
Courtesy of the Historical Society of Pennsylvania.

7. A FLORIDA SETTLEMENT

*A*fter establishing the groundwork for the settlement/school, Moses Levy departed for St. Augustine, East Florida, where he arrived on 25 July 1821.[1] The formal change-of-flags ceremony between Spain and the United States had taken place fifteen days earlier. Since Levy's U.S. citizenship would have been granted immediately had he been in Florida at the time of the ceremony, it is not clear why he waited so long. Apparently, last-minute business in Philadelphia and Charleston coincided with adverse conditions at sea and caused his late arrival. Regardless, Levy's appearance in the former Spanish provincial capital caused many to take notice, and his reputation as a man of wealth with high-ranking connections to the Spanish government preceded him. Yet the town that Levy entered, with its three hundred houses and quaint, narrow streets, had suffered significant neglect. According to one contemporary, "the Spaniards, having contemplated quitting [St. Augustine] . . . had neglected most of the precautions of cleanliness which they usually adopt, so the great accumulations of filth were formed in the streets and different yards and lots."[2] Many of the Spanish inhabitants had abandoned their property and emigrated to Cuba, further contributing to the town's forsaken image. A contingent of adventurers, most without ample means of support, filled the dilapidated boardinghouses. Amid this rather desperate scene, persons of Levy's stature were a distinct rarity, and he rapidly made the acquaintance of St. Augustine's small cadre of leading citizens, most of whom were recently appointed government officials. Soon Levy made preparations for an expedition to his property on the St. Johns River, about sixty miles to the south.

95

While there is no record of Levy's impressions of this trip, the remarks of an anonymous observer, written for the benefit of the newly established territorial press, can be taken as a good indication of the scene that Levy encountered on his river journey: "You see almost every where, charming perspectives, magnolias, laurels of every species, and water oaks, in the shade of which the citron and orange grow naturally, forming an evergreen curtain the whole length of this fine river." In a place where oranges grew "spontaneously," where mulberry trees (used for silk production) were "found every where along the banks of the St. Johns," and where "Indigo springs up under the pines," East Florida presented itself as an agricultural paradise that was ripe for immense rewards.[3] Obviously, Levy's enthusiasm for the region was shared by a small but growing number of new arrivals.

In addition to the dense canopy of trees that lined the river, Levy would also have seen a profusion of subtropical wildlife as well as the occasional, unsettling presence of Seminole Indians—a population that had every reason to resent and fear the arrival of American settlers. Further on, the moldering ruins of Rollestown, a failed endeavor of the previous century which sought to employ the beggars and vagrants of London in an ill-conceived utopian experiment, would have been clearly visible on the eastern bank. Despite these ominous signs, Levy was genuinely impressed with his "fertile and happily situated" property located to the south of Lake George, and he did not hesitate to send his positive evaluation to his loyal colleague Frederick Warburg.[4]

Pleased with his prospects, Moses Levy was nevertheless prepared to dispose of his lands in order to abide by the wishes of the American Jewish community. He placed the founding of the *Chenuch* as paramount and expected that Jewish leaders would choose a northern locale, presumably rural Pennsylvania. He postponed Warburg's arrival until all elements of doubt about his intended settlement were resolved. In the meantime Levy resolved to increase the value of his holdings by erecting plantations upon the land. While on a brief visit to Cuba, he hired Antonio Rutan, an experienced sugar plantation manager, to supervise his Florida operations. By the time of Levy's return it was obvious that support for the *Chenuch* was dwindling. The reasons behind this setback can only be conjectured, but his large expenditures in Florida and frequent absences were certainly contributing factors. Furthermore, as Jacob I. Cohen surmised, while Levy's ideas were admirable and worthy of implementation, he was, nevertheless, a foreigner who did not fully understand "the peculiar character of the native Hebrews of the United States."[5] As this comment suggests, Levy made at least a few tactical blunders. His proposal that the Baltimore society—which Cohen led—merge under the leadership of the Norfolk society offended the wealthy and influential Cohen. Levy's knowledge of American culture may have been limited, but it is also true that the country's "native Hebrews" still bore strong familial and regional allegiances, and any outsider, no matter how well intentioned, would be especially vulnerable to criticism. Moreover, the perceived threat of the American Society for Meliorating the Condition of the Jews may have subsided, reducing the need for a Jewish response. Ultimately, however, at a time when Jews numbered only several thousand and immigration was still limited, the conditions that would allow for a bona fide "National Institution" simply did not exist.

Undeterred by this additional setback, throughout 1822 Moses Levy launched a full-scale effort to establish a plantation infrastructure. He also sent for his eldest son, Elias, in England and enrolled him at Harvard College, where he expected that the young man would benefit the colony by earning his medical degree.[6] After Levy realized that support from the Jewish community would not be forthcoming, he informed Warburg that their final destination would in fact be Florida. Despite his arrival after the change-of-flags, on 4 March Levy swore allegiance to the United States before the mayor of St. Augustine and assumed U.S. citizenship—an event that would later arouse much controversy. A few months later he returned on a schooner that was laden with Cuban sugarcane, "the first brought to the country," according to the local inhabitants. The cultivation of sugarcane, a minor crop during the Spanish and English periods, had dissipated to such an extent that many East Floridians believed that Levy was responsible for its introduction.[7] While still a novelty in Florida, sugar had attained great profitability elsewhere and was regarded as the foremost plantation crop in the New World. Levy's status as an agricultural innovator was augmented by the "quantity of tropical fruits, roots, and seeds" which he brought with him as well as his attempts to "cultivate the vine, the olive, and other products of the South of France."[8]

Awaiting Warburg and the first settlers, Levy built a modest plantation and planted sugarcane on a twelve hundred–acre estate located at the intersection of Moses Creek and the Matanzas River, about ten miles south of St. Augustine. Much farther to the south, in the region of present-day

Astor, he established the four thousand–acre Hope Hill plantation and ordered Antonio Rutan to oversee construction of buildings on a hammock
bluff overlooking the west bank of the St. Johns River. Levy acquired more
acreage and started yet another enterprise named Pilgrimage.[9] This property, located a few miles from the small, inland settlement of Micanopy in
Alachua County, eventually became the focus of Levy's attention despite its
considerable distance from any navigable waterway.[10] Situated near present-day Levy Lake, the plantation had an adequate supply of fresh water.[11]
In addition the soil was augmented by a "rare" source of natural fertilizer
that was found floating in abundance on a nearby lake. Levy considered
these "Islets" of "vegetable decomposition mixed with the dung of Alliga-
tors" as a special asset for his farming endeavor.[12] Agents commenced with
the construction of a viable plantation, complete with various dwelling
houses, a sugar mill, a saw mill, and a blacksmith shop.

The ambitious newcomer quickly established himself as one of East
Florida's largest landowners and continued to acquire vast tracts, eventually amounting to over 100,000 acres.[13] Moses Levy fully expected that his
investments would prove profitable, thereby providing an additional revenue stream for his extensive venture. Leading citizens not only applauded
Levy's sense of industry but noted his humanitarian impulses as well. His
ultimate goal of establishing a refuge for oppressed European Jews in the
sparsely inhabited interior did not provoke concern. On the contrary, his
motives were judged far "superior to the selfish views of a mere land specu-
lator." Soon his "laudable object of converting an uncultivated wilderness
. . . into fields of plenty" was brought to the attention of Secretary of War
John C. Calhoun, who, it was assumed, would aid Levy in his dealings with
the Indians.[14]

Moses Levy's presence was deemed of major importance to the fledgling territory, and he maintained close and cordial relations with the local
gentry. Alexander Hamilton Jr., the founding father's son and newly appointed U.S. attorney for East Florida, considered Levy a "gentleman of
much respectability" and acted as his lawyer for a time.[15] Another New
Yorker, Colonel James G. Forbes, U.S. marshal for Florida and also mayor
of St. Augustine, joined Levy in a subsequent land investment scheme and
served as Levy's agent during his absence.[16] Acting Governor William G. D.
Worthington, recently arrived from Maryland, pronounced Levy "one of
the most useful settlers in this Province" and allowed him the rare privi-

lege of trading directly with the Indians.[17] Worthington was a strong advocate of Jewish civil liberties and took pride in his subsequent support of Maryland's so-called Jew Bill, which fully enfranchised the state's Jewish residents, when he returned home after his brief tenure in Florida.[18]

Elsewhere in the South, Levy's dual status as a foreigner and Jewish visionary would have roused suspicion, if not open hostility. While he continued to hold his most extreme views in check, he did not refrain from making his colonization plans known. In more typical areas of the South, where the perception of order rested upon a rigid social hierarchy, such nonconformity and social innovation would not have been easily tolerated.[19] Therefore, Levy's initial support among the territorial elite can best be explained in terms of the atypical nature of the region. Immense and underpopulated, the former Spanish borderland was physically and culturally isolated. Moreover there was an influx of new citizens from both North and South as well as an exodus of Spanish inhabitants. In fact, "Yankees" constituted a distinct and often contentious faction in St. Augustine.[20] Overall the region still lacked a rigid plantation caste system, and, after years of Catholic monopoly, residents began to experience a newfound sense of religious freedom.[21] Within this transitional milieu Levy's philanthropic motives as well as his finely honed interpersonal skills enabled him to pursue his unorthodox scheme relatively unencumbered, at least amid St. Augustine's unusual provincial social structure.

While Levy was welcomed by leading officials, his experience on the frontier was quite a different matter. Two years after his arrival, Levy admitted his grave concerns about the nature of the Florida interior to Moses Myers. "Oh my good Sir!" Levy exclaimed. "I have embarked myself in a wild country peopled with wolves instead of men."[22] The violent tendencies of the few white inhabitants as well as the Indians caused Levy real distress. Such apprehensions, however, were eventually quashed by Levy's sense of divine mission. After such a lengthy period of planning, the colonization process itself—once implemented—carried a certain momentum that could not be easily put aside. In contrast, Moses Myers had adopted a much more conservative stance. While he sincerely admired Levy's intentions, he privately dismissed the Florida venture as "too speculative & sanguine."[23]

Moses Levy's first experience with what one historian has called the "maelstrom of contention"—the volatile, frontier environment where legal authority was nonexistent and diverse factions vied for control—remains incomplete and somewhat mysterious.[24] But enough evidence has emerged that indicates Levy's initial efforts at plantation building resulted in both hostility and major losses.

The first indication of trouble was at Hope Hill, Levy's newly established sugar plantation on the St. Johns River. In January 1822, with a start-up budget of twenty thousand dollars, Antonio Rutan assumed responsibility for the initial construction.[25] Two shipments of Cuban sugarcane and "sundry other articles" were brought in by schooner, and two thousand dollars' worth of "utensils for the manufacture of sugar" were delivered from Savannah.[26] A store was set up for the Indian trade, but Levy forbade any dealing in animal pelts. Despite this restriction, which apparently stemmed from his objections to killing animals for the frivolous dictates of fashion, Rutan ignored the orders. Most troublesome was Hope Hill's close proximity to Volusia, an isolated residence and trading post located on the opposite shore of the relatively narrow upper St. Johns. Because Volusia was the home of the Anglo-Spanish Indian trader Horatio Dexter, any competing trade would have created serious tensions and defied the traditional "one trader–one town" arrangement on the frontier.[27]

Horatio Dexter was a former Spanish subject who maintained important contacts with both Seminole and Miccosukee Indians, the latter being comparative newcomers to peninsular East Florida. In fact, Dexter's influence among the principal chiefs was unequaled, and, as a result, he became a figure to be reckoned with in the interior. Far from being an uncouth frontiersman, however, Dexter was actually a literate man with gentlemanly airs who maintained a facade of respectability by virtue of a second residence in St. Augustine. Despite his aspirations toward the genteel, he also possessed a malevolent side and could be extremely vengeful. Dexter felt slighted by some of the large Spanish grant proprietors, especially Fernando Arredondo, and Dexter's waning influence in the Indian territory undoubtedly contributed to his rancor.[28] Although there is scant evidence, a peculiar reference to Hope Hill, an "accident that has occurred to Mr. Rutan's houses," appears in Dexter's correspondence and suggests that he came under suspicion for foul play.[29] The circumstances must have been severe. After Levy's considerable investment, he was forced to abandon the plantation in June 1822 because of "various and many unforeseen [troubles]." Since it is known that Dexter once led his Indian allies in threats of violence and coercion and that Levy subsequently became quite enraged toward Dexter, it appears that Hope Hill was deliberately destroyed, presumably by fire. As a consequence, Rutan's responsibilities were shifted to Pilgrimage plantation, and farming implements and supplies were salvaged for use in the Alachua country, some fifty-five miles to the northwest.[30]

Notwithstanding Levy's massive losses at Hope Hill, he focused once more on his mission. His previous experience in remote areas of the West Indies, locations where equally menacing outlaws often held sway, undoubtedly played a part in Levy's remarkable tenacity. At forty he was still in good physical condition and possessed an uncommon determination. While he may have been greatly influenced by Protestant culture, he certainly did not accept the Christian ideal of turning the other cheek, an axiom that Levy considered quite unnatural. Indeed, he developed a righteous anger over this incident as well as other crimes. Finding himself without legal remedy, Levy confronted Dexter in St. Augustine, where he publicly denounced him as "an assassin, an incendiary, a scoundrel and a rascal." By all accounts these epithets appear to have been entirely accurate, but Dexter feigned innocence and claimed to be criminally maligned. Denying any complicity in "murder" and "house burning," he proceeded with a ten thousand–dollar slander suit against Levy, the final outcome of which is unknown.[31]

As this episode illustrates, the appearance of wealthy and intrepid individuals such as Moses Levy presented a challenge to the old order, and, in the process, frontier dynamics were altered. Prior to the U.S. cession, few men ventured beyond St. Augustine or the coastal areas, and, as most of the peninsula was considered Indian territory, any type of exploration was avoided. Therefore, the introduction of an orderly and well-financed settlement effort in the interior, with Levy at the vanguard, represented nothing less than revolutionary change. These activities were a compelling demonstration that the lifestyles of the native Indians, the runaway slaves, and those "profligate characters" who lived among them, as Andrew Jackson once labeled Dexter and his cronies, would soon be inexorably transformed.[32]

Antonio Rutan certainly did not possess any previous experience with either renegade frontiersmen or Indians, and his inability to speak or understand English added to his difficulties. After Hope Hill, Rutan became exceedingly fearful of all Indians, and he soon deserted his responsibilities at Pilgrimage and sought the safety of St. Augustine. Supervision of the Alachua plantation temporarily reverted back to Edward Wanton, a longtime resident of East Florida who, unlike his former associate Horatio Dexter, was much more willing to make a peaceful transition to United States rule. Wanton had been entrusted by Arredondo and his partners with the management of the nearby hamlet and trading post of Micanopy and lived in the area with his black wife and children.[33]

As early as February 1822, Wanton worked as Levy's agent in transforming the isolated lowland hammock area, located a few miles west of Micanopy, into a modestly productive plantation. According to the observations of Dr. William H. Simmons, physician, author, and chronicler of early territorial Florida, most of the work at Pilgrimage was accomplished by slave labor, and, of the thirty persons employed on the land that year, only eight or nine were white.[34] It should be noted, however, that black laborers, in actuality Seminole "slaves," were often hired by Levy's agents in the early stages of the settlement, and payment was in the form of Indian trade goods.[35] Although technically regarded as slaves by their Indian masters, these blacks—many of whom were runaways from Georgia and other states—were permitted a great deal of personal liberty and were not bound into forced labor.[36] "There was a range of tenements," Simmons remarked, "which would accommodate nearly all the persons there." In addition there was a corn-house, a stable, and a blacksmith's shop as well as "a good crop of corn" which he judged sufficient for "the whole establishment for a year." Of Pilgrimage's 1,000 acres, 120 were immediately cleared for planting crops.[37]

Clearly, the massive expense and risk of forging self-sustaining settlements in inaccessible and dangerous locations was a formidable task for any single individual. Fortunately, Levy's endeavors on the Alachua frontier were greatly facilitated by his decision to join a business consortium. His participation in this venture is yet another example of his capacity to enact compromise solutions. For the sake of the greater good, Levy deemed it necessary to step away from utopian isolation and resume his business career, at least temporarily.

After the United States assumed jurisdiction of Florida, Fernando Arredondo sought investors in his extensive Alachua holdings, which amounted to over 289,000 acres. When in 1822 Levy exchanged other property for a one-eighth share of this grant, he became one of four major proprietors who were obligated to fulfill the original Spanish stipulations, the foremost being the settlement of two hundred families within three years.[38] Such an endeavor would have been improbable during the declining days of the Spanish empire, but the United States offered substantial advantages, including the presence of capitalists who were not adverse to high-risk undertakings. Levy's entry into the Arredondo partnership coincided with the formation of the Florida Association. This company was based in New York City, the residence of the largest investor, General Jasper Ward. By virtue of his substantial New York business connections, Levy played a pivotal role in the company's founding. Portions of the Arredondo grant were subdivided and sold to various people in New York and New Jersey—including Mordecai Noah. The Florida Association assumed responsibility for colonization, and the newly established hamlet of Micanopy became the nucleus of the intended settlement. On 4 November 1822 Levy represented the Florida landholders' interests at a company meeting that he arranged at Lewis Tavern in New York's elegant Bowery district.[39] In what was surely the earliest Florida development corporation, taxes were levied, town lots divided, roads and mills planned, settlers recruited, and a generous allowance allocated for both a physician and a clergyman. Although Levy's main objective was Jewish colonization, he also had a vested interest in the town's success. Micanopy provided access to supplies, livestock, laborers, skilled carpenters, and a physician, all scarce commodities. Therefore, it is significant that, although Levy's initial efforts at Hope Hill were short-lived, his Alachua plantation endured until the commencement of the Second Seminole War, a period of thirteen years.

By February 1823, under the auspices of the Florida Association of New York, a forty-five-mile road was completed linking the village of Micanopy with the site of present-day Palatka on the St. Johns River. Essentially an expanded Indian trail with eight newly constructed bridges, the road greatly facilitated the transportation of supplies and settlers. Pilgrimage was the actual terminus of this frontier passage, and for a few years the plantation remained the farthest point west in peninsular Florida which could easily accommodate wagons and carriages.[40] After the road's completion, Frederick Warburg arrived with twenty-one other settlers, who had departed New York harbor by ship a few months earlier. Most of these adventurous homesteaders had responded to advertisements placed in the New York City newspapers and were under obligation to the Florida Association to stay in Micanopy for at least a year. Also accompanying the group were fifteen slaves destined for Pilgrimage plantation. Six years after Moses Levy first conferred with Warburg in London, the two men finally met again in the East Florida wilderness. Whatever idealistic form their initial plan may have taken, one wonders if the rudimentary frontier scene that unfolded before them could have truly matched their earlier expectations.

In addition to Warburg, Levy also arranged for the transportation of a French immigrant named Hipolite Chateanneuf, who was hired to supervise vine and olive production. The main contingent of Pilgrimage settlers arrived at a later date, but complete records are woefully lacking.[41] Warburg stated that a scarcity of housing prevented "forty to fifty" potential colonizers from departing Europe. No doubt, the destruction at Hope Hill contributed to the shortage of accommodations.

As events would demonstrate, the Jewish settlers' late arrival proved fortuitous. The sudden influx of colonists greatly agitated the Indians throughout the region. While Edward Wanton and his mixed-race family were welcomed, the Indians perceived the newcomers as a threat. Adding to the tension, the irascible Horatio Dexter entered the scene and, aware of the escalating anger among his Indian cohorts, once more enticed them to serve his own ignoble ends.

Following the Hope Hill scenario, Dexter entered Micanopy with a dozen Indians, some of them chiefs, and threatened to burn the entire town. But Wanton had been alerted to Dexter's intentions and was prepared to respond. Moses Levy, recently appointed as one of the town's superintendents, joined Wanton, and they both managed to halt hostilities by holding a formal "talk" with the Indian leaders. Wanton surely reminded the Indians of their valued trading relationship as well as their promises of protection for him and his family. Records indicate that the chiefs were routinely awarded "presents" of trade goods—including demijohns of rum—during the early years of the town, so it is fair to assume that these items were present during the negotiation. As a result, the Indians were dissuaded from carrying out their threats and left the town unmolested.[42] The Florida Association's reliance on northern colonists rather than on Georgian frontiersmen proved propitious in this situation and actually eased tensions. Had Georgians been present, as they were in other isolated sections of East Florida, they would not have tolerated any such threats from their longtime adversaries and would have been quick to draw fire and to retaliate forcefully. Fortunately, calmer dispositions prevailed. This time at least, Dexter had clearly been outmaneuvered.

In spite of the positive outcome, this episode underscored the precarious position of the neophyte settlers. Some individuals, such as the newly arrived physician Samuel R. Ayers, reached the same conclusion as Antonio Rutan before him and left Micanopy because of the Indian unrest.[43] Most of them, however, bravely elected to complete their commitment to the company, and soon additional arrivals joined the fledgling settlement. Within six months the number of houses in town increased from thirteen to twenty-five, with materials ready to build an additional ten. In addition to Pilgrimage, two other plantations were established in the vicinity.[44]

In the fall of 1823 Moses Levy hired Reuben Charles, another seasoned Florida resident, to take over the management of Pilgrimage.[45] With his establishment in capable hands, Levy divided his time between St. Augustine and the Alachua country. While the majority of Jewish colonists remained in Europe, some had already arrived in the United States and waited only for the best opportunity to travel. In 1824 Warburg acknowledged his hard-won success in establishing "five heads of families on Mr. Levy's settlement," all of whom were given land as well as accommodations.[46] In addition, Levy's correspondence confirms that these Jewish newcomers represented a broad economic spectrum and that none had previous agricultural experience. Their urban background also proved to be a significant handicap. "It is not easy," Levy complained, "to transform old clothes men [street peddlers] or stock brokers into practical farmers."[47] In addition to this unlikely group, Elias Levy, who greatly disappointed his father after he abandoned his studies at Harvard, joined the others at Pilgrimage and was given his own residence.[48] Unlike many utopian endeavors, Levy's did not require that all colonists share living quarters under one roof or hold property in common. While Pilgrimage had a very specific communal identity, each family had its own private accommodation and held its own parcel of land—all courtesy of the benevolent Mr. Levy.

Moses Levy's initial losses and his great expenditures in land acquisition, construction projects, transportation, livestock, and a wide array of costly plantation hardware and supplies hampered his ability to accommodate more colonists. Furthermore, legal questions arose involving the legality of his land titles, and Levy—as well as all other purchasers of Spanish land grants—was unable to sell his substantial holdings until the matter was settled in the courts. This last obstacle became Levy's most pressing problem. Since he assumed that land sales would offset expenses until his plantations could operate profitably, any disruption in this strategy could herald financial ruin. In fact, his situation rapidly deteriorated. Because the issue of the Spanish grants would not be resolved until many years after Levy's colonization venture, the total number of Jewish families probably never exceeded Warburg's initial figure. Much later, the broad discrepancy that existed between Levy's vision for a vast refuge for European Jews and the actual low turnout caused him to regard the whole effort as a failure.[49] In actuality, although Levy was never cognizant of its significance, he managed to form the first Jewish farming settlement in the United States, albeit on a drastically reduced scale. Pilgrimage's status as a humanitarian refuge adds to its importance. Levy's philanthropic gesture was an innovative response to centuries of Old World repression. Considering his many misfortunes, it was a true wonder that Pilgrimage existed at all.[50]

Regardless of the disruption in Levy's business plan, he saw no other choice but to turn the Alachua plantation into a moneymaking venture and to consolidate resources. In 1824 he sold his plantation on the Matanzas River to Achille Murat, a French émigré and nephew to Napoléon Bonaparte. Evidently, the deed to this particular tract of land was never in dispute. Interestingly, the aristocratic Murat, undoubtedly inspired by the writings of Jean-Jacques Rousseau and others, was also taken with romantic notions of pastoral simplicity and found the rudimentary living conditions at the plantation much to his liking, at least for a while.[51]

Although Murat may have shunned the accepted norms of the privileged class, he harbored no notions of the impending millennium, nor did he adhere to any communitarian ideal. Nevertheless, despite his slight amusement at this "Hebrew visionary" and his "colony of Israelites," Murat probably would have found life at Pilgrimage to his liking.[52] While Levy designed his Alachua dwellings to conform to what he considered a higher moral standard, one that shunned displays of luxury and privilege, he made sure there was at least a modicum of comfort. It can be assumed that the majority of the Pilgrimage settlers, certainly the former peddlers, did not share either Levy's or Warburg's wealthy background, so the relatively simple accommodations were hardly a deprivation. Levy's own residence, however, offered an opportunity to implement an unpretentious lifestyle. His two-story, wooden frame house had porches on either side and a separate kitchen and was of relatively modest dimensions (thirty-six by twenty-four feet). While undoubtedly a dramatic step above the average dwelling in the area, it was furnished quite simply and lacked the accoutrements of wealth which usually distinguished persons of Levy's class. The accommodations certainly did not constitute a mansion, as one historian has claimed.[53] Nevertheless, this six-room residence had eighteen windows and shutters, a gabled roof, and two small hallways and rose to a height of twenty feet. In addition, the house had its own garden, a fenced-in "fowl yard," and a well. A storehouse, stable, and blacksmith shop were in close proximity as well as seven "negro houses."[54] In comparison, Warburg's residence remains something of a mystery, although local Micanopy history places him in close proximity to Levy, on an estate near present Lake Wauburg.[55]

The recent appearance of the Reuben Charles papers and other records as well as a thorough examination of archival documents have provided vital new information regarding Pilgrimage. Yet much remains obscure, especially details concerning the Jewish families. The manner in which these settlers may have adopted Levy's strictures concerning religion, education, and the communal rearing of children is simply not known. Nevertheless, in spite of Levy's natural reticence, news of the unconventional arrangements at Pilgrimage eventually reached public notice. An 1841 St. Augustine newspaper editorial, written in response to David Levy's controversial entry into national politics, cast Moses Levy as "a man of eccentric ideas" whose earlier efforts to "establish colonies of 'Harmonites' upon utopian principles, in Alachua county" had led to ruin.[56] Such a direct reference to Levy's utopianism, although rare, suggests that at least some of the more radical aspects of his communitarian scheme were implemented and that news of this arrangement eventually became common knowledge in the territory.

During Pilgrimage's early days, however, life went on with slight interest from the outside world. With land sales at a halt, sugar production attained even more importance. Unfortunately, the only plantation records that have survived date to 1824, a year that evidently predates actual mill operations. Yet by 1829, despite setbacks and long absences abroad, Levy expected "60 to 80 acres of excellent sugar cane" that would yield one ton of sugar per acre—a most productive level for the time.[57] Levy also made substantial investments in a wide array of agricultural equipment and residential supplies and kept two hundred head of cattle as well as an adequate number of horses, sheep, oxen, and hogs. The latter were apparently raised for slave consumption, since Levy, and presumably other Jews at Pilgrimage, abstained from eating pork.[58] Nothing has surfaced which can shed further light on Levy's experiments in vine and olive culture, although the plantation eventually had about one hundred "fruit trees"—probably an orange grove.[59]

Quite unexpectedly, records show that Levy established a trading relationship with Chief Micanopy's band of Seminoles, located about sixty miles to the south in present-day Sumter County. Although Miccosukees lived in the immediate area of Micanopy, the original Alachua Seminoles had long departed for a safer and more remote locale. The naming of the company town after Micanopy was an early effort to appease the chief and to acknowledge his original authority over the land and did not indicate his actual presence in the town itself. Therefore, the trading relationship that developed between Pilgrimage and the chief's distant band, particularly his "slave" town of Pelaklikaha, or "Abrahams Old Town," is significant.[60] Pelaklikaha was under the leadership of Abraham, a former slave and an advisor to Micanopy who would latter attain distinction during the Second Seminole War. As a result of this association, Levy acquired much needed livestock and occasionally hired Black Seminoles as laborers.

The number of actual slaves at Pilgrimage fluctuated from a low of ten to a high mark of thirty-one—the total Levy held when he divested himself of all his slaves in 1839.[61] From an account in the *Niles' Register* the average number of slaves on three unidentified Alachua County sugar plantations in 1833 amounted to twenty-six, so Pilgrimage was certainly within the norm. Although the identities of these planters were not revealed, leading candidates include Colonel Duncan L. Clinch and Colonel John H. McIntosh Jr., two prominent individuals who followed Levy's lead and established nearby sugar estates. The income generated by the average bond servant in Alachua was rated at $387. "A great deal more," the newspaper observed, "than the average product of free labor in the North." The largest of the plantations, with forty-seven slaves, produced 160 hogsheads of sugar, 14,000 gallons of molasses, 4,000 bushels of corn, and fodder, rice, beans, and peas valued at $1,000.[62] One can surmise that Levy's operation had a similar range of crops and that its potential profit was high.

Quite distinct from all other Alachua planters, however, was Moses Levy's philosophical position vis-à-vis slavery. Freedom, Levy believed, should be given to the children of slaves at the age of twenty-one and only after they had completed both agricultural training and a basic education. After a lifetime of bondage, he concluded, slaves would suffer more if left to fend for themselves. In time, he assumed, technological advancements would enable non-slave-dependent agriculture to displace slavery. While a few southerners may have concluded that slave labor was inherently inefficient, Levy was motivated by a biblical standard of morality which was not concerned with classical economics or regional and state interests.[63] Although he did not adhere to immediate abolition and there is no evidence that he was able to implement his plan, his ideas would have been viewed as highly threatening in the territory and could have placed his entire settlement in jeopardy. Irrational fears often led to the vehement condemnation of any form of abolitionist sentiment.[64] As a result, while news of Pilgrimage's utopian lifestyle managed to spread, Levy succeeded in keeping his antislavery views out of public notice in Florida.

To the casual observer the practice of slavery at Pilgrimage probably did not appear that unconventional. Yet brutal excesses were certainly not a part of the plantation regimen. Levy abhorred the "wantonness and caprice" of those slaveholders who inflicted "horrible cruelty." Not unexpectedly, he looked to the Hebrew Bible and its humane laws that prohibited such abuse as his paradigm.[65] Moreover, as in Cuba, Levy believed that all persons would benefit by keeping slave families intact and was convinced that "conjugal affection, parental and filial love, are the best guarantees for good conduct."[66] To what extent he was able to alleviate work conditions and to turn the typical bond servant's plight into his ideal "instrument of blessing" remains unclear. Cane growing and the transformation of cane juice into valued granulated sugar was a labor-intensive process. In any case it is hard to imagine that he would ignore one of the primary goals of his self-proclaimed "ministry," that of providing a practical education as well as a basic understanding of the Bible to both slaves and free men alike.

The very thought of chattel slavery coexisting within an egalitarian environment runs counter to most historical assumptions and deserves further clarification. As historian W. Fitzhugh Brundage has noted: "One cannot conceive of a contemporary utopian vision to reconcile the racial hierarchy inherent in slavery with the pursuit of equality central to communitarianism."[67] For this very reason most utopians avoided the South, a region that was viewed as anathema to egalitarian concepts. Indeed, as one member of Robert Owen's New Harmony experiment in Indiana put it, the contrast between life at the utopian community and visits to the slaveholding South was nothing less than "disgusting."[68] To be sure, Levy's heightened notions of social justice led him to challenge slavery. Among abolitionists of the 1820s, however, the tide had not completely turned in favor of immediate emancipation, and gradualism was still looked upon as a respectable and proven method of ending slavery. Furthermore, Levy took a more literal view of the Old Testament than those abolitionists who were swayed by immediatism. In the biblical model Israelites did indeed hold slaves, but their behavior toward them was guided by a stringent code of ethics which was far more progressive than anything practiced in the South.[69]

In addition to this scriptural justification, Levy's lengthy experience as a slave owner led to his own distinct notions about the institution. The greatest sin, according to Levy, would be to free those who were "indolent" and "unaccustomed to think for themselves"—the inevitable result of straying from the biblical injunctions. This paternalistic outlook led him to conclude that most slaves were irreparably damaged by their "abject state"; he never imagined that adult slaves could part company with their masters and thrive on their own.[70]

Once again, Levy's dual nature was poised between expediency and visions of utopia. Since Levy's messianic expectations were so intertwined with his identity as a Jew, any sense of immediacy was clearly cast in favor of his coreligionists. On the other hand, the best that could be done for slaves was to provide a humane atmosphere and to prepare the way for future generations. Once this intellectual partitioning is understood, the apparent anomaly at Pilgrimage becomes less perplexing. Despite his continued slave ownership, Levy saw no contradiction when he published his plan for "abolishing slavery, destroying prejudice, and effectually improving the condition of millions of unborn souls" while in England. In fact, because of his firsthand knowledge of "the weaknesses and infirmities, the temptations and passions, which are incident to slave-owners," he believed he was better able to construct a viable scheme for the complete eradication of slavery.[71]

The key to understanding Levy's ethics, however, resides in his unique interpretation of both Torah Judaism and Christian tenets. In Genesis he was able to set a moral framework for slaveholding as well as to establish the need for its gradual demise. Central to his logic was that inequality was inevitable, given mankind's fall from grace and the subsequent banishment from the Garden of Eden. The "curse that was inflicted as the consequence of that transgression," Levy believed, became the very "source of slavery"— a statement reminiscent of the Christian doctrine of original sin. "Thus sin gave rise to an inequality in power," Levy concluded. "That inequality produced dependence, or servitude, and servitude degenerated into slavery." While slavery was indeed sinful, so was virtually every other aspect of life. Mankind was living in disharmony. Rather than degenerate farther, Revelation demanded that sin be banished and that all people should again assume "the power and the desire to do the will of God." A period of time was needed, as well as appropriate instruction, so that man could truly "love the Lord with all his heart, and his neighbour as himself." Once this was accomplished, man "would again be perfect." The world, as Levy saw it, was the result of spiritual cause and effect. Slavery was merely an outgrowth of the fall from God. Once the cause of mankind's misfortunes was remedied, the effects would end. As Levy would later postulate while in London: "The Almighty did not say, do not have slavery or servitude, because it was the effect of a cause still existing; the aim of the law was, to make the love of God the spring of action in all the circumstances of life, and therefore to destroy the very evil from which that state of things took rise; to suppress the cause, rather than restrain its effects."[72]

Simply to announce the end of slavery would only result in misery because blacks would continue to be abused by a sinful world that reveled in inequality. Similarly, man-made laws did not stop wrongs from happening, and neither did invoking the sternest punishment. It was Levy's utopian ideal of perfectionism, based on the Hebrew Bible, which informed virtually every aspect of his life. His idea of transitional training, or apprenticeship, in which Jews, Gentiles, and slaves would improve their nature and eventually live in agrarian harmony, was also central to his thought and shows a certain similarity to the monastic tradition. Finally, as far as the specific practice of slavery is concerned, Levy depended to such a large degree on the biblical accounts in Leviticus, Exodus, and Deuteronomy that he concluded that God had clearly devised "the means by which the master and the slave shall be rendered a mutual benefit to each other." Slaves were considered part of the master's household, were allowed to own property, and could inherit the estate if the slave owner was childless. Overwork, physical mistreatment, even verbal abuse, was strictly banned. Exactly how Levy implemented the ancient model, with its many holidays and Sabbath observances, in which the slave was viewed "as a poor brother" and the master was as duty-bound as the slave, may never be known.[73]

Moreover, Levy's belief in perfectionism should not be confused with the later notions of utopian John Humphrey Noyes and the radical abolitionist William Lloyd Garrison. More than likely, Levy was influenced by the eighteenth-century ideas of John Wesley, the founder of Methodism, who called for vanquishing all sin. In the process sinners would indeed be transformed into saints and reach Christian "perfection." Also, the Shaker concept of perfectionism, in which followers claimed to follow God's will and not their own selfish desires, almost certainly played a major role. In addition, Levy was familiar with the messianic teachings of Rabbi Joseph Crooll in England, about whom more will be said later. As an autodidact who was always on the margins of traditional centers of learning, Levy's awareness of a full range of religious and secular ideas was impressive, and he used this knowledge to fashion his own distinct synthesis. To be sure, Levy maintained close relationships with some notable and sophisticated figures during his lifetime, but he had no illusions about his essential outsider status. This sense of alienation certainly contributed to a rather unorthodox blend of the progressive and the reactionary.

Levy's elaborate theological construct notwithstanding, the more mundane affairs of his frontier operation needed drastic attention. Just three years after his arrival in the territory, Levy recognized that his utopian experiment was in economic shambles. He may have been the first Jew to establish a communitarian settlement in the United States, but Pilgrimage's dire financial situation was by no means unique. In fact, most of the ninety-one utopian communities that were established between 1780 and 1860 failed within four years. Sociologists have determined that the few that did endure, such as the Shakers, enacted a more regimented and idiosyncratic lifestyle and maintained a strict code of separation between their community and the outside world. Additionally, in contrast to Pilgrimage and other undertakings, individuals were expected to pool their resources and to perform manual labor in exchange for housing and other necessities—a complete communism of sorts. Pilgrimage, therefore, belonged to a more flexible and less demanding category. Sometimes these communities attained historical significance not through longevity or financial success but by virtue of certain intellectual innovations that influenced society at large. This group, represented by such renown utopian experiments as Robert Owen's New Harmony (1825–27) and George Ripley's Brook Farm (1841–47), were decidedly progressive in character.[74]

In comparison to more rigid utopian models, it is doubtful that the Pilgrimage colonists, such as the Brook Farmers and Owenites, ever submitted themselves to authoritarian discipline. As we have seen, Levy's homesteaders found food, housing, and land for the taking and were, in some respects, catered to. The "triune" relationship that Levy envisioned did not include harsh demands upon those who had recently fled European persecution. Furthermore, Levy accepted a disproportionate share of the colony's financial burdens, a paternalistic benevolence that cost him dearly. Despite the sectarian nature of Levy's Alachua settlement, its messianic orientation, and its reliance on slaves, the day-to-day environment probably did not differ that much from secular communitarians. The absence of religious rituals, distinctive dress, and a traditional synagogue resulted in few outward signs that would have set Pilgrimage immediately apart. Based on Levy's own behavior, there was no attempt to maintain stringent social boundaries between Pilgrimage and Micanopy or the rest of the territory for that matter. Yet, despite the additional burden of hostile Indians, Levy defied the norm, and Pilgrimage managed to survive until 1835.

By summer 1824, having spent all his "ready means," Moses Levy assessed his situation and felt that he had no other alternative but to seek additional funds in Europe. Once abroad he hoped he could persuade affluent members of the Jewish community to contribute to his cause. Long-standing business connections would also facilitate the mortgaging of his lands, despite the uncertainty attached to their titles. Determined to continue his settlement, no matter what the cost, in August he left the plantation management to Reuben Charles and the bookkeeping to Frederick Warburg and departed for the North. Levy spent some time in New York City, where he was able to secure a loan from a former business associate. While there, Levy probably conferred once more with Mordecai Noah, by then an investor in the Florida Association, and brought him up-to-date

on Pilgrimage's rather precarious position. Levy also learned of Noah's renewed interest in the Grand Island property, the ownership of which had
finally been granted to New York State. On 20 May 1825, as Levy boarded
the ship *Crisis* bound for London, a frenzy of land speculation erupted after
Noah's intentions of purchasing Grand Island became public.[75] The episode
soon escalated into a full-blown colonization and land investment scheme,
the likes of which Americans had never witnessed before. Although Levy
disapproved of Noah's penchant for publicity, Levy's own ideas, while he
was in England, would soon take on a much more public form.

8. A JEWISH ACTIVIST ABROAD

*A*mong the many peculiar characteristics of London during the 1820s, the loud refrain of the Jewish peddler was one of the most ubiquitous and scorned. In the minds of Englishmen and visitors alike, the constant chorus of "old clothes, old clothes" issuing from the ragged peddlers was more than an incessant nuisance: it was also an explicit reminder of the lowly and undignified status of most Jews. The proverbial "Levi of Holywell Street," to quote Samuel Taylor Coleridge, was a reviled stereotype who often wore a dark, long-robed caftan and wide-brimmed hat, kept an untidy beard, and was an aggressive sort.[1] Unseemly as they may have appeared, Moses Levy felt a special sympathy for the old clothes men. "Excluded by law from all Universities," Levy wrote, "and by prejudice, from even the more common seminaries of learning," these men could hardly be expected to be refined or cultured gentlemen. As Jews were also prohibited "from all honorable professions," occupational choice was certainly restricted. According to the divine plan, however, Jews had an essential and elevated part to play. If only Christians would repent and act humanely toward God's chosen people, Levy reasoned, Jews would cease "being venders of old clothes, [and would] sell without price, the waters of the fountain of life to the sons of man."[2]

When Moses Levy arrived in London during the summer of 1825, the city of 1.5 million was home to a substantial Jewish population—15,000 by Levy's reckoning.[3] Most resided in the rough environs of the East End, far removed from genteel society. At this time all Jews were, in fact, excluded from English universities and from professional careers (medicine being the sole exception), and they could not vote or hold public office.[4] Nevertheless, in contrast to the Continent, Jews enjoyed certain advantages in England. They were, by and large, free to travel and to reside wherever they wished, were not subject to special taxes, and could openly practice their religion without harm. Moreover, the growing merchant class had unprecedented access to Gentile society, although prejudice was still rampant. For the small cadre of elite bankers, financiers, and stockbrokers whose fashionable appearance and lavish estates differed little from the rest of the upper class, full acceptance was only possible through conversion to the Church of England.[5]

Britain, with its unprecedented wealth and industrial might, masses of urban poor, and often discordant notions of social justice, presented Levy with a host of paradoxes. Liberalism, reform, and the performance of "good works" were, however, on the ascent. London was home to an abundance of philanthropic organizations, and most were the special concern of evangelical Protestants: the General Association of the Friends of Civil and Religious Liberty, the Society for Superceding the Necessity of Climbing Boys [chimney sweeps], the London Missionary Society, the Religious Tract Society, the Aged Pilgrims Friend Society, to name a few. Wealthy evangelicals routinely supported twenty or more organizations at a time. "This is the age of societies," a youthful Thomas Babington Macaulay noted sarcastically. "There is scarcely one Englishman in ten who has not belonged to some association for distributing books, or for prosecuting them; for sending invalids to the hospital, or beggars to the treadmill; for giving plate to the rich, or blankets to the poor."[6] Nonetheless, the plethora of British charitable and missionary societies, both large and small, far exceeded any other country.

The evangelical movement—with its strong activist tradition, philosemitism, and unremitting support for the abolitionist crusade—would eventually offer Levy a distinct outlet for his ideas. The movement itself, however, represented a wide spectrum of religious beliefs: from millenarian sects, Primitive Methodists and itinerant Baptists, to the conservative Anglican elite.[7] On all levels evangelicals contributed much to London's position as the world center of the reform movement, but it was the Anglican faction that eventually became the mainstay of the London Society for the Promotion of Christianity among the Jews, an organization that was fairly aggressive in its conversion tactics. Prominent abolitionists such as

William Wilberforce and Zachary Macaulay were active members. Given this environment, any Jew with reformist ambitions, especially an outsider such as Levy, would have to possess exceptional diplomatic skills as well as sterling religious credentials in order to find any acceptance within most evangelical circles. In comparison, Anglo-Jewry was fairly notorious for their lack of religious piety and learning, and they were not, as a whole, committed to any particular social issue. The conversionists themselves presented a major obstacle to any discourse; the very concept of apostasy offended even nominally religious Jews.

Several months after Levy's appearance in London, his quest for financial support was dealt a serious blow when news of Mordecai Noah's "Ararat" fiasco reached Britain. True to his desire for maximum publicity and theatricality, on 15 September 1825 Noah declared himself "governor and judge of Israel" during a so-called ecumenical service in a Buffalo, New York, church. Arrayed in a Richard III costume—complete with somber robe and gold medallion—Noah exhibited a curious blend of self-promotion and religious hokum in his now infamous "Proclamation to the Jews." Not content to limit himself to the formation of a Jewish colony, he appeared to abandon all restraint. Among other oddities, Noah tried to impose a worldwide Jewish tax, outlawed polygamy, named leading Jews as his commissioners without their knowledge or consent, and proclaimed that the Indians were descendants of the lost tribes of Israel. Not long after the sound of the ceremonial cannon shots had receded, Noah's attempt to capture the attention of the worldwide Jewish community actually succeeded but hardly in the manner that he had hoped. Faced with criticism and ridicule from both Jews and Gentiles, he was forced to abandon his grand ambitions for a "City of Refuge for the Jews."[8] The aftermath of this "early American public-relations scheme," as one scholar has generously described the debacle, would present yet another impediment for Levy.[9]

Moses Levy was fully aware that the grandiloquent New Yorker had greatly exceeded the boundaries of good taste and common sense and that the mocking commentaries that issued from both sides of the Atlantic, although well deserved, could hinder his own cause. This situation far surpassed his worst fears concerning the perils of needless publicity and contemptible "vain-glory." Nevertheless, in an attempt to distance himself from Noah and to attract interest in his Florida venture, Levy wrote to Isaac Lyon Goldsmid, a bullion broker to the Bank of England and to the

East India Company who held an envied position at the Royal Exchange. Goldsmid later became one of the few communal leaders to promote Jewish emancipation actively. In his letter Levy condemned Noah's "folly and sacrilegious presumption" and listed the merits of his own plan. Apparently written in great haste, it is unknown whether this correspondence elicited any positive response from Goldsmid. The same month Levy also placed ads in the German Jewish newspapers soliciting settlers to come to Florida. Again, it is not clear whether these notices accomplished their goal.[10]

In January 1826, after taking up residence in Paris, Levy succeeded in mortgaging a large portion of his Florida land for fifty thousand francs. The mortgagor was a widow named Seraphina Chauviteau, whose recently deceased husband, Salabert, had left a considerable inheritance of two million francs. The Chauviteau family were longtime friends of Levy and had known him in Cuba, where Salabert had established himself as one of the premier coffee planters.[11] In fact, it was Salabert's firm of Hernandez & Chauviteau which initially held title to Levy's Florida landholdings in Cuba. Although Seraphina Chauviteau was certainly cognizant of the value of Levy's land, the transaction was not without risks. According to Madame Chauviteau's son, the loan was viewed as an honorable attempt to do "justice to the constancy of an old friend" who had abandoned "matters of self-interest" and was engaged in more high-minded pursuits.[12]

Also during this time, Levy experienced another religious milestone when he developed his spiritual doctrine of "operating and being operated upon." He defined this "law" as an interdependent relationship that existed on three levels: with individuals, the human community, and God being linked together in a constant bond. As a result, Levy could no longer consider his deeds as being disconnected from the rest of man. No matter how trivial a person's actions, everything—for good or for ill—reverberated within this "triune" association. As a result, Levy rededicated himself to advancing only the highest and loftiest goals, as "communicated to [him] by the spirit."[13] Levy's adherence to this mystical principle permeated all his thinking, and it became a motive force behind his subsequent decision to embark on an activist career. Accordingly, instead of returning to the United States after his monetary windfall, in 1827 Levy resided once more in the West End of London, at No. 1 Park Lane, Knightsbridge. This same year Joseph Delevante, an affluent merchant and confidant from Levy's St.

Thomas days, lent him an additional 2,110 pounds. Undoubtedly, although much of this money went to meet his obligations in Florida, it also allowed him the freedom to pursue his reform causes abroad.

In May Levy received the distressing news that his seventeen-year-old son David, after complaining of "languor and apathy," had abruptly left Norfolk and was bound for his mother's home on St. Thomas. David's actions may not have come as a complete surprise, since the boy's behavior had been a problem for some time. According to Moses Myers, David's unruly conduct required the "full attention of [the] family." Disappointment regarding Elias's episode at Harvard convinced Levy that a college education would not benefit David's character and that a trade would teach him proper values. Therefore, David was not allowed to follow his Norfolk Academy classmates into higher education and was required to work as a clerk in one of the Myers's countinghouses instead—a situation that the teenager resented. David's sudden departure caused great distress, and Levy feared for his son's future. It is not clear whether Rachel or Rahma remained in England at this time or if they had returned to St. Thomas. In any case Levy's finances were in "a frightful state," and he fully realized the precariousness of his position. Despite the increasing pressure of indebtedness and his premonitions of financial collapse, Levy decided to heed what he considered to be a higher calling. He opted to stay in London to pursue a life as a social and religious activist—at least for as long as he was able.[14]

To understand Levy's decision fully, it is important to consider that he felt a personal obligation to improve society as a whole, and in many ways the metropolis offered the best platform in which to advance his views. As a result of Levy's implementation of his "Sacred Cause" in Florida, a variety of issues still appeared feasible elsewhere. Educational reform, abolitionism, a restructuring of Judaism, and challenges to antisemitism came to the forefront. Despite his problems, as long as Pilgrimage endured, it became—to paraphrase historian Arthur Bestor—a working model of a good society.[15] Judged within the communitarian mind-set, the size of the endeavor did not matter as much as the fact that it was up and running. To be sure, there was always hope that the Florida settlement would expand, attract more colonists, and reap a rich sugar harvest. In the interim Levy decided to take advantage of the interest that was given to him by an increasing number of Protestant activists as well as Jews. From his Park Lane address, with its facade of Georgian respectability, he was poised to enter the prestigious circle of the London reformers. Also of continued importance was the necessity of finding fellow philanthropists who would come to his aid.

Perhaps more than at any other time in his life, now Levy's dichotomous nature was brought to the fore. While still adhering to Jewish separatism, pragmatic considerations led him to seek closer relations with certain Christian organizations. Specifically, Levy's interest was drawn to the newly formed Philo-Judaean Society, a more liberal offshoot of the London Society for the Promotion of Christianity among the Jews. In contrast to the latter, the Philo-Judaeans did not focus on conversion per se. Rather, their agenda centered on the performance of charitable acts, and they were, by and large, far more respectful in their relations with practicing Jews than the London Society. The goals of the Philo-Judaeans included physical assistance to the sick and aged, establishment of schools, financial contributions, promotion of full civil liberties, and public admission of Christianity's past transgressions. The last item certainly spoke directly to Levy's belief in atonement, and there was no doubt that impoverished Jews had much to gain from even a modicum of assistance. Nevertheless, the society still hoped that by alleviating the suffering of Jews and making restitution, they eventually would be more inclined to convert. Also according to theory, by loosening the bonds of alienation and admitting Jews as full citizens, a great step would be achieved, since assimilation—so it was thought—would surely lead to more baptisms.[16] The millennialist spirit was, after all, fully in force. Although the theme of "amelioration" was certainly well-known and mistrusted by many in the Jewish community, Levy concluded that Jews would hardly relinquish their religious identity after being treated with mere compassion and kindness from Christians, their spiritual "children."

Certainly, the Anglo-Jewish lay leadership—split between Sephardi and Ashkenazi factions—failed fully to address the needs of the growing masses of Jewish poor, most of whom were Ashkenazim from the Central European ghettos. One historian of the Georgian period has attributed this lack of support to the "frontier boom town" quality of London; the rapid influx of newcomers quickly overwhelmed existing communal institutions.[17] Collectively, the Spanish and Portuguese congregations were more prosperous than their Yiddish-speaking brethren and held higher status, a situation similar to the United States. Because each community was expected to take care of its own, slim charitable resources were reduced even more. Levy, however, saw the deplorable Jewish slums and the lack of education as symptomatic of a much more pervasive problem. The needless tension and division among the Sephardim and Ashkenazim were just two aspects of the quandary. He attributed the dearth of benevolence to the legacy of persecution, a systematic humiliation that made the "Israelite . . . insensible to the state of his nation." Levy was not alone in assigning blame to the Jewish psyche. After details of Levy's Philo-Judaean activities became widespread, a well-known Ashkenazi rabbi had the courage to chastise the lay leadership in a London newspaper: "Our faces ought to be covered with shame, when we see daily the Christians join, the rich and the poor together, to instruct their poor, and sparing no expense. But we, who are the children of Abraham, the friend of God, and the people with whom God made a covenant, are lying in a deep sleep. . . . Let us not be ashamed to learn of Christians; take an example of them, and do the same."[18]

In fact, the few Jewish attempts at educating the poor, such as the Jews' Free School (1817), were founded in direct response to earlier Christian-conversionist schools. But the meager number and small scale of the Jewish academies had scant impact. While a sizable portion of the Jewish community may have understandably regarded the Philo-Judaeans with suspicion, if not outright animosity, there was a growing awareness that needs were not being met.[19]

Filled with a magnanimous spirit, and holding great expectations for hastening the Second Coming, the Philo-Judaeans went about their formidable task of confronting the material, social, and educational requirements of the Jewish lower class. Chaired by Viscount Mandeville, the society met regularly at London's Freemasons' Hall, a grand and elegant venue located on Great Queen Street. The organization's charter admitted both religious dissenters and members of the Church of England, and the group also formed a separate Ladies' Association. Prominent members of Parliament, such as Robert Grant and Lord Bexley (the former chancellor of the exchequer), were active in the society and promoted its causes. The preeminent banker, former Tory MP, and radical evangelical Henry Drummond acted as treasurer. Levy trusted that the organization would not overstep its bounds and proselytize; as long as they were willing to help the majority of Jews who lived in squalor, all would benefit. His participation was also in accordance with his universalist tenets; he was convinced that all believers in the divine authority of the Bible were united in the same spirit. Just as Levy distinguished between the actions of individual "Israelites" and the greater "house of Israel," he also divided Christians into two groups: the "real" and the "nominal." Of course, he was predisposed to assign the Philo-Judaeans to the first category. His decision to support the society was only partly indicative of his alienation from orthodox Judaism. To a large degree it represented a genuine belief that the Philo-Judaeans would do "great things" for the "distressed and necessitous Israelite."[20]

Levy's first major address to the organization was a genuine triumph. The speech was subsequently published in the London evangelical newspaper the *World* not once but twice—the second, a two-part unedited version. He stressed the commonality of the Judeo-Christian heritage, condemned antisemitism in all its forms, pleaded that everyone "apply to the Bible and feel its spirit," and used inclusive terms such as *Divine Providence* and *Revelation* to such a degree that the Anglican divine Hugh McNeile admitted that he was confused: "He knew not whether he was a Christian or a Jew, or whether Mr. Levi was a Jew or a Christian." Most important, McNeile noted that "love had been spoken of" and that made a "deep impression on his heart." Levy knew his audience well and addressed them with passion and persuasion. The difficult subject of conversion, however, had to be dealt with: "If, indeed, the Jews must ultimately turn, the Almighty seems clearly, by their dispersion, to have placed it beyond the power of man to effect, who can at best only convert one here and there; the work he evidently reserves for himself. Clearly, then, this is but a subterfuge which the enemy of man puts into the mouth of *soi-disant* believers, in order to keep alive that hatred towards the Jews."[21]

This statement was so adroitly delivered, inserted as it was between praise for the society's "persuasive language of love" and its "unremitting exertions," that many listeners and readers alike took what they wanted from Levy's speech and reached their own positive conclusions. His words and spiritual orientation defied all the negative stereotypes. Notably, there was no discussion of the despised Talmud, which, in contrast to the "pure and undefiled Sacred Word," was deemed by evangelicals as "strange and monstrous."[22] There was certainly no hint of the ghetto about Levy, nor was there any connection to the other end of the spectrum, the taint of the stock market, gem trade, or a lifetime's obsession with mere mammon.

In short, he met the lofty British standard of gentility, a complex set of behaviors that went far beyond fashionable dress, verbal acuity, and subtle comportment.[23] Well-to-do Sephardim had a reputation for being more so-phisticated and acculturated than their Ashkenazi counterparts. But Levy transcended neat categories and appeared once again as the very same "benevolent Stranger" and "compassionate Being" whose altruism was so lauded by the Jews of Curaçao. Because he considered himself reborn in the spirit, Levy had much in common with most persons gathered at Freemasons' Hall. His noble concerns were seen as pure and motivated by a love for God, the Bible, and his fellow man; his self-confidence and spiritual zeal was worthy of the most accomplished Protestant preacher. Remarkably, Levy did not shun the media. In addition to the *World,* other leading papers, such as the venerable *Times,* covered Levy's speeches and lectures in detail. As a result, London's literate classes soon became intimately familiar with this charismatic Jew from Florida. Significantly, attendance at the Philo-Judaean meetings grew to about a thousand people.[24]

Certainly not all evangelicals relished Levy's views. At one meeting sponsored by an organization called the Society for Investigating the Prophecies, Levy was interrupted several times by a "few uncontrolled persons" and was unable to continue. His main intent was "to prove from the New Testament, Daniel and Zechariah, that Israel's continued existence as a separate nation is still the will of God; that they will return as a distinct nation, to accomplish the as yet unfulfilled redemption of man." The rude behavior at this meeting drew forceful criticism from the editors of the *World.* Nevertheless, Levy's unprecedented activism and popularity among the Philo-Judaeans created a distinct backlash. Some Protestants contemptuously objected to any Jew quoting from the New Testament and even disputed the phrase "God's chosen people." Statements such as these demonstrated that a palpable hatred of Judaism was still very much in force, especially among the High Church faction of Anglicans. This was also seen in the divided British reaction to a Russian *ukase,* or imperial edict, which was given much notice in the London papers. Among other things, this decree—or, more precisely, a series of decrees—from Czar Nicholas I dictated the forced removal of Jews from their homes in the Russian province of Grodno and singled out peddlers and rabbis as especially worthy of ousting. Later all Jews were ordered to leave the city of Kiev. Ironically, new legislation that drafted Jews into the imperial army—a convoluted statute that contained 157 articles—was not initially recognized for what it really was: a brutal, conversionist policy that targeted Jewish youngsters as young as twelve.[25]

A few prominent Londoners reacted to the news from Russia with a callous contempt and cloaked their indifference by comparing the "exclusive character of Judaism" to "popery" and other "human inventions." Some vented their wrath at rabbis, who were accused of everything from promoting "gross idolatry" and superstition to bringing on the "destruction of Jerusalem, the Temple, and the long train of incalculable misery and slaughter."[26] Predictably, Levy reacted with indignation and expressed genuine dismay that any Christian would "betray such cold and indifferent feelings." Was it appropriate, he asked, to diminish the suffering of "thousands of poor naked and starving families, helpless widows, and still more helpless orphans, hurried on by the merciless *venal* officers of an *arbitrary* power through the inhospitable wilds and rigorous climate of an extensive empire? Great God! Is this Christianity?"[27]

Criticism also came from certain Jews who were reluctant to register any complaint without tangible proof that suffering was indeed taking place. This skepticism rankled Levy's sensibilities, and at one public meeting that included a number of his coreligionists he dared to suggest that, if the issue had been a "money-making" scheme, "the stock-jobbers would have adopted every means to obtain the earliest intelligence; and they would have speculated upon it even before its promulgation." Such condemnation drew cheers from Levy's Jewish supporters. Finally, he compared any form of persecution to a wound received in the collective body of Israel and then asked: "But what would they conclude if this body betrayed no sensibility to the effects of the wound?" As Levy paused for an answer, several replied in unison: "In a state of mortification." Such scenes were routinely reported on—with relish—by the city's journalists.[28]

The questions Levy posed disturbed many who believed that the restoration of the Jews was being horribly subverted in Russia. Among others Levy gained the public support of John Aquila Brown, secretary of the Philo-Judaean Society, geologist, and author of several influential tracts on Bible prophecy. Jewish advocates included Selig Newman, a progressive Ashkenazi leader and learned Hebraist who had been a Hebrew instructor at Oxford University.[29] Newman joined Levy in a series of unprecedented weekly meetings that were held between Christians and Jews. These discussions, which were, according to one observer, "attended by a great number of Jews" as well as evangelical Christians, began at Salvador House in Bishopsgate and subsequently moved to the King's Head Tavern. In addition to the Russian persecutions, topics included Oral Law, Bible prophecy, and scriptural references to the Messiah. Such interfaith exchanges, while at times heated and contentious, generally observed the rules of decorum and became a unique and much publicized experiment in Judeo-Christian dialogue. The Anglo-Jewish elite, however, scrupulously avoided such encounters. As a whole, they resented Levy's leadership at these gatherings and criticized his "sanguine interference." Rather than risk any publicity that could offend the Tory establishment, most communal leaders sought to maintain an image of "a harmless, unmeddling people."[30] Nevertheless, more liberal-minded Jews admired Levy's forthright stance. For instance, Selig Newman took many of Levy's admonitions to heart and, in conjunction with Dr. Joshua Van Oven, a noted scholar, physician, and progressive communal leader, and Michael Josephs, an eminent Hebraist, founded the Light of Torah Society. Their main objective was to establish a free, adult night school in the metropolis. Indeed, though short-lived, a school was founded with the sanction of the chief rabbi, and a Sabbath afternoon lecture series continued for several years.[31]

Of all the issues that Levy tackled in 1827, the Russian edicts assumed utmost urgency. He was quick to seize upon the affair as a means of stirring his fellow Jews from their apathy and uniting them behind a common cause. Because the oppressions concerned a foreign power, none could accuse any protestor of sedition. Like Protestant dissenters, the last thing that Jews desired was to have their patriotism and loyalty questioned. Furthermore, it played into Levy's vision of a unified Jewry that transcended state boundaries. Also of consequence was his ability to curb his radical opinions in order not to alienate any potential followers. He even defended, on several occasions, the value of rabbis and of Oral Law—although he always asserted the primacy of the Torah. As the leader of a special public meeting of the Jews which was convened to challenge the Russian *ukase*, Levy declared "that his wish was to rouse once more the spirit of nationality in his brethren." "If this could once be done," he concluded, "their oppressions would cease."[32]

On 5 December the Jews who gathered at the opulent City of London Tavern—at Levy's behest—approved a series of resolutions that protested the actions of Nicholas I. The last of these articles requested that "an address be presented to the various congregations of the Jews in Great Britain, representing the sentiments of this Meeting and requesting their cooperations in such measure as may be likely to arrest the calamities which we universally deplore." "M. E. Levy, Esq., of Florida," who was unanimously appointed chairman, was selected to write the declaration. The significance of this moment would be discussed in London for some time, for a major portion of the speeches and arguments were duly recorded in the papers. Public activism and protest of this kind was unheard of among Anglo-Jewry, so this undertaking was deemed extremely newsworthy. Compelled to address any apprehensions, Levy admitted that some Jews may indeed have been "afraid of expressing their sentiments, least they should arouse the indignation of the governments." Such timidity, he asserted, "could only arise from want of faith in their Almighty King." For the wealthy Jewish elite, whose absence was noted, Levy heaped significant scorn. Imagining they were otherwise engaged "in the improvement of their fortunes or in fashionable amusements, or else were so much in dread of exciting any hostile feelings in persons possessed of power," he considered these monied individuals a lost cause. Thoroughly inspired by the evening's events, with the few opposing voices having been quelled, the group scheduled to meet again. Evangelicals in attendance promised to take more action and were quite pleased at this sudden show of defiance against Russian brutality.[33]

The second "Public Meeting of the Jews" met again on 19 December. Chairman Levy opened the session and requested that the most recent *ukase* be read in full as well as his own address to the Jews of Great Britain. In fashioning his appeal to the various synagogues, Levy hoped he could sway the most conservative elements by highlighting the plight of rabbis and of families who would be left without the benefit of religious instruction. Being politically astute, he knew the value of framing his arguments behind a cause that he judged to have the greatest support among the orthodox. In so doing, he became a defender of the very rabbinical tradition that he privately condemned: "Most deeply do we lament this regulation, as depriving such families of all religious instruction and consolation under their sufferings, which will unavoidably produce woeful consequences upon their moral and spiritual character: thus spreading the contagion of infidelity among a people hitherto characterized by devoted adherence to the religion of their forefathers. But alarming as we consider this decree in its effects, upon those on whom it mediately or immediately operates, we cannot but consider that it will be still more disastrous in its influence on generations yet unborn."[34]

After enumerating similar examples of European persecution in Germany and elsewhere and reinforcing his premise that only a concerted Jewish action could effectively counter such threats, a motion was entered to approve the address as written. Selig Newman seconded this, and Levy's address was carried by a show of hands.

Afterward, one person in attendance became visibly agitated, and, as he stood to express his views, he turned to a group of newspaper reporters and pleaded with them to be "fair" and not take advantage of the situation. After denying that such severe conditions could exist and asserting that "there were no Jews in Russia, only in Poland," the man was met with jeers and cries of "turn him out!" Still he continued, and his next comments revealed the real source of his anxiety: "I advise all innocent Jews to abstain; they [Russians] would only make the restrictions worse—do they want to have all the Jews throats cut?"

Thus was fear-driven denial, a legacy of generations of pogroms and humiliations, allowed expression. Several others voiced similar sentiments, with one explaining that the loss of rabbis was not so bad, since it was the responsibility of fathers to instruct their families. Levy had long recognized this unpleasant tendency among his fellow Jews, but he allowed all to express their opinions. Later, after stepping down temporarily from his role as chairman and fully aware of the journalists and stenographers who were present, Levy decided to confront the issue head on: "There are people among us, who say, 'O, this Ukase—O, it is nothing; it is what has been done for ages; they have a right to make what regulations they will in their own country.' It appears as if they were like the negroes in the West Indies, who are so accustomed to look up to and receive every thing at the hand of their master, and their master only, that even when the cart-whip is unmercifully laid on their backs, they mechanically shriek at the smart of every lash, 'Thank ye, Massa!' I do think the spirit of the times, combining with that of persecution, is favourable to our rising and becoming once more a united people."[35]

Such a sentiment, with its correlation of Jewish acquiescence with "a slavish state of mind," resonated deeply with most in attendance, and Levy's call for action was cheered and applauded. Of course, news of these events soon spread beyond London. One anonymous commentator considered the recent "Public Meetings of the Jewish Nation" as "the first time for many centuries" that Jews have considered their "external relations . . . with all the nations of the earth." Indeed, in his view "the eyes of England, of Europe, and of [a] great part of the civilised world, seem to be directed towards us."[36]

The next protest came on New Year's Day 1828, at a gathering of Christians and Jews led by the prominent decorative glass manufacturer Apsley Pellatt. This group approved a series of resolutions lauding Levy's actions. Furthermore, it was decided to post these remarks in the newspapers and to forward them to "the various congregations of Jews in the British dominions."[37] For unknown reasons these lively and indignant responses to the Russian *ukase* had a short duration. Despite the enthusiasm and publicity, notices of subsequent meetings were not forthcoming, and there is no indication that any synagogue acted upon any of these proclamations. Based on the level of anxiety which was expressed by some in attendance and the almost revolutionary fervor of Levy's oratory, perhaps government pressure came to bear. In fact, Britain had recently forged a military alliance with Russia and, together with France, successfully launched a naval campaign against Turkey a few months before. Such heated and well-publicized rhetoric leveled against their Russian ally may not have been tolerated by government leaders.

Another question arises regarding Levy's newfound enthusiasm for entering the public domain. In retrospect the episode did serve to offset the embarrassing spectacle of Mordecai Noah's previous "folly," an affair that reinforced rampant stereotypes of Jewish self-interest. When viewed as a public relations venture of a different sort, the media coverage actually succeeded in promoting positive qualities of altruism, strength, and cohesion—and with absolutely no taint of profit motive, land speculation, or egotistical claims. Regardless, Levy would have seen the entire effort as a much needed training exercise. Once awakened, he believed the pride of the Jewish people would soar again and "the noble faculties of the mind" would rise above the unremitting "persecution of contempt." Furthermore, the concept of a benevolent Jewish nationalism that transcended borders and attended to the welfare of the less fortunate had finally been aroused. This ideology would not be given full expression until the founding of the Alliance Israélite Universelle (Paris, 1860) three decades later.[38]

References to Levy's call for action among the Jews managed to surface in the press several months later, but any further mention of the Russian *ukase* was very limited. Nevertheless, a clergyman from Bristol expressed his view that the recent activity among Jews and Christians represented "certainly extraordinary signs of the times and shew that something most singular is approaching." It appeared, to some at least, that Levy's activities may have heralded the millennium.[39] A letter by Rabbi Joseph Crooll, a Cambridge University Hebrew instructor, was especially solicitous and praised Levy for his struggle toward the "restoration" of the Jews. "We have of late observed a man by the name of Mr. Moses Elias Levi who endeavoured to bring in motion the Jews, that they might rise and shew themselves men; that they might find favour in the sight of God and men."[40] Crooll had gained recognition in his own right as the author of *The Restoration of Israel* (1812), in which he refuted the claims of conversionists and announced that the promised reign of the Messiah was near. In fact, he brazenly set a date for this miraculous occurrence, based on his interpretation of Scripture, as the year 1840. Whether Levy accepted this as fact is by no means certain. It is obvious, however, that Levy had much in common with Crooll, and it is likely that Levy's own assumptions regarding the Messiah—even his perfectionist beliefs—were influenced by the writings of this idiosyncratic scholar. After years of teaching Hebrew to earnest evangelicals, the Hungarian-born rabbi adhered to his own distinct brand of millennialism. He predicted that the messianic age would be "a world of perfection, of wisdom; a world of peace and happiness, and of long duration, the life of man will be restored to the degree as it was in the time of Adam."[41] It is also noteworthy that Levy's Philo-Judaean supporter, John Aquila Brown, arrived at a similar date for the Second Coming based on his interpretation of the Book of Daniel, as did others.[42] In any case Levy believed that the "purposes of revelation [would] soon be accomplished," a momentous event "which the world is fast approaching."[43]

Levy and Crooll's belief that the day of Redemption was near should be considered in the context of a Jewish messianic movement that emanated from Eastern Europe. In fact, Crooll referred to "the opinion of one great and eminent Rabbi" in order to justify his belief that 1840, or the year

5600 according to the Hebrew calendar, would mark the arrival of the Messiah. While Crooll did not identify this learned rabbi, there is little doubt among scholars that he was referring to Rabbi Eliahu of Vilna (1720–97), commonly known as the Vilna Gaon.[44] During his lifetime the Gaon (or "genius") was considered the preeminent Ashkenazi rabbi; his scholarship was without peer, and his authority extended far beyond Lithuania. This ultraorthodox rabbi stood in contradistinction to his Berlin contemporary, Moses Mendelssohn (1729–86), the founder of the Haskalah movement and a proponent of the German Enlightenment. While *maskilim* championed civil liberties and attacked rabbinical authority, followers of the Vilna Gaon relished their separateness and adopted a potent messianic fervor. The Vilna rabbi's influence remained undiminished even after his death, and thousands flocked to Palestine (Eretz Yisrael) to await the Messiah—an event that was noted by well-informed Jews from across the diaspora.[45] Consequently, Moses Levy managed selectively to blend elements from both the orthodox and the *maskilim* into his personal belief system, and it is hardly surprising that Levy attracted followers and admirers from both camps while in London. Undoubtedly, Levy's own traumatic experience in Morocco deterred him from any immediate move toward Palestine, then under Ottoman rule, and he focused his intended gathering of Jews in Florida instead. According to the Bible, however, an eventual return to the Holy Land would parallel the messianic age, an event that Levy would surely have relished. As it happened, Levy's avoidance of Palestine was well served; the disciples of the Vilna Gaon were confronted with deadly plagues, earthquakes, and repeated assaults by Muslims—all of which created immense suffering.

More moderate Jews and Christians preferred to keep their distance from the rise in millennial fervor. Nonetheless, whether motivated by ancient messianic prophecies or by Enlightenment ideals, the goal of all reformers was to affect practical change in society as a whole. The "good works" tenet of evangelicals, as expressed in a myriad of causes including abolitionism, penal reform, and the missionary/conversionist movement, was a manifestation of a deep shift in thinking. As historian David Brion Davis has posited: "for the first time in history the more enlightened nations were beginning to understand that morality, self-interest, and human progress were mutually interdependent and were to be achieved by the same means."[46] Especially as it pertained to the plantation system of the British West Indies, moral progress (abolition) was seen as taking precedent over economic interests, or mere mammon in evangelical parlance. This concept was most revolutionary, and, from its rudimentary start in the late eighteenth century, abolitionism had achieved a tremendous degree of popular support in Britain. One historian has concluded that the ardor and enthusiasm of the antislavery crusade almost reached the status of a religion, albeit an overwhelmingly Protestant one.[47] The resultant propaganda campaign that equated abolitionism with Christian morality spurred an uncommon response from Wesleyan Methodists, Baptists, Congregationalists, as well as evangelical Anglicans and inspired the greatest surge of parliamentary petitions in British history.

Levy attended antislavery meetings throughout his tenure in London. Because of his reputation as a public speaker and his unusual background as a plantation owner, Levy was invited to voice his opinions at several meetings, including the well-to-do Surrey Anti-Slavery Society, chaired by the influential Philo-Judaean Henry Drummond. While certainly not immune from recounting horrific tales of slave abuse, Levy preferred to base his arguments in broader terms. He emphasized that his practical, long-term goals were "offered to the consideration of those actuated by principle, and not by feeling." It should be noted that abolitionist meetings as well as the bulk of antislavery literature were usually highly charged with emotion and inevitably castigated the slave owner as being both morally degenerate and cruel. Levy assumed that this strategy would only solidify the opposition of Parliament, an institution that was still under the sway of West Indian plantation owners and their allies. Therefore, Levy sought a different approach. The "great question," he concluded, "was not whether criminal abuses existed but "whether they were to keep some thousands of their fellow-creatures in their present state of debasement," a condition that not only injured blacks but—in both a moral and a spiritual sense—injured whites as well. He placed final responsibility on society as a whole: "The slave-holder had a right to turn round upon them and say, 'If you all wish to remove slavery, you are all bound to come forward and assist. The evil, such as it is, was introduced by your fathers, but the money gained by it has found its way into your pockets.'" Abolitionists could rail as much as they wanted; what was needed was a general plan that addressed economic realities as well as the moral good and could be implemented immediately. "Many found fault of the system of slavery," Levy admonished his audience, "many were ready to petition against it; but few were inclined to come forward and help to remove it."[48]

Levy's words were eloquent, and his twenty-year experience in the slaveholding Caribbean certainly contributed to his standing as an expert— something that few abolitionists could claim. But his stature as a *Jewish* abolitionist, a distinction that was unparalleled during the development of the British antislavery crusade, suggested that "something most singular" was indeed happening, although to what end was still open to debate. At least in the minds of Henry Drummond's group in Epsom, Surrey, and to the growing number of evangelicals who believed in the prophetic character of the Bible, Levy's mere presence invoked a certain reverential respect. After all, within a very short period this previously unknown American activist had achieved great celebrity among reform circles, a feat difficult enough for any foreigner, let alone a Jewish outsider from the Florida frontier. Moreover, Levy's notions concerning the gradual abolition of slavery were deemed quite reasonable and impressed many by his emphasis on pragmatic action. As a result of his increasing influence in the abolitionist cause and the encouragement that he received, Levy decided to put his ideas into concrete form and to publish a pamphlet that could be distributed throughout England.

In fact, during July 1828 Levy's treatise, *A Plan for the Abolition of Slavery, Consistently with the Interests of All Parties Concerned,* was released and gained significant notice. Although his associates in the reform movement were aware of his authorship, Levy believed that much would be gained by withholding his identity from the pamphlet. As we have seen, a burgeoning nationalism as well as a legacy of antisemitism pervaded British culture, and by remaining anonymous his ideas would be judged on their own merits and reach as wide an audience as possible. Keenly aware of his status as both a "stranger and a Jew," he saw little reason to alienate potential readers.[49] Additionally, any gesture of anonymity was highly valued as an act of piety and humility within religious circles, and Levy's motives would be seen as divorced from personal aggrandizement—an impression that Levy always strived to maintain. Finally, and perhaps most important, unlike England, abolitionists in the American South were universally reviled, and dire consequences would certainly have ensued had the author's identity been discovered and his controversial views been exposed in the United States. Pilgrimage's very existence, as well as Levy's own welfare, would have been placed in jeopardy.

In Levy's valiant attempt to appeal to "all parties" he revealed many of the inconsistencies in his own character. His narrative may have utilized many conventional themes, such as invoking the inevitable doom of slave insurrections as well as the moral imperatives of the Bible, but the scope and complexity of his plan greatly exceeded the norm. Not surprisingly, his pamphlet presented a unique blend of utopianism, biblicism, business-like pragmatism, agrarian and educational reform, and travelogue. Despite his observation "that only those persons who both acknowledge *and feel* the influence of Divine Revelation (and not the mere philanthropist) are capable of undertaking the work proposed," it is apparent that he wished to reach beyond his evangelical supporters. Therefore, contradictions were inevitable. His prose could at once be extremely sensitive and caring toward the "benighted sons of Africa," while a sterner persona reminded readers of harsh realities. Slaves were, after all, "habitually indolent, deceitful, and vicious"—a result of their "abject state." Freedom, therefore, could only be given to their children.[50] Any criticism of slaves was very unusual within the abolitionist community, and most authors limited negative characteristics to their collective enemy, the slave traders and plantation owners. Absent are any specific references to the humane strictures of Levy's cherished biblical model, a paradigm that he evidently considered beyond the capability of most slave owners. Notably, unlike other tracts that linked the abolitionist cause with the supposed moral supremacy of Christianity, such as Rev. Andrew Thomson's *Slavery not sanctioned, but condemned, by Christianity: A Sermon* (London, 1829), Levy did not offer a single reference to Jesus Christ but invoked the Old Testament instead. All things considered, while a good number of his core beliefs do appear in his plan, the pamphlet was designed as a compromise solution, one that Levy believed could still set the stage for eventual emancipation.

A key component of his plan was the establishment of commercial-philanthropic companies in "every civilized nation." Social change, rather than large profits, would be the group's main goal. Plantations would be constructed in the West Indies and the Americas, and, while carrying on the tenets of Levy's scheme, these enterprises would also engage in the development of non-slave-dependent agriculture. As model communities of reform, each operation would be open to inspection from outsiders and offer firsthand proof of its practicality. The relationship to Levy's Florida endeavor is clear. "The communitarian point of view," according to Arthur Bestor, "was the idea of commencing a wholesale social reorganization by first establishing and demonstrating its principles completely on a small scale in an experimental community."[51] The "plasticity" of New World society, or so it was assumed, would offer the requisite freedom for such experimentation.

Characteristically, educational reform was also central to Levy's abolitionist strategy. "[Emancipation] must begin with children," Levy proclaimed, "let them emancipate their minds, and when they have education and virtue, they [will] become free."[52] Therefore, not only would these "chartered companies" develop a new form of agriculture, but a more accessible educational agenda would also emerge. Following the ideas already established for his Jewish colony, the children of slaves would be instructed in the basics of the arts and sciences as well as being trained in agriculture. Classical Greek and Roman literature, so much in vogue among the higher classes, would be excluded. Bible studies—both Old and New Testament—would become an integral part of this "general and consistent system of education," and the combination of "practical religion and useful knowledge" would mold the characters of slave children so that they could carry on productive, free lives. In a variant of Levy's idea of the communal raising of children, young pupils would be taken from their families and raised separately under the guiding efforts and watchful eyes of their instructors. Cut off from any connection with their slave past, children would acquire a lofty and harmonious nature, and at the age of twenty-one they would be awarded their freedom. "Retributive justice," or the scourge of the earth by slave insurrections, would thereby be averted: "By commencing a system of improvement, founded on the solid basis of practical religion, you will attack prejudice with the only weapon likely to subdue it; you will then avert the vengeance of retributive justice; and atone by the labours bestowed on succeeding generations, for the cruelties inflicted on their forefathers; and you will then ward off the calamities, with which that hemisphere is threatened, and introduce such a state of society as will be a blessing to it and to the world at large."[53]

Another distinctive feature of Levy's abolitionist plan was his advocacy of miscegenation. He called for the diversion of British convicts to the West

Indies, rather than Australia, to accomplish this goal. It must be noted that penal transportation was generally seen as a progressive step in criminal justice, and the horrors of the journey to New South Wales were either suppressed or ignored. In fact, Levy reflected the high degree of misinformation about the institution when he wrote of the supposed desire of ordinary men for "free passage to a good country." Because it was regarded as "wise and humane," a reformer such as Moses Levy would naturally consider the merits of transportation within his own ambitious scheme.[54] He theorized that intermarriage between white convicts and the resident slave population would be of immense value in reducing the polarity and inherent conflict between the races. Such ideas, of course, were especially common in Cuba and elsewhere in the Caribbean. At the core of this scheme was an attempt to recognize the deep-seated racism that was so characteristic of the nineteenth century. As Levy acknowledged:

> The charity of Englishmen may give freedom to the slaves of their own colonies; but it will avail nothing, as against the general feeling entertained towards this unhappy race all over the world. Will their charity mould their own nature, to view with equal complaisance the symmetrical form and the fair skin of an European, and the disproportioned figure and black skin of an African? the long auburn tresses, and the woolly hair? the well-shaped and polished forehead, and a depressed one? the finely-shaped nose, and the short, flat, wide nose? the cherry lips of an European, and the thick black ones of an African? It is within the power of legislation or money to emancipate 800,000 slaves; but is there any legislative act, *except that of God,* that can counteract such insurmountable prejudices?[55]

Levy pressed this "most delicate question" further. Holding American Quakers as worthy exemplars of abolitionist zeal, he noted there was "no instance of their taking a genteel coloured family or person by the hand of unqualified friendship, intermarrying with them, or even mixing in social or convivial pleasure."[56] Therefore, it appeared that whites, no matter how high-minded, would always discriminate against blacks. The only solution, according to Levy, was that "the black skin [should] be lost with slavery in the gradual shades of improvement."[57] Significantly, Levy never asserted the inherent inferiority of blacks, but his notions stemmed from a concern for social equality. Considering Levy's literal-mindedness regarding the biblical account of creation, it is striking that he did not entertain the more common idea that God had created racial differences according to his own design and that racial intermixture would be antithetical to the natural order.

The worldwide network of philanthropic companies that Levy proposed also offered an irresistible opportunity to enact his universalist tenants. He proposed that a "United Association" be formed that would "inquire into and suggest to government the best and most effectual means of annihilating the slave-trading system." Levy believed that a common fleet of specially designed sailing vessels would constitute a formidable force in halting the "inhuman traffic" that continued off the coast of Africa. This "uninterrupted cruize against slave traders" would be manned by African natives and commanded by "able and expert men from the same place." Such a collective endeavor would prove invaluable in intercepting slave ships and would greatly surpass the individual efforts of Britain, or so Levy reasoned. Again, communitarian ideals of the collective good would triumph over individualism (autonomous states).[58] Also of note, Levy envisioned that power would reside in the philanthropic consortium, not in government.

The United Association of companies—a supranational organization reminiscent of the United Nations—would also promote "the emigration of white people" to the West Indies and to the Americas for the purposes of intermarriage as well as fix a time for universal emancipation. Any future date would have to be of sufficient duration to allow for the plantation economy to shift to free labor, a time that Levy figured should be measured in Jubilee years—that is, either "50 or 100 years."[59]

Levy certainly went much farther than any of his abolitionist colleagues in proposing wide-scale, systematic changes within the proven (and lucrative) New World plantation system. According to his reasoning, any simple declaration of emancipation, gradual or otherwise, was bound to fail because the source of all difficulty was nothing less than the structure of society itself. While the plantation may have been a microcosm of larger societal ills, it also represented a mighty force for economic and social change—a fact that Levy was extremely cognizant of. Historian Richard Sheridan aptly described the plantation system as "a combination of African labor, European technology and management, Asiatic and American plants, European animal husbandry and American soil and climate."[60] The Industrial Revolution may have achieved dominance in Britain, but the older Caribbean sugar revolution had long served as a model for the large-scale exploitation of labor, the accumulation of vast amounts of capital, the massive migration of people, and the emergence of a politically powerful planter/mercantile elite. Planters were also manufacturers because the production of crystallized sugar depended on the specialized factory regimen of the sugar mill. The influence of this slave-based system was far-reaching and complex. By utilizing the moral suasion of the antislavery crusade, Levy hoped to enlist others to transform the very core of plantation society so that it would adhere more closely to his utopian model. It must be emphasized, however, that change would be gradual and that the traditional slave economy would coexist, at least for a time, with the new, enlightened order.

Levy's plan heralded the emergence of an educated group of free, mixed-race farmers who exemplified the best Christian attributes. Each family would have a small plantation, between two to ten acres, and "for every two or three hundred of these plantations" Levy foresaw a large communal sugar mill that would serve their needs. During harvest season all families would work together in cutting and transporting the cane to the mill. A reasonable toll would be charged for the refining process, and in return each individual farmer would be given a portion of sugar, based on a liberal spirit of "neighbourly consideration." Thereby sugar, long stigmatized and boycotted by many abolitionists as being the unsavory product of brutal West Indian slave regimes, would be transformed into the respectable bounty of a free and God-fearing people.[61] Similarly, the image of the mill was altered to incorporate only the most humane and benevolent feelings of brotherly cooperation and enterprise. This system of enlightened agriculture would serve as a beacon of righteousness which others would surely emulate.

Despite its utopian character, Levy's *Plan for the Abolition of Slavery* did achieve favorable notice. The London *Literary Chronicle,* swayed by the anonymous author's reasoned exposition and his gradualist approach to abolition, recommended the tract "to the serious attention of the legislature and the public."[62] The *World* newspaper devoted an entire column to Levy's treatise. "We are much pleased to find that the writer of this pamphlet takes a rational view of the subject," the paper observed. "For while he is fully alive to the monstrous evil of slavery . . . he deprecates the idea of inflicting an additional evil on the unhappy race who are its subjects, which no one at all acquainted with the character of the slaves can reasonably doubt would be the result of full and immediate emancipation." Furthermore, the unnamed author was entitled to "a respectful hearing" not only because of his "great benevolence of soul, and [his] deep and enlightened piety," but his "twenty-four years in slave-holding countries" imbued his views with the wisdom gained by practical experience.[63] Most impressive was the formation of a new antislavery organization that incorporated Levy's innovative proposals into its charter, including a provision to divert the transportation of criminals to the British West Indies. While Levy's United Association was not mentioned specifically, the group promised "to promote the establishment of similar Societies all over Europe and America." Notably, this organization met every week at Salvador House, Bishopsgate, the same location where Levy had initiated meetings between Jews and Christians some months before.[64] There is no indication, however, that any Jews actually joined Levy in the abolitionist cause.

After the pamphlet's appearance, Levy's celebrity status attained new heights. As one prominent evangelical observed, "Mr. Levy has by his conduct and discourses at the meetings of Jews and Christians over which he presided, and by his writings on the subjects of discussion at those meetings, as also by his plan for the abolition of negro slavery, made his name so well known, as to render any further introduction of him to public notice unnecessary."[65] Yet admirers of both faiths soon became disappointed after Levy denounced an unexpected side effect of his social and religious activism: increased Jewish interest in British civil liberties. Levy's conviction that Jews could only claim the nationality of the "House of Israel" caused a great deal of consternation—especially in light of the publicity that his opinions generated. As Samuel Levy Keyzer, one of Levy's most ardent supporters, expressed in the *World*: "Though Mr. Levy's learning, humanity, and unwearied exertions, to ameliorate the deplorable condition of our brethren in faith, entitle him to the esteem of every religiously enlightened person, whatever his persuasion may be, and though the honour of knowing this excellent man personally, has given me the greater opportunity to appreciate his high qualifications, yet believing I obey the talmudic maxim: 'Love Aristotle, love Socrates, but truth more.'"[66]

According to Keyzer, his friend's "alarming presentiments, with regard to emancipating the Jews in the British empire" were extremely perplexing. Levy, however, was convinced of something that Keyzer was not: that the restoration of the Jews as a distinct and separate nation was essential for the new messianic era. To this end Rabbi Crooll heartily agreed. "Instead of doing the will of their God," Crooll asserted, "they [emancipationists] go and walk a dreaming to petition Parliament to make them equal in liberty with the Christians of the land. Have they forgotten that prisoners have no right to be equal with the inhabitants of the land[?]"[67] Outright persecution was one thing and should be adamantly condemned, but entitlement to vote and to hold office under a Protestant monarchy was quite another matter. According to both Crooll and Levy, assimilation would only lead to the loss of Jewish identity. Ultimately, the real source of suffering was the desolation of Zion. This conservative position, far from unique, was actually commonplace among the Jewish community. For instance, Chief Rabbi Solomon Hirschell also feared the repercussions of full participation in British society, but, for political reasons, he did not publicly voice his concerns. Despite the announced disapproval of Levy, Crooll, and others, momentum for Jewish civil liberties rapidly assumed a life of its own. On 18 August, at the same London Tavern where Levy had organized protests against the Russian *ukase,* Jews gathered once more, this time to write a petition to Parliament to claim "Equal Civil Rights with their Christian Fellow Subjects."[68] An increasing number of Jews were now joining Protestant dissenters and Catholics in the cause for civil emancipation. This change in mood could not have gone unnoticed by the Jewish elite. In fact, Isaac Lyon Goldsmid and Nathan Rothschild both engaged in their own maneuvers to remove Jewish disabilities during this period. Levy's series of protest meetings as well as the public dialogues between Jews and Christians had unleashed a new spirit of confidence and activism. As a result, Levy became an important—albeit unwilling—factor during the early campaign for Jewish emancipation in Britain.[69]

Despite Moses Levy's disapproval of the emerging Jewish civil rights movement, both Jews and evangelical Christians continued to praise Levy for his reform contributions. As a result of his efforts, interfaith discussions continued unabated, and initial conflicts eventually gave way to a remarkable atmosphere of brotherhood. According to one observer: "We have seen in our Meetings those Jews and Christians, who have been the most thoroughly opposed to each other on the particular question under discussion, almost weeping over each other, and would it have been of any avail, each ready to sacrifice his life—to give his heart's blood for his brother!" As a direct result of these meetings and the "deficiency . . . in learning" exhibited by some in attendance, a learned Jew called for the formation of a college that would be open to "the Jews of the whole world." While a college would not be forthcoming, at least for the immediate future, the Jewish community did establish a highly popular public lecture series, an adult school, and a Tract Society for the circulation of religious publications. It was quite obvious to all that Levy had awakened a latent pride and imagination and stirred others to action.[70] Protestant reformers could no longer complain that Jews always "kept themselves within certain strong holds, and inaccessible recesses" or that their leaders never "attempted to lead forth their troops into the open field of fair argument."[71]

Shortly before the release of *A Plan for the Abolition of Slavery*, Levy wrote to John Forster, an evangelical minister with whom he had been conducting a long theological debate, "I have been, and still am unwell, both in body and mind."[72] This brief personal comment, so much in contrast to the more formal but enthusiastic nature of their correspondence, could very well have been the result of news from the United States—bad tidings indeed. Continued Indian unrest, lack of business profits, scarcity of settlers, even the questionable validity of his landholdings—all these difficulties foreshadowed even bleaker times for the cosmopolitan reformer. By the end of summer Levy had moved from Knightsbridge to a temporary residence in the City which was offered to him by Robert Miller, the publisher of the *World*. On 28 August Levy presented Reverend Forster with a copy of his "pamphlet on the slave question," confiding that he was much hurried, "being on the eve of my departure for America." He also suggested that Forster publish their lengthy correspondence.[73] In fact, these letters were published the following year. Levy and Forster's *Letters Concerning the Present Condition of the Jews: Being a Correspondence between Mr. Forster and Mr. Levy* (London, 1829) covered many of the same arguments in defense of Judaism which Levy made during his numerous public appearances. Yet another book, *Letters to the Jews: Particularly Addressed to Mr. Levy of Florida* (York, 1829) by Thomas Thrush, included the full text of a speech—described by Thrush as "extraordinary and impressive"—by Moses Levy at a meeting of Christians and Jews in 1828.[74]

One can safely assume that other accomplishments would have ensued had Levy elected to stay in the metropolis. During a comparatively short period he had certainly proven his mettle as an orator, writer, and a leader of righteous causes. In the *World* Levy's excellent character and

"unbounded philanthropy" were equated with the great Christian philanthropist William Wilberforce.[75] Characteristically, Levy denied himself any
thought of personal triumph and was consumed with the harsh reality of
his finances. He had failed to attract support for his Florida colony—one of
the most crucial aspects of his stay abroad. Because assimilation was key to
the Philo-Judaean strategy, there was certainly no interest in removing Jews
to a frontier wilderness. Regardless, Levy persisted in his self-appointed
"ministry," despite the slim chance of receiving any material relief. As a result, he remained deeply burdened by debt. Pilgrimage was in dire need of
his attention, so necessity required that Levy's remarkable London crusade
come to a close.

After Levy's return to the United States, the passage of reform laws
in Great Britain cleared the way for a Whig majority in Parliament, and
slaves enjoyed emancipation in the British colonies between 1833 and 1838.
A five-year "apprenticeship" was imposed in order that slaves and their
former masters could transition into a free economy. After a hard-won
victory by a broad coalition of activists, England could justly feel a sense of
moral leadership regarding slavery. As Levy predicted, however, many of
the freedoms implemented on paper did not exist in practice. Soon planters colluded to set the minimum wage at the lowest possible level, and for
many years former slaves and their descendants were excluded from full
participation in society.[76]

In Britain legislation was passed which gradually awarded Jews more
civil rights. In 1858 Lionel de Rothschild was allowed a seat in Parliament,
and in 1871 Sir George Jessel became the first Jew to hold a British ministerial position. In the popular mind, however, the image of the Jew as "other"
was still very much the norm. As the earl of Derby stated: "though among
us, they are not with us . . . they retain their laws . . . their political customs
. . . they do not generally associate freely with their fellow subjects . . . they
have interests wholly apart."[77]

9. RETURN TO FLORIDA

For ten years Moses Levy avoided the subject of Moses and Samuel Myers's debts. Only after he considered his funds "exhausted beyond measure" did he broach this sensitive issue. Finally, his mounting financial pressures forced him to request some form of payment on the ten thousand–dollar obligation. On the positive side Levy's return to the Alachua country in January 1829 left him with "60 to 80 acres" of sugarcane as well as a mill, boilers, and all the ancillary equipment required for sugar manufacture. Levy judged that "the Plantation [was] now in a way to give excellent returns." For unknown reasons the number of slaves had been reduced to ten during his absence—an inadequate workforce to harvest and process the entire crop—so much of the cane would be lost. As a remedy, Levy proposed that Moses Myers send "25 field negroes in families" so the mill could be properly manned and the debt canceled. The elder Myers may have actually complied with Levy's request, since the slave total tripled in the following years.[1] As we have seen, Levy certainly decried the inhumanity of the slave trade and contributed much toward the abolitionist cause, but his religious philosophy did not immediately preclude slave ownership. In addition, the seasonal demands of sugar production made slave labor appear to be a practical necessity, at least until technology could advance enough to supplant it. In Levy's view, as long as he upheld high standards of treatment, kept families intact, provided religious instruction, and prepared the way for eventual emancipation through his reform agenda, he believed that his slaveholding status was both moral and beneficial.

A few months after his arrival in Florida, Levy received word that Samuel Myers had passed away. While in Pensacola, Samuel had been fortunate
to escape the ravages of a yellow fever epidemic, a disease that claimed the
lives of over five hundred people—mostly newcomers like himself. Myers
considered this calamity as "decisive" and was greatly affected not only by
the loss of life but by the overall poverty of the town itself.[2] Despite these
adverse conditions, he managed to establish a small law practice, served
as a city alderman, and was appointed as a lieutenant colonel in the local militia. Ultimately, however, he became disillusioned with his financial prospects in West Florida, and his initial expectation that Pensacola
would become "the New York of the South" failed to materialize. Rumors
concerning the old Richard Bowden affair continued to plague Myers and
hampered his career. After two years in Pensacola, Colonel Myers returned
once more to Virginia, where he died on 21 February 1829. Levy sent a brief
letter of condolence to Moses Myers and expressed his concern over this
"additional dispensation of providence."[3]

Unlike Levy's well-documented London years, records were sparse on
the East Florida frontier. There is no doubt, however, of Levy's mounting
displeasure toward his sons. David's St. Thomas sojourn lasted only a few
months, apparently the result of the turmoil surrounding his mother's second marriage. Hannah Levy's new husband had become both physically
abusive and progressively insane.[4] Understandably, David decided to join
his brother, Elias, at Pilgrimage—a plan of last resort. The two brothers had
both rebelled against their father's wishes and were viewed as wayward and
undisciplined. Friction, therefore, was inevitable. For the first time father
and sons actually lived together as a family, and in this capacity they were
able to judge each other more accurately. In addition to their unease toward their father's Jewish causes, Elias and David would have regarded any
abolitionist activity with genuine horror. Furthermore, they were greatly
opposed to Moses Levy's other unconventional views—his "condition of
religious socialism," as one of Levy's grandchildren later phrased it—and
were generally ill suited to life on a communitarian settlement.[5] Animosity
was especially strong between Levy and his eldest son. According to Levy,
Elias's stay at Pilgrimage did little to alter the young man's conventional
and rather pampered outlook. After Elias demanded a stipend to carry
on "a gentleman's trade," which Levy equated with doing "nothing," the

two parted ways—apparently for good. The twenty-five-year-old lived for several years in St. Thomas, where he married a cousin. Then he returned to the United States and became an adherent of the eighteenth-century Christian mystic Emanuel Swedenborg. In time Moses Levy's eldest established himself as an attorney and as an educator of some prominence in Savannah, Georgia.[6]

In contrast, nineteen-year-old David was more tactful in his relations with his father, at least during these early years. But his steadfast ambition to enter the legal profession became yet another source of contention. Clearly, David was unmoved by his father's religious mission and was hardly content to limit himself to the confines of the East Florida wilderness. The boy's two-year stint on the frontier stirred his imagination, however, and he became convinced of Florida's political and economic prospects. In addition, Elias had introduced David to St. Augustine society during their father's absence, and the outgoing teenager quickly made a positive impression. While in Norfolk, the Myers family "found it impossible to call his serious attention to the most simple duties." Now David transformed himself into an earnest and astute worker. He contributed toward the management of the plantation while he pursued an independent study of law. Not long after his father's arrival, and in response to the increasing frequency of Indian raids in the region, David joined other Alachua County residents and petitioned President Andrew Jackson for the establishment of a military post in Micanopy.[7]

Earlier federal policy had produced the Treaty of Moultrie Creek (1823), by which the Indian chiefs ceded much of their former holdings and withdrew to the more remote and less fertile regions to the south. Over the years tensions were exacerbated as the Indians' reduced circumstances were compounded by drought; the resultant starvation prompted some bands to leave the reservation and turn to cattle rustling and other theft. While settlers experienced losses, even occasional killings, the Indians had not yet resorted to full-scale war. Despite increased tensions, the Alachua plantations were still able to survive and profit. But Levy's troubles mounted when the Florida Association decided to suspend further settlement—the inevitable result of land title uncertainties. True to form, Levy still clung to his Pilgrimage ideal, seemingly oblivious to his own personal and financial welfare.

As a leading landowner and planter, Moses Levy maintained substantial political connections in the territory. Indeed, Levy was on familiar terms with most of the prominent figures in East Florida, including Zephaniah Kingsley, a well-known planter and former slave trader. Kingsley traced his tenure in Florida to the second Spanish period, and he shared his isolated island plantation on the St. Johns River—near present-day Jacksonville—with his African wife, Anna, and their mixed-race children. Kingsley manumitted all of his immediate family, including other slave women with whom he maintained relationships. His was an unconventional lifestyle by any standard, but interracial "marriages" had been fairly routine among white males in Spanish East Florida. Despite Kingsley's proslavery convictions and his secular outlook, Levy remained on cordial terms with the one-time St. Thomas ship's captain.

Kingsley, one of the first presidential appointees to the Legislative Council of Florida, grew increasingly concerned about the repressive laws enacted by the new territorial government—especially as it related to the precarious position of free blacks and to the issues of manumission and miscegenation. In response, Kingsley advanced his own ideas regarding these controversial topics, and, in doing so, he mirrored the more permissive policies of the previous Spanish colonial administration. In 1828, while Levy promoted his abolitionist scheme abroad, Kingsley published his own tract: *A Treatise on the Patriarchal, or Co-operative System of Society, As it Exists in Some Governments and Colonies in America, and in the United States, Under the Name of Slavery, With its Necessity and Advantages.* While a proponent of slavery, Kingsley nevertheless pleaded for a more humane and "patriarchal" system in which the slave would be considered "as a member of [the] family." Although it is unknown to what degree Kingsley and Levy may have exchanged their views, certain similarities appear in both their publications. For one, Kingsley and Levy championed miscegenation at a time when the very thought of racial intermingling was considered repellent in most areas of the United States. Kingsley saw this practice as a way of improving the stock, as it were, and as a way of maintaining a separate class of free persons of color—much like the West Indies tradition. "The intermediate grades of color are not only healthy," Kingsley claimed, "but when condition is favorable, they are improved in shape, strength and beauty."[8] Quite unlike Levy, however, Kingsley idealized slavery and saw no reason for ending it. Kingsley also studiously ignored any reference to the Bible, religion, or formal education; such innovations only fomented discontent, or so he thought. His brief *Treatise*, while a call for racial tolerance and legal reform, clearly lacked the complexity and moral suasion of Levy's utopian scheme. While Levy's abolitionist strategy would have placed him in real danger in Florida, Kingsley believed that his proslavery status provided him with certain protections and that he would not, in his words, "be suspected of any membership or community with manumating societies."[9] Not unexpectedly, Kingsley's efforts failed to alter the deep-seated prejudices of the new territorial inhabitants, and his ideas and lifestyle were considered quite scandalous and unacceptable. At a time when cultural mores increasingly reflected the rigid, two-tiered slave system of the South, both Kingsley and Levy were representative of a more lenient West Indian sensibility that was becoming less tolerated in the region. Eventually, out of concern for the welfare of his wife and children, Kingsley felt compelled to move his large family to Haiti.

This episode would certainly have reinforced Levy's sense of caution. Nonetheless, he did not abandon all thought of social reform while in Florida. In particular, the issue of public education was one topic that could be safely championed without fear of retribution. On 22 January 1831 Levy's efforts on behalf of "the sacred cause of education" resulted in the formation of the Florida Education Society—the territory's first organization devoted to "the establishment of such a general system of instruction as is suited to the wants and condition of the Territory."[10] The 1830 census revealed a white population of only 18,385, with vast counties averaging only 1,300 persons. Therefore, any form of education would have been a welcomed improvement in one of the poorest and least populated regions of the United States. Levy served as vice president of the society, while Davis Floyd—the treasurer of Florida and a prominent St. Augustine attorney who had once looked after Levy's business interests while he was in Europe—was appointed president. Nine other leading people of the territory joined Levy and Floyd as officers. The board of directors met each month in the new capital of Tallahassee—barely a village at the time—and various branches were established throughout Florida. One of the most active of these affiliate groups was the St. Johns and Mosquito County society, which included St. Augustine. This organization determined that of the "341 children, between the ages of 5 and 15, there are but 57 who are likely to obtain elementary education; 80 receive but precarious instruction; and 204 are left to grow up in ignorance and its attendant consequences." In response to the dire situation in St. Augustine, Levy, with the backing of the society, played a direct role in soliciting support for a free public school. In fact, a school was in operation by 1832, the first of its kind in Florida. In order to fund the school, however, the city council increased taxes, a move that soon created adverse feelings. Well-to-do citizens particularly resented the new tax burden, since they were already paying private school tuition for their own children. The St. Augustine city council, still convinced that it had acted for the public good, was forced to close the philanthropic endeavor despite the school's five months of successful performance and the appointment of a well-qualified and popular teacher.[11]

Convinced that education was "the patrimony of all men, be they poor or rich," Levy persisted in his worthy cause. Earlier in 1831, Governor William P. DuVal appointed Levy as one of three education commissioners charged with determining "the condition of the existing schools in the Territory, the wants of the People in regard to education, and the means calculated to relieve their wants." The commissioners were also expected to report to the Legislative Council on the precise number of schools, the number and qualifications of teachers, the subjects taught, as well as the proportion of school-age children who attended these private institutions. Such a comprehensive study had never been attempted in the territory. Finally, each commissioner was also required to submit a proposal for the "best system of general instruction."

In a separate report submitted to the governor and the Legislative Council in January 1832, Levy outlined the benefits of adopting the new Fellenberg model, a progressive, vocational-technical school system that had garnered much attention abroad. Based on the theories of Philipp Emanuel von Fellenberg—a former disciple of Pestalozzi—and the success of Fellenberg's school in Hofwyl, Switzerland, similar efforts were just beginning to appear in the United States, such as New York's Rensselaer School. Fellenberg offered technical training in agriculture and manual arts and provided basic academic instruction in an effort to help the poor and to reduce class differences. This endeavor would have been a significant innovation for any frontier region, especially one that was as bereft of "internal improvements" as Florida. An early forerunner of the widespread agricultural and technical colleges of the later part of the nineteenth century, Levy's Fellenberg proposal was regarded by at least one conservative member of the legislature as an unnecessary risk. "Experiments requiring innovations upon the settled habits and systems of a Country," it was claimed, "are rarely successful."[12] Nonetheless, Levy generated enough interest in the Fellenberg system that a prominent group of Tallahassee citizens established a sizable fund and campaigned for their own "Manual-Labour School" in the district.

This educational reform movement, however, was short-lived. Once again, financial considerations halted all progress toward the establishment of any public school system. After Florida became a U.S. territory, the federal government allotted a certain amount of land to help with the funding and construction of schools. Many assumed that the sale of this land would generate adequate capital for an entire system of Fellenberg schools, but permission was only granted to lease the land, not to sell it outright. Because the aborted St. Augustine school project amply demonstrated a great reluctance toward any additional tax burden, this shortfall came as a great setback for Levy and the early public school movement. The Florida Education Society, as well as the various affiliate groups, suffered a premature demise in a scene reminiscent of Levy's earlier Hebrew societies.[13]

Meanwhile, Levy's troubles, especially the unsettled issues regarding his land purchases, steadily mounted. In 1832, despite a positive ruling by the Supreme Court which validated the Florida Association's Arredondo title, Levy's legal quagmire grew even more complex. At issue was the determination of the center of the grant, a point that was left fairly vague by Alejandro Ramírez's decree of 1817. The court focused on the nebulous wording of the grant which alluded to "a place known as Alachua inhabited in other times by a tribe of Seminole Indians." In order to follow the spirit of Ramírez's original stipulations, the "place known as Alachua" would be considered the center and would delineate the boundaries of the entire grant. Up until this time the Florida Association had agreed that the town of Micanopy was the midpoint. As it happened, it was left to a deputy surveyor of Florida, Henry Washington, to investigate the matter and to survey an area equivalent to "four leagues to each wind," or just over 289,645 acres.[14]

Unable to find a Seminole village that bore the name of Alachua, Washington decided to ignore the grant's reference to an Indian habitation and focused on a more general geographic interpretation. The proprietors, in-

cluding Levy and his son David—newly admitted to the Florida bar—tried
to dissuade Washington, but their efforts proved futile. According to the
landowners' perspective, the immediate history of the area should have
been given much more credence.

Micanopy itself was the site of Cuscowilla, the original Seminole "capital" mentioned by eighteenth-century naturalist William Bartram. Paynes
Town (Pueblo de Payne), a mile away, grew into importance after King
Payne assumed leadership of the Alachua band, and it achieved even more
notoriety during the Patriot War. While the village's substantial log cabin
dwellings, large herds of cattle, and productive farmland were destroyed
during the war, the same locale became the destination of Patriot (Georgian) settlement, an aggressive move that further violated the territorial
integrity of the Spanish colony. In fact, the Georgians built their own military blockhouse, which they named Fort Mitchell, to serve as their self-appointed capital of the "Republic of East Florida." In short, the Paynes Town
/ Fort Mitchell location was the most recognized feature of the Alachua
country, or the "Tierras de la Chua," during the time of the Arredondo
award.[15]

After Paynes Town was destroyed by U.S. forces in 1813, Spanish officials in St. Augustine reverted once again to the generic "Alachua" when
mentioning the area. For instance, the governor's clerk, Antonio Alvarez,
noted Indian objections to "the establishment made by Mr. Wanton on the
Alachua" during the spring of 1821—a clear reference to the future town
of Micanopy.[16] Finally, it was the opinion of Fernando Arredondo himself that the grant's center was the Micanopy / Paynes Town site. As noted
previously, it was Arredondo's service during the Patriot War as well as his
unpaid tenure as Indian commissioner which qualified him for the award.
Arredondo was quite familiar with the region and well understood its at-
tractions; he was the least likely candidate to initiate a settlement in the
wrong location, thereby jeopardizing his rightful claim.

All this information was undoubtedly discovered by Washington, since
he visited the area, conducted numerous interviews, and was familiar with
the original wording of the grant as well as the records that were delivered
to the land commissioners. A personal animosity developed, however, between the surveyor and the grant proprietors. In particular, Washington
thoroughly resented David Levy's efforts on behalf of his father. Instead
of confirming Micanopy, or perhaps recognizing the nearby Paynes Town

site, Washington arbitrarily moved the grant's center to the swamps of the Alachua prairie, a location seven miles to the north which was conspicuously devoid of any history of Seminole habitation. This decision placed a large portion of Levy's holdings in the least desirable section of the grant.

Despite the new grant boundaries, the matter was still unresolved. The property of each investor in the Florida Association had to be delineated, and individual surveys were needed to subdivide the grant. This complicated task fell once more to Henry Washington some twelve years later, but the surveyor neglected to connect the private grant lines with the various township surveys, an oversight that resulted in his dismissal.[17] In the end the entire Arredondo grant was sold at auction, a legal requirement that was designed to clear all titles. This exasperating, time-consuming, and expensive exercise in litigation became a substantial burden for Levy, especially at a time when he could ill afford any delay in validating his land claims. The whole affair was symbolic of the unrelenting volley of misfortunes that plagued Levy's Florida venture almost from its inception.

Also during the 1830s, the territory was set on a direct course of conflict with the Indians, the length and breadth of which was unparalleled in U.S. history. Sparked by President Andrew Jackson's desire to transport the Seminole and Miccosukee tribes to the Arkansas Territory, a policy that abrogated the previous Treaty of Moultrie Creek, the Second Seminole War caused catastrophic loss of life and property. The Indians—it should be noted—were actually divided on emigration, but the resistance faction, which included most of the black leaders, eventually gained the upper hand.

The escalation of hostilities began in the summer of 1835 and continued throughout the fall. Widespread destruction and panic became so commonplace that in early December Levy's fellow Alachua sugar planter— Duncan L. Clinch, now a brigadier general and military commander of Florida—advised his superiors in Washington, D.C., of the necessity of four additional companies to protect the frontier from continued "war, murder, and plunder." Furthermore, Clinch was greatly distressed by the sufferings of "the white frontier inhabitants."[18] Bands of Indians gained sanctuary in the swamps and hammocks and ventured forth to burn homesteads with impunity. Clinch correctly assumed that, if the Indians and their black allies were not "promptly put down," the destruction would inevitably extend to the major plantations. Many settlers moved with their families to places of safety, so it is not surprising that Moses Levy took up residence once more in St. Augustine.[19] The whereabouts of the Pilgrimage settlers is uncertain. Nevertheless, as the following excerpt from the *Tallahassee Floridian* indicates, at least a few individuals were at the plantation during the fateful early morning hours of 23 December, perhaps in a final effort to protect their own hard-won assets.

> From the west we are informed by Mr. Rose, who left Micanopy on the 28th ult. that . . . The sugar works of Moses E. Levy, Esq. whose plantation is situated 2 miles N.W. of Micanopy were destroyed on the 23rd. Ult. Mr. Rose, who was manufacturing sugar at Mr. Levy's plantation near Micanopy, arrived at this place on Saturday last. This gentleman gives the following account: "That on Wednesday, the 23d. at 2 A.M. a cry of fire was heard and on getting up the flames were observed just rising, but by the time he could go out, the whole building was on fire; he directly rode to Micanopy for help. At the day dawn, many persons went to the plantation, but saw no Indians, but they traced 2 tracks from the sugar house, to an oak tree in the woods, near the place in a westerly direction, where the persons appeared to have rested, with the dent of a gun next to the footsteps."[20]

According to the *Jacksonville Courier*, Levy's plantation was set fire by Black Seminoles rather than Indians, but this assertion was not based on actual eyewitness reports. Later independent appraisers set Levy's losses at twenty-five thousand dollars—a rather staggering sum.[21] Fortunately, no one was harmed during the conflagration, and, unlike the thousand or more slaves who chose to escape during the chaos in the territory, none of Levy's bond servants took flight.[22] Pilgrimage's humane environment may have accounted for any reluctance to pursue the uncertainties of liberty. Unlike Clinch's Lang Syne plantation and McIntosh's Oakland plantation— both located about seven miles to the southeast—there weren't any armed military guards at Pilgrimage to deter escape. In any case Levy and his new manager, Mr. Verhain, were spared from an even greater catastrophe. Verhain moved the slaves to a place of safety and also salvaged some equipment for transport to Micanopy. The town itself had been barricaded and turned into a fort, but Micanopy's fate also ended in calamity after the U.S. Army elected to abandon the area. On 24 August 1836, rather than allow anything of value to benefit the enemy, Micanopy was ordered burned to the ground.[23] After fourteen years of persistent struggle, nothing remained of Levy's utopia other than vast tracks of land that he could not sell and from which settlers fled in terror.

Following the first wave of conflict, an entire industry lay in ruins—some two dozen sugar estates were destroyed south of St. Augustine alone. Levy thus joined a long and tragic roster of planters whose fortunes collapsed during the Second Seminole War. Ironically, it was Levy's early expenditures in costly sugar mill technology as well as his importation of Cuban cane which helped launch the East Florida sugar boom, a phenomenon that defied traditional prudence concerning large investments in unsettled Indian territory.[24]

The loss of Pilgrimage heralded a period of significant economic decline for Moses Levy. He was, to use the common adage, land-rich and cash-poor. The haunting specter of fiscal doom which plagued Levy in England had finally manifested itself, and he soon felt the full burden of a massive fifty thousand–dollar debt. By his own admission this final blow to his long-held spiritual quest caused much "want and misery," but Levy's intense religious convictions were far from broken. Regrettably, the fate of the former "old-clothes men" and stockbrokers remains a mystery, although it is clear that Levy's former protégé, Frederick Warburg, left Florida and returned to Altona. Warburg never married and died as a pensioner in 1844.[25]

10. THE RISE OF SENATOR YULEE AND THE END OF A REMARKABLE LIFE

*D*uring the early war years St. Augustine was crammed with back-woods refugees, all of whom sought the safety of the city walls as well as the large military presence at Fort Marion—formerly known as the Castillo de San Marcos.[1] Levy was fortunate to board with his newfound friend, Dr. Andrew Anderson. Anderson, a wealthy New York City physician, businessman, and aspiring planter, arrived in 1829 out of concern for his ailing wife—St. Augustine being widely extolled as a healthful destination for the sick—and quickly found an amiable companion in Levy. Anderson's twenty-acre "Markland" farm, located west of town, proved quite productive, and the retired doctor soon experimented with planting mulberry trees to meet the increasing demand for silk production along the eastern seaboard (a subsequent blight eventually put an end to this lucrative market). Anderson's wife died in 1837, and, not long afterward, in the fall of 1839, the doctor himself fell victim to a yellow fever outbreak. While it is not known how long Levy may have lived with the Andersons, he most certainly endeared himself to the entire family, including Anderson's second wife, Clarissa (née Fairbanks).[2]

By late 1837 St. Augustine was sufficiently removed from the main theater of war to allow a relative calm to descend upon the inhabitants. The more peaceful milieu, coupled with the friendship and hospitality of leading citizens, offered a much needed respite for Moses Levy. After the loss of Pilgrimage, he mortgaged his thirty-one slaves for the sum of five thousand dollars, an amount that allowed him at least some semblance of financial stability. Eventually, in 1839, Levy divested himself of all his slaves when he sold them to his friend Dr. Anderson.[3] By virtue of this sale Anderson became one of the largest slave owners in the county. The doctor was a humane master who, as one historian has noted, "maintained a sincere human relationship—even friendship" with his bond servants.[4] Anderson died soon after this transaction, however, and for a few years Levy managed the family's widespread business interests, traveling frequently to the North.

Moses Levy's continued high standing in St. Augustine was confirmed by the personal observations of Henry Summer, a young attorney from South Carolina who made favorable note of this "very interesting" and "learned man" when he visited in 1837. Additionally, according to Summer, St. Augustine did not lack in either congenial society or fine food, a finding that apparently took him by surprise. The once seamy town had made steady progress since the cession, but old ruins still marred some sections, a curious and unsettling novelty for someone used to the tidiness of Charleston. Wild rumors connected to the military campaign were a constant reminder of the ongoing struggles elsewhere in the territory. Yet, toward the end of Summer's stay, despite the influx of officers and enlisted men from throughout the country, the near carnival-like demeanor of the local eccentrics, and a dramatic tar-and-feathering incident, the young visitor grew tired of St. Augustine and pronounced it "extremely dull."[5]

In September 1838 Levy was once again in New York City, apparently on a business venture with General Joseph M. Hernandez and other prominent St. Augustinians. Hernandez, commander of the East Florida militia, had achieved notoriety during the previous year by the capture of the famed warrior Osceola. Acting under orders, Hernandez disregarded Osceola's white flag of truce, thereby establishing an ignoble precedent in the military's conduct toward the Indians. While in the company of the noted general, Levy completed his last will and testament. After much deliberation he disinherited both his sons—awarding each a token one hundred dollars—and left his estate to his daughters and to his sister Rachel, all of whom lived in St. Thomas at the time. Hernandez witnessed the document, and other St. Augustinians, such as Major Benjamin A. Putnam and Colonel John M. Hanson, were listed as executors. Coincidentally, all were bitter opponents of a rising young politician named David Levy.[6]

Moses Levy, then fifty-six, felt fully justified in this ultimate parental rebuke. While he did not acquit himself of all responsibility for his sons' supposed shortcomings, he still believed that he had been a good provider and went to great lengths to steer his children away from negative influences. If Levy had been physically absent as a father, such was the fate of many boarding school youths in the nineteenth century. In the case of his youngest son, David Levy had once vowed that he would forgo law and politics in favor of a humble life in agriculture. Not only did he break this promise, but he severed all connections with Judaism. As a result, David exemplified the very attributes that his father most abhorred: assimilation, individualism, and unrestrained ambition and vanity. Moses Levy concluded that his son had forsaken his own people as well as God's covenant. Consciously or not, Levy followed a well-known communitarian tactic when he began to shun his two sons. As a Shaker hymn intoned: "Of all the relations that ever I see, my old fleshly kindred are furthest from me."[7] Although Levy undoubtedly felt an enduring fellowship, even a mystical bond, with his fellow Jews, it was evident that this one-time colonizer had become increasingly isolated from both his coreligionists and his own children. For someone who deeply yearned for a communal life, it was a tortuous fate.

Apart from David Levy's Whig adversaries, many in St. Augustine disapproved of Moses Levy's actions. Word of the alienation that existed between father and son quickly spread throughout the territory, and Moses Levy was widely cast as an "unnatural father." Especially in the South, family honor, lineage, and parental respect were virtues that were held in such high esteem that the severance of kinship bonds could have resulted in a kind of social death. Consequently, a public display of disinheritance was something that was reserved only for the most troublesome and recalcitrant, who brought considerable dishonor to the family. In relegating David Levy's growing political prestige to disrepute, Moses Levy delivered a weighty insult to many Floridians. As for David Levy's estrangement from Judaism, this was hardly thought of as a negative attribute in an overwhelmingly Christian region.[8]

Despite his troubles with his notable son and his increasing isolation, Moses Levy still claimed a position of respectability. After all, for two decades he had retained a close network of friends and associates who showed remarkable tolerance toward his personal beliefs. When needed, Levy could easily muster the requisite displays of charm and intelligence which so captivated his St. Augustine contemporaries. This ingratiating aspect of his character—the Jewish courtier personality—served him well during these difficult years. Like his father before him, Moses Levy was certainly adept at living in two worlds. Disaster may have befallen his utopia, but he still had to make do in a society whose essential values were diametrically opposed to his own.

While the elder Levy's fortunes declined, it was apparent to most Floridians that David Levy was poised for certain political success. Of course, any career in territorial politics would be fraught with bitter party rivalries and would risk his father's condemnation. Notwithstanding, David Levy calculated that the region was in dire need of talented leaders, and he knew that by filling that void he could establish himself as a major force. Unlike the more established areas of the South, East Florida politics were largely unfettered by intricate family alliances. Free to forge his own strategic associations, the astute young man chose to ignore his father and to follow his own ambitions. Also, like many other men of the time, David Levy was drawn to Andrew Jackson's brand of populism and determined that his best interests lay within the emerging Democratic Party. It did not take long for Levy to gain substantial recognition in the territory.[9]

In April 1829—just months after his father's return from England—David left Micanopy to assume a full-time position as a clerk to the Legislative Council of Florida. After further experience in the Alachua County Circuit Court in Newnansville, he was admitted to the bar in the Eastern District of Florida in 1832. Afterward Levy resided in St. Augustine and formed a close rapport with Robert R. Reid, the federal judge for East Florida and future territorial governor who recognized the young man's political potential. At the commencement of the Second Seminole War Levy held the rank of a militia lieutenant, although it is doubtful that he actually saw action in the war. Between 1836 and 1837 he was elected to the Legislative Council; the following year he served as a senator in the new bicameral legislature. Levy demonstrated a mastery of grassroots politics and frequently engaged in public receptions and gala barbeques, complete with toasts and grand speeches. During his participation as a delegate to the territory's Constitutional Convention of 1838, however, Levy experienced the clashes between the rising Democratic Party, of which he was an important member, and its ideological opponent, the Whigs, whose members represented the planter and banking interests. As a result of this hostility, the twenty-eight-year-old first heard "the odious charge that [he] was not a citizen of the United

States"—an accusation that threatened to end his promising political and legal career.[10]

Curiously, this "odious charge" could be traced directly to Moses Levy. During this time the elder Levy suddenly expressed doubts about the legitimacy of his own citizenship. This newfound apprehension took root among the company of his prominent Whig friends.[11] It must be said that Levy was hardly a Whig partisan or a proponent of any political party for that matter. To be sure, he was at ease with the refined manners and customs of the elite merchants and planters, the group that he had associated with for most of his life. Also, the Whig's vehement opposition to the emerging cult of the common man—the Jacksonian ideal—also spoke directly to Levy's disdain for individualism. One must remember that Levy's egalitarianism was forever linked under the banner of religion and communitarianism, a standard completely opposed to what he considered selfish motives.

Another of Moses Levy's friends, General Peter Sken Smith, an affluent developer and financier from New York, actually held abolitionist sentiments. The general's views were certainly the exception in St. Augustine, and, like Levy, he tried to keep them to himself. Nevertheless, word of the New Yorker's abolitionist leanings did manage to surface. In fact, it was David Levy who first leveled the charge during the Constitutional Convention. In order to save himself, Smith publicly renounced any association with the antislavery movement. This abrupt turnaround enabled him to evade such consequences as tar-and-feathering—or worse—but the general's days as a political candidate were doomed. While always a controversial figure, as long as Peter Sken Smith repudiated any sympathy for abolitionism and his considerable investments continued to enrich the St. Augustine elite, the newcomer retained solid backing from his fellow Whigs. Smith's impressive pedigree certainly aided in this regard: his father owned over a million acres of New York real estate and had been John Jacob Astor's business partner. Due to his adroit political moves and his extraordinary wealth, the general averted serious calamity, but the incident turned him into one of David Levy's most vocal opponents. More than any of his contemporaries, Smith seized upon the question of David Levy's citizenship and was prepared to go to any length to denounce his adversary.[12]

The source of Moses Levy's sudden misgivings about his own nationality was his late arrival during the summer of 1821. Technically speaking, he had not been present during the actual change-of-flags ceremony, the standard by which the former inhabitants of Florida were automatically awarded U.S. citizenship. Previously, local officials granted Levy considerable leeway in this matter, and he was able to circumvent the letter of the law. Yet Levy never mentioned the original naturalization application that he made in Rhode Island in 1818. According to this document, his request for citizenship was made not only with his land purchases in mind but to make certain that his children could enjoy U.S. nationality as well.[13] The time required for naturalization was five years. Since it was most improbable that Levy could have forgotten this episode, either his application was denied, or he deliberately withheld mention of it in order to cast doubt on his own—and consequently his son's—national affiliation. In any event, because Florida statutes allowed foreigners to own land, the forfeiture of his citizenship hardly mattered, and it would teach David a grave lesson. Moses Levy always considered his Jewish nationality as sacrosanct and above all others. "In politics," he admitted, "I have neither portion or lots." He acknowledged voting only once, and that was because "the candidate had pledged himself to do something for the establishment of schools."[14]

This issue took on new relevance during David Levy's 1841 bid for congressional delegate. Florida was entitled to a single, nonvoting seat in the U.S. House of Representatives—the territory's most prestigious post. The Whigs were at a special disadvantage because the party ticket was split between two rivals. Furthermore, the financial downturn caused by the Panic of 1837 resulted in the insolvency of many banks, a bitter episode that created an immediate opportunity for the "Anti-Bank, Anti-Bond" candidacy of David Levy.

Despite a ruling from the Court of Appeals in Tallahassee which upheld David Levy's U.S. citizenship, the issue continued to plague him, and the charge was renewed during the campaign. Not only was Levy accused of being an "alien," but there were efforts to excite antisemitic prejudices as well. In response, David Levy's supporters reminded the electorate of their candidate's personal struggle for religious choice: "With the unflinching fortitude of the proscribed race from which he sprung, he has suffered bitter persecution and disinheritance because he would and could not adhere to the religious dogmas of his ancestors."[15] Religion and family discord were now used in the electioneering process. Although David Levy won the election, the outcome was immediately contested. A petition to Congress, backed by Peter Sken Smith, asserted once more that Levy, as an alien, could not legally serve his term. A House committee was formed to examine the matter.

During the subsequent investigation Moses Levy testified on several occasions about his 1821 arrival. While he may have privately concluded that neither he nor his son were entitled to U.S. citizenship, Moses Levy was reluctant to swear to this under oath, and his vague recollections failed to give much solace to either Democrats or Whigs. The passage of time, or so he stated, blurred many details. Foremost on his mind during this earlier period was his colonization project; ships' names as well as departure dates hardly mattered to someone who was engaged in such a high-minded and extensive enterprise. Furthermore, he testified that he had been at sea on over one hundred occasions and had owned many vessels. How could he possibly be expected to recall his travel itinerary of twenty years earlier? Despite Moses Levy's hazy memory, a majority of committee members concluded that his initial intentions were quite clear and that a delay at sea—caused by lack of wind—resulted in his late arrival. Therefore, David Levy was allowed his seat in Congress and was officially recognized as Florida's delegate.[16]

Remarkably, this was still not the end of the affair. As one can imagine, the election of David Levy to the House of Representatives represented a historic milestone. Albeit a nonprofessing Jew, Levy had become the first person of Jewish heritage to serve in Congress, and, as such, he was especially vulnerable to antisemitic sentiment. For example, a published legal decision upholding the favorable committee ruling was ridiculed as the "Book of Levy" in the St. Augustine party organ, the *News*. Whigs characterized themselves as "Protestants" and "true Americans" who were staunchly united against "unnaturalized foreigners" in public office.[17] New elements were brought into the melee as well. Moses Levy, perceived as protecting his son's interests during the congressional investigation, was now a suitable target. He was not only accused of leaving Cuba under the taint of illegal business practices, but he had to endure the charge that both his sons were the progeny of an interracial tryst in St. Thomas. Supposedly half-black, it was again surmised that David Levy was unable to serve as territorial delegate. In his first address before the House of Representatives David Levy forcefully assailed the initial charges against him as emanating from "bitter, reckless, and malignant enemies" who had hoped to pursue him "to destruction, without regard to the means."[18] Over the next few years this blunt assessment proved to be uncannily accurate.

Of course, news of these rumors circulated widely. Distinguished members of Congress, John Quincy Adams among them, evidently made up their own minds regarding the controversy. Adams privately referred to David Levy as the "alien Jew Delegate" and also conjectured, albeit sarcastically, that, if Levy's "dash of African blood" were proven, it would be "a far more formidable disqualification." The northern press was not immune from indulging in caricature and in one instance declared Florida's delegate—who stood over five feet seven inches—a "sweet little dandy . . . well-perfumed in ladies' essences, with hair well-curled" who was "the smallest man, physically and perhaps intellectually, of the House."[19] Nevertheless, as long as David Levy retained his seat in Congress, such comments could easily be endured. But for Moses Levy deliberate fabrication and insults were felt to a much larger degree and confirmed his worst opinions regarding society at large.

What started as a lesson in humility for his son escalated into a most disagreeable public spectacle for the father. Moses Levy refuted all accusations in a series of articles in the *Florida Herald and Southern Democrat* which included documents from his days in Cuba as well as a letter written by Zephaniah Kingsley which "indignantly" denied that Levy's sons "were of coloured origin." The irony of Kingsley's statement was not lost on the *News*. Nevertheless, Levy demanded that the Whig editor stop his slanderous accusations: "He only furnishes me with additional pebbles to put into my Kaleidescope to exhibit the hideous design society presents."[20] Most fortunately for Moses Levy, neither his *Plan for the Abolition of Slavery* nor his published speeches in England ever surfaced during the fiasco. Ultimately, however, most Florida voters—burdened by protracted war and financial calamity—did not care if David Levy was an alien, Jew, or even an illegitimate mulatto. What mattered most was whether he could bring some relief to the territory, especially in the form of federal dollars, an expectation that Levy fully met.

The final flurry of political squabbling took place in 1843. Moses Levy used the forum given to him in the Democratic paper not only to refute Whig assertions but also to address the larger issues involved. In Levy's mind political mudslinging and falsehoods merely reflected the faults of "a social compact [that] is based on self." This "soul destroying principle" was responsible for the "degraded and degenerate" publications that were proliferating in the United States. Instead of striving toward harmony and peace, as God intended, selfish individuals inflicted great harm to society at large:

> A selfish man will in his reasoning make the good or benefit of himself tantamount to that of the whole nation; and a party spirited man is apt from degree to degree to border in his ratiocination, upon the reasoning of a maniac. He hesitates not to call that which is bitter, sweet, and that which is sweet, bitter; that which is holy, profane, and that which is profane, holy. Though his wife and children, or even all his generation are morally ruined and his country sinks, it matters not, "live my party forever," is the motto. I write, I argue for it—the stimulus must be kept up—the intoxicating drug must be administered to the multitude, and daily the doses must be increased until frightful ruin insues, ending in bloodshed and revolution like that of Robespierre.[21]

Moses Levy's series of articles were quite unlike anything that had been seen before in East Florida. The rising tide of individualism was firmly denounced, while Bible-inspired communitarianism, although never mentioned by any name, was extolled as the panacea for all of mankind's ills. In fascinating detail Levy even explained what he perceived as the futility of inductive and deductive logic when compared to the ultimate truth of the Bible. "Truth," he claimed, "can never be expected as a result from the reasoning of beings so defective."

The *News*, hardly in the mood to discuss metaphysics, derided Moses Levy's missives as "senseless cant and hypocritical raving."[22] Levy, however, did manage to score some significant points, especially after he released details concerning his former relationship with Alejandro Ramírez. Old letters of recommendation and statements from government officials in Havana further substantiated Levy's position as a man of honor who had left Cuba in good standing. As in England, Levy never faltered in presenting himself as a Jew, and his appeal to all "believers in Revelation" allowed a common bond between him and his Christian readers. These articles alleviated tensions to some degree, but the mudslinging was finally put to rest after David Levy's reelection rendered personal aspersions irrelevant. Delegate Levy emerged as the leader of the Florida Democratic Party, and two decades of political domination by the landed gentry of Middle Florida came to an end.

Unfortunately, it was also during this time of heated electioneering that Moses Levy lost whatever marginal financial stability he had possessed. His previous slave sale to Andrew Anderson resulted in Levy's acquisition of a number of shares in the Southern Life Insurance and Trust Company, an enterprise for which Anderson once served as president. The bank's demise in 1843, a result of mismanagement as well as a cascade of troubles brought on by the Panic of 1837, finally left Levy "pennyless" at the age of sixty-one.[23] Impoverished and betrayed by former friends—such as General Smith—Levy fell into a state of depression reminiscent of his earlier years in Gibraltar.

Despite the magnitude of Moses Levy's predicament, he managed to gain some relief through a business proposal that brought him a small stipend. In fact, this arrangement would eventually prove to be Levy's salvation. Many people believed that his land titles were hopelessly mired and would, in all probability, be declared invalid. So, it was fortuitous indeed when George R. Fairbanks, a neophyte attorney, decided to take on Levy's case in return for five percent of his holdings. The case would clearly take years to complete, but Fairbanks was braced for the challenge and was optimistic enough to advance money to meet his client's drastically reduced living expenses.[24] Unfortunately, young Fairbanks was not always prompt with his payments, causing Levy even more anguish. In the long term, however, Levy's trust in his lawyer would be vindicated.

In the meantime Moses Levy lived alone in what he referred to as the "obscure village" of St. Augustine on fourteen dollars per month. After twenty years of continual disappointment, burdened by legal fees and taxes on land he could not sell, he felt oppressed "beyond endurance." In a letter to his daughter Rachel, Levy confided: "I am at times half mad & truly accept death rather than to live, hedged in by a labyrinth of trouble." Suicide, however, was out of the question, so he became resigned to his misery. At an advanced age, he found himself "without family, friends, or society in a land I perfectly detest."[25] In an attempt to pay his creditors Levy was forced to sell whatever he could, including the "sugar boilers & mill" that remained undamaged after the attack on Pilgrimage. "Insatiable Lawyers," Levy complained, were "daily getting more ravenous" as they sensed his desperate state.[26] In addition to depression and chronic "dyspepsia," a condition for which he took a variety of patent medicines, he was burdened by what he believed was his own spiritual disharmony. Like many radical reformers and progressives of the period, Levy drew inward and was captivated by new and exotic beliefs, including spiritualism, mesmerism, phrenology, and water cures.[27] Of course, these "sciences," like the noxious content of most patent medicines, were of questionable benefit and probably augmented his troubles.

Understandably, Levy's status as a single, divorced man also added to his burden, and he privately yearned for at least a spiritual intimacy with the opposite sex. In this realm Rebecca Gratz still loomed in the distance as Levy's ideal expression of Jewish womanhood—even during his darkest moments. On a rare visit to Philadelphia in 1843, Levy described an encounter with Gratz which encapsulated his awkward, unfulfilled attraction: "I saw Rebecca walking at some distance before me with her cousins . . . my affections towards her were excited & so strongly operated upon her that she turned her face to look at me."[28] According to Levy, Gratz never shared his ardor, and therefore she remained an alluring, unattainable fixation. Levy's feelings toward her were just as intense as when they had first met in 1818. He was attracted to other women as well, albeit to a much lesser degree, but he despaired that he would never remarry and surmised that "once a man joins so with a woman he is incapable of doing the like with any other female."[29] Much more at ease in the company of men, Levy's idealized notions concerning women and marriage apparently compensated for an innate shyness and reticence toward the opposite sex. Regardless of deeper motivations, Levy preferred to view himself in a virtuous guise and—always the romantic—he transformed Gratz into the embodiment of a pure, ethereal love.

Additionally, Levy's unfulfilled messianic expectations certainly played a role in his psychological state, but to what degree is uncertain. In all likelihood his anticipation of the Messiah was of a more general nature than that of either Rabbi Crooll or the followers of the Vilna Gaon, and therefore Levy would have been less affected by the failure of the 1840 prediction—a year, incidentally, which Crooll did not live to see.

Moses Levy's sense of estrangement was greatly eased by his reconciliation with David Levy in 1845. "The resumption between us of our natural relations," David was keen to point out, "[was accomplished] without any compromise in our respective views of duty & life."[30] The reasons behind this turnaround had much to do with David Levy's upcoming marriage to Nannie Wickliffe. The attractive daughter of the former governor of Kentucky and postmaster general in the Tyler administration, Nannie Wickliffe was not a typical southern belle. Her willingness to marry David Levy reflected an uncommon independence. She was also an exceptionally devout Presbyterian, a characteristic that earned her the sobriquet the "Wickliffe Madonna" in Washington social circles.[31] Such religiosity was bound to make a favorable impression upon the elder Levy, and he was, in fact, quite taken by her. Nannie encouraged her fiancé's efforts toward reconciliation, as did Moses Levy's attorney, George Fairbanks. Moved by David's heartfelt pleas and suffering in self-imposed isolation, Moses Levy relented, and both of them established at least an outwardly cordial relationship. A similar rapprochement never occurred between Elias and his father.

David Levy's marriage corresponded with his election as senator. Florida's transition from territory to actual statehood followed a carefully crafted strategy set by Levy while he served as territorial delegate. Before he assumed office, the Florida legislature responded to his unusual request for official recognition of his change of name. Thereafter, the former David Levy (whom the legislature had previously honored by naming Levy County after him) became known as David L. Yulee. Moses Levy, who no longer felt compelled to keep his Moroccan past hidden, relayed details about his background—including the existence of the Yulee surname— during a conversation with George Fairbanks. Fairbanks was so captivated that he promptly passed on the particulars to David Levy. The fact that *Yulee* did not carry any particular Jewish connotation in the United States would certainly have factored in the formal name change. When asked to comment on his son's decision, Moses Levy admitted that "some of my people find the name [Levy] an inconvenient one, even in the most tolerant countries in the world." Such an overtly Jewish surname, however, became, in Moses Levy's view "an additional reason, and a strong one it is to my mind . . . to have retained it."[32]

Many years later an elderly George Fairbanks recalled that Moses Levy had told him that his father had been the "grand vizier," or prime minister, of Morocco. Such overstatement, however, was hardly in keeping with Levy's character. More than likely, Levy had merely recalled significant details from his childhood, and the opulent courtier's life was subsequently transformed by others into a still higher realm. In any case such a unique lineage—noticeably lacking any reference to Eliahu's disgrace—certainly served David Yulee's political ends. At the same moment he was elected senator, Yulee's exalted Moroccan pedigree was brought forth as dramatic proof of a natural predisposition toward greatness. He had transformed himself from humble beginnings on the Alachua frontier, "clothed in the garb of the most ordinary peasant," into a patrician—albeit a rather unorthodox one.[33] Such a scenario suited David Yulee's natural penchant for showmanship, and it added a distinct *Thousand and One Nights* aura that obscured his actual Jewish roots. In addition, Moses Levy was sometimes referred to in the newspapers as an "old Turk" whose unusual ideas and "singular" qualities—if not truly understood—at least became slightly more fathomable. This fascination with Morocco, as well as the general tendency toward embellishment, became indelibly associated with David Yulee and, as previously stated, continues today in Florida folklore.

Although Moses Levy and his youngest son may have been on speaking terms, their relationship apparently did not extend to financial affairs. By this time David Yulee enjoyed a certain degree of affluence and could have easily aided his father. Whether any such offer ever surfaced remains hypothetical, but it is clear that Moses Levy's desperate financial condition continued unabated until 1849. After George Fairbanks's efforts succeeded in clearing all of Levy's land titles, the years of privation suddenly ended. Levy's properties had been off the market for twenty-five years; now he gladly journeyed throughout Florida, contacting individual buyers, who eagerly sought his most fertile lands. Of course, the wetlands on the Alachua prairie were virtually worthless, but much of Levy's property, bought in Cuba at seventy-three cents an acre, had gained substantially in value. Soon he started to pay off his debts, most notably to his exceptionally patient friend Seraphina Chauviteau. While dutifully recording Levy's mortgage at 6 percent interest, Madame Chauviteau never sought legal remedy for this long overdue note and accepted whatever payments Levy could muster through the years. After liquidating assets, Moses Levy still retained about seventy thousand acres located in Orange, Clay, Alachua, Marion, Volusia, and Sumter counties. From his former bleak position Levy not only resurfaced as one of Florida's largest landowners, but his holdings were deemed as some of the "most valuable lands in the State."[34]

When Moses Levy turned seventy in 1852, he decided to propagate his communitarian ideas in pamphlet form. Earlier that year he had spoken before a temperance group in Micanopy, once again a prosperous little town that had been completely rebuilt after the destruction of the Indian war. Levy often visited the area during his land transactions and, as one of the town's original founders and a gentleman of means, was awarded some deference. In his *Address Delivered Before the Temperance Society of Micanopy . . . Containing Thoughts and Suggestions on a System of Reform, the Chart and Guide of which is the Holy Bible* (Jacksonville, 1852) Levy elucidated his reform agenda to a most unlikely audience—the majority of whom probably included the wives of moderately successful merchants, farmers, and cattle ranchers and almost certainly a few Protestant clergymen as well. Although he never attempted to form another agrarian settlement, his belief in his self-proclaimed "law of operating and being operated upon" was very much intact. While there is no record of what this temperance group had to say about Levy's speech, it can be safely assumed that most in attendance were not especially taken with his arguments.

For one, Levy doubted the very validity of societies such as theirs and did not hesitate to say so: "You can no more effect a cure by attacking a single evil that besets man, than you can cure the leprosy by applying a patch to one of its sores, instead of attacking the disease which lies in the vitiated blood." Similar to his earlier abolitionist arguments, Levy saw alcoholism as symptomatic of a society that was based on individualism rather than the harmony of the "triune love." Without "annihilating" the self and becoming united in love, mankind was doomed to serve satanic ends; injury, pain, and "intemperance" were the inevitable result. By following such a direction, people would "never arrive at that state promised in the Bible, that the whole human race will 'serve the Lord with *one consent.*'"[35]

Furthermore, Levy asked: "Look back upon the history of these temperance societies: did they originate in principles?—principles whose province it is to regulate feelings? No. They originated in the speeches of orators calculated to excite feelings—feelings originating in the excitement of the faculties most developed, and which are in reality as intoxicating to the noble mind as Alcohol is to the organization." And, as far as their membership was concerned, "ninety-nine out of a hundred" were not intemperate, and for the few who were, most—Levy declared—would take up spirits again. While slavery was not mentioned, Levy's rebuke to the entire temperance movement was indicative of his alienation from the abolitionist crusade in the United States and for the very same reasons that he had enumerated in Micanopy. Driven by his own logical assumptions, any deviation or compromise was simply not acceptable, for his ideas concerned nothing less than the divine order of the universe.

Unlike his earlier writings and oratory in England, Levy's *Address* was far too condemnatory of society to attract many adherents. His writing style had become less accessible and more pedantic in tone, and his attached "Appendix" was hardly more than a series of anecdotes. Although Levy had his own misgivings about this publication, he nevertheless distributed copies to his friends, acquaintances, and fellow Masons in the hope that some of his points would make an impression. His personal correspondence revealed what was probably the main cause of this sudden show of activism: a strong preoccupation with his own mortality. His seventieth birthday was an especially difficult milestone, and his increasing frailty convinced Levy that he was "a dying man." Now that he possessed the means, he felt obligated to share his spiritual truths. This extended to his letters as well, as the imprint on his stationery attests:[36]

THE IMPOSSIBILITIES OF ALL IMPOSSIBILITIES:

To speak the Truth—that is in our hearts: To LOVE our fellows as OURSELVES, in GOD: And to make the will (or, more properly speaking, the delight) of GOD the *motive power* of action.

Far from negating these "3 virtues" of the Bible, Levy merely attempted to dramatize their impracticability, given the "radical errors" of both traditional Judaism and Christianity. He concluded that Christian theologians as well as rabbis, with their different dogmas and teachings, had turned "the religion of the Bible" into something totally apart from the true spirit of God's written word. In Levy's view the inevitable result was mankind's utter failure to adhere to the basic tenets of Scripture. Among other things "unconquerable self love" made the aforementioned virtues "impracticable." No doubt, Levy was struggling with his own imperfections as well as his mortality. In addition, he had not forgotten the failure of his sacred cause. Despite his very best efforts, there was still no Jewish nation and no Promised Land.

Levy conveyed his frustrations and disappointments in his continued correspondence with Rebecca Gratz. Gratz, now also in her seventies, must have been a good friend indeed, for Levy sent long letters detailing not only his unique religious perspectives but also recounting the milestones of his life, beginning with childhood. This correspondence survives in the form of extracts transcribed by David Yulee; none of Gratz's replies were noted. Nonetheless, based on the personal nature of his letters and the length of their friendship, one must conclude that Gratz harbored some fondness for Levy. In addition, it is hard to imagine that he would have failed to convey his passionate ideas concerning education and philanthropy to Ms. Gratz over the years; she certainly would have been a prime candidate, as her own charitable organizations and innovative Hebrew Sunday School attest. Sadly, no additional documents have surfaced which can shed more light on this intriguing relationship.[37]

Also during this period, Levy maintained a steady correspondence with his daughters, both of whom had moved to New York with their husbands and children. Unlike the well-documented, tempestuous relationship between Moses Levy and David Yulee, only a comparatively small number of letters to his daughters, Rachel Pretto Henriques and Rahma Mendes Da Costa, have surfaced. They reflect an intense love and concern, but Levy's general tendency was to send very intellectually demanding, and at times somewhat obscure, correspondence. Inevitably, he would include criticism of his daughters' husbands, especially as it related to their role as providers. It can be said that Levy was quite generous in his support in his later years. Perhaps Levy's propensity toward depression was passed on to some family members, since he once referred to Rachel's "alarming . . . state of mind" as well as her "morbid feelings."[38]

Rahma appears to have fared better, although in one of two extant letters to her father she wrote of her husband's ill health and thanked her father for his financial assistance, which she admitted was their "sole support." Also reflected in her comments was a rather forceful intellect that was well prepared to tackle sensitive issues—including Levy's separation from her brother Elias. "He [Elias] expressed a great desire to see you," she wrote, "and appears to suffer much grief that you have forsaken him." She hoped for a reconciliation. Unlike the staunch independence of her brothers, however, Rahma claimed that "her heart is firm in my people" and was quite adept at mirroring her father's criticism of traditional Judaism: "The Jew finds but the mockery of prayer and outward imagery with no sincerity of heart."[39] It was perhaps inevitable that her children became Christians, but she still insisted to her father that she had not renounced her own Jewish identity.

Rahma also spoke fondly of her son, Jacob, who had just finished his studies at Jefferson Medical College in Philadelphia. It appears that Moses Levy, who once had hoped that Elias would become a doctor, contributed funds for his grandson's medical education, including postgraduate work in Paris and Vienna. Jacob Mendes Da Costa (1833–1900) eventually became one of the most distinguished physicians in the United States, and through his lectures, research, and publications was instrumental in the formation of internal medicine as a specialty. During the Civil War he initiated one of the earliest systematic studies of shell shock, which in his day became known as "Da Costa's syndrome" or "Irritable Heart." Among other accomplishments his *Medical Diagnosis* (1864) became the first text of its kind and underwent nine editions during his lifetime. It is recognized as one of the classic texts in medical literature.[40]

By 1854 Moses Levy's declining health was remarked upon by Clarissa Anderson, who met him while traveling by steamship on the St. Johns River. "We met Mr. Levy at the river on his way to Jacksonville," Mrs. Anderson noted to a relative. "The old gentleman looks very feeble. He is really an object of pity."[41] Her comment not only confirms his ill health but adds credence to the idea that Levy may have actually moved to Jacksonville by this time. Since a fire destroyed most city records of this period, the question of his residence is quite difficult to resolve.

Despite his frail condition, in a few months Levy joined a group of friends for a summer excursion to the fashionable White Sulphur Springs resort in Virginia (present-day West Virginia). The resort had achieved a national reputation as the destination of choice for affluent southerners, and the composition of the springwaters was greatly touted for its medicinal effects. Reflective of the social conventions of the day, summer residents assembled themselves according to their respective states and maintained separate group lodges. The actual White Sulphur Spring was encircled by columns, and an arched roof supported a statue of Hygiene, the "Goddess of Health." No doubt, Levy would have been perturbed by such a "heathenish" display. Nevertheless, at a set hour each day residents lined up to have their glasses filled by a "bright-faced, dark-eyed boy." As one observer noted, this fellow served the "bubbling sulphurous liquid" with "the mechanical precision of a steamboat piston." The whole scene had an other-worldly quality, with fashionably dressed "cavaliers" and ladies interspersed with the old and young.[42] There were other springs, of varying temperatures, which were also used for bathing.

On 7 September 1854, after an entire summer spent at the mountain resort, Moses Levy died peacefully, and, contrary to his fears, he was not alone. According to witnesses, he "died somewhat suddenly and without struggle" and was "carefully & kindly tended by friends who were present." Among this group was Levy's old companion John M. Hanson, who informed David Yulee that the funeral was "attended by a large number of persons."[43] The gravesite was almost certainly in the vicinity of the springs, probably the old cemetery at the present-day Greenbrier resort. Scarcity of records and the lack of a headstone hamper any definite conclusions concerning Levy's remains.

Unlike his more flamboyant contemporary, the controversial Mordecai Noah, prominent Jewish publications did not eulogize Levy or even note his demise. His reluctance to promote himself in the United States, coupled with his social withdrawal during his financial crisis, resulted in a degree of anonymity, and he passed from the scene relatively unnoticed.[44] In contrast, Mordecai Noah's 1851 funeral elicited the attendance of "representatives of the bench, the bar, and the mart . . . doctors, authors, musicians, comedians, editors, mechanics, professionals and non-professionals" at Shearith Israel's Twenty-first Street Cemetery in New York City.[45] Noah's "Ararat" fiasco had long been forgiven by the Jewish community, and his reputation actually grew in prominence over the years.

After Moses Levy's trunks and personal belongings were shipped to St. Augustine, David Yulee fully expected to discover a new will that would have reinstated his inheritance. Whether Moses Levy had actually declared this as fact seems improbable. Evidently, their reconciliation led Yulee to reach his own conclusions, especially after his father made reference to updating his will to George Fairbanks. Such was not the case, however. The only document that surfaced was Levy's 1838 will, which appeared in the possession of David Yulee's political adversary, Benjamin A. Putnam. After finally conceding that no other document existed, Yulee started a bitter and protracted effort to invalidate the will, charging temporary insanity, an affair that pitted David and Elias (who also changed his name to Yulee) against their sisters and aunt. While Rahma and Rachel had moved to the United States, Levy's sister, Rachel Benlisa, remained in St. Thomas. David actually met his sisters for the first time when he traveled north to contest the will. Eventually, the family reconciled and reached an out-of-court settlement; all shared in a large legacy.[46] Senator Yulee's formidable political power and wealth—he had become president of the Florida Railroad and a large-scale sugar planter—as well as Moses Levy's well-documented, unorthodox views certainly aided Yulee in nullifying his father's final wishes.

This event further marginalized Moses Levy in the eyes of his descendants. David Yulee's son, Charles Wickliffe Yulee, reflected his father's prejudices in a brief biography of Senator Yulee which was published in 1909. Among other things Charles cast his grandfather, whom he knew only as a very young child, as an erratic dreamer whose "sophistic self-reasoning" led him to suddenly "cast adrift" both his sons while they were still in school and let them fend for themselves. Other bits of misinformation included the assertion that Moses Levy's mother had been an "English Jewess," that Levy had been educated at an English university, and that his father—allegedly of Portuguese extraction—was a Moroccan "prince" and a "Mahometan." Also published without disclaimer in one of the first issues of the *Florida Historical Quarterly,* this "sketch" cast a most unflattering portrait of Moses Levy and obscured any resemblance to legitimate history.[47]

EPILOGUE

*R*ecently, historian Robin D. G. Kelley joined with other noted scholars in a plea "for the kind of history that follows people back and forth across the physical borders of the United States, a history in which the boundaries are determined not by geo-politics but by people and their movement—physical and mental, real and imagined."[1] Such a liberating philosophy, which intends to free professional historians from the confines of a self-limiting, parochial outlook, appears especially relevant to any serious study of Moses Elias Levy. Anything less than a transnational or Atlantic World context would inevitably fall short, for Levy was a character who—in a very literal sense—transcended nationality. Any attempt to mold his significance strictly within the context of the United States would be to miss the point entirely.

This is not to deny Moses Levy's importance to U.S. history—far from it. His was a unique and largely unacknowledged contribution. To appreciate the true significance of his actions, however, one has to check constantly both sides of the Atlantic.

In addition to his achievements in the United States, in England Levy stirred his coreligionists from "a deep sleep" and awakened a latent Jewish nationalism. In an unprecedented series of speeches, newspaper articles, and public rallies, and from his position within the Protestant dominated abolitionist movement, Levy emerged as a Jewish social activist without peer. As such, he did not confine himself to purely Jewish causes but challenged authority and championed broad reforms in the public square—issues that affected blacks and whites, Jews and Gentiles. In many respects

172

his behavior resembled the activism of a much later generation, especially the radical reform rabbis during the beginning of the twentieth century. But there was certainly no parallel for Levy's conduct among the Jews of Europe or the United States during the 1820s.

This singular event, however, was largely ignored in the historical literature. Why, then, did Levy fail to engage the interest of historians? Were his activities really that elusive, or was there something intrinsic to all his actions which obscured his importance?

The answer lies, at least in part, in the statement from Professor Kelley. The exclusive character of physical borders and nationality has indeed shrouded Levy's achievements abroad. Implicit in this situation is the daunting specter of intellectual turf. Given Levy's transnational agenda, scholars who had invested themselves in a specific nation or region were hardly likely to go beyond their field. For historians of British Jewry, Levy was merely a transient and perplexing figure about whom little was known. For American Jewish historians British history was best left to the British.

Similarly, Jonathan Sarna of Brandeis University has defined American Jewish history as an amalgamation of two historical traditions: "one Jewish, dating back to the Patriarchs, the Prophets, and the rabbis of the Talmud, the other American, dating back to the Indians, Columbus, and the heroes of the Revolution." Sarna builds a clear message that invokes patriotism while still holding a reverence for "the rabbis of the Talmud." He further notes the inevitable tensions involved in any such synthesis but concludes that this distinctive history "is also unified by a common vision, the quest to be fully a Jew and fully an American."[2] Given such a restrictive standard, what becomes of complex characters such as Moses Elias Levy, whose vision rejected patriotism as well as the Talmud? Is he less worthy of recognition? Indeed, did Levy's rejection of his own citizenship make him less "American"? Such questions are most relevant, especially in light of the fact that Levy was, until recently, considered a very minor character in American Jewish history.

The fact that Moses Levy was simultaneously attracted to two of the most radical movements within Ashkenazic Jewry, the Haskalah movement and the messianic, anti-assimilationist stance of the ultraorthodox, certainly didn't help his case. Far from the typical middle path chosen by most of his Sephardic contemporaries, Levy gravitated toward the extremes. It must be remembered, however, that, in his merging of what he called "the true Spirit of our Holy and abused Religion" with "liberal and enlightened Principals," Levy had to make significant alterations.[3] He dropped the assimilationist goal from Haskalah and severed the rabbinical tradition from the ultraorthodox. Once this radical surgery was complete, Levy may have been significantly less encumbered by contradictions, but he certainly did not endear himself to the mainstream.

While Levy's religious amalgamation contributed much to his alienation during his later years, it also served him rather well during his activist period. First of all, the inherent dualism fit his own predisposition. His outsider status also gave him tremendous freedom, especially in London. As "Moses E. Levy of Florida," he could say and do things that British Jews would normally never have attempted. Because he believed in the imminent reign of the Messiah, delay and compromise were hardly options; immediate action needed to be taken. As a Jew of the Enlightenment, Levy recognized that he could not restrict himself to only Jewish concerns: all of mankind also had to be served. Universal education, the abolition of slavery, interfaith dialogue—all these reforms not only prepared the way for the Messiah, but they were worthy and humane goals in and of themselves. As for his Jewish colony, communitarianism was simply a Bible-inspired life. In returning to the dictates of Scripture, mankind would eventually reach the perfection described in Genesis. The Messiah would reign, and the world would be saved. In other words, no matter how divergent his ideas, Levy always subsumed them under the unifying authority of the Bible.

Adding yet another layer of complexity is the matter of Levy's utopianism. The fact that he chose to live in frontier isolation—at least for a time—further marginalized his character. Indeed, until fairly recently, most discussions on utopianism emphasized the participants' negative characteristics, their supposedly aberrant psychological makeup, their "outcast" status, peculiar beliefs, and the relatively short duration of most communities. Thankfully, this attitude has modified, and scholars have been far more interested in the positive contributions that these social experiments added to the American experience. To be sure, many of the cast of characters included some very odd fellows. Although Levy, toward the end of his life, may have followed the conventions of the spiritualist movement and claimed to have communed with the spirit world, he was certainly not the madman of David Yulee's imagination. Despite Levy's messianic expectations and his desire for a communitarian haven, there was actually little about his outward demeanor which immediately set him apart from the mainstream. Nevertheless, the utopian label is still a difficult obstacle to overcome. Notwithstanding, Levy's substantial achievements demand a thorough, impartial, and open hearing. He should be judged not only by his own distinct attributes but also within the context of his times.

If Levy's merging of biblicism with Enlightenment ideals predisposed him toward activism—just as it did for his evangelical contemporaries—then Pilgrimage became the physical manifestation of this convergence. Like similar ventures, Pilgrimage existed in backwoods isolation in order to be free from the contagion of the prevailing current. To use Arthur Bestor's classic analogy, Levy's settlement became a kind of "Patent Office Model of the Good Society." Just as a nineteenth-century patent was awarded only after a working model demonstrated the invention's functionality, utopian experiments became their own best proof of their practicality or, as the case may be, their impracticality.[4] Even before Pilgrimage existed, the very idea was enough to drive Levy to promote his agenda. As a result, he was planning innovative educational institutions and settlements in the United States as early as 1818. Levy's tenure in Curaçao, Cuba, and England also reflected his heightened concern for reform and social justice. It is no co-incidence that, after Pilgrimage was destroyed, not only was Levy's utopia building never rekindled, but he gradually withdrew from society. Poverty was a factor, but there is little doubt that he also suffered from the loss of his dream.

Despite Levy's own pessimistic assessment of his life, a more objective view reveals substantial accomplishments. Using the same international approach of his merchant years, Levy replaced his goods and stock with what he regarded as the higher currency of reform. He became a "benevolent Stranger," a gentleman who preferred anonymity, but, when compelled to take up the torch of leadership, few individuals could match his gift for oratory and powers of persuasion. He became one of the first Jews to enter the world stage as a respected spokesman for Jewish nationalism and as a militant denouncer of antisemitism. In fashioning an activist role for himself and in taking on the cause of abolitionism, he became the spiritual progenitor of those modern Jews who marched for civil rights and who risked their own welfare for a broad spectrum of social causes. No longer was the Talmudic maxim—"the law of the land is the law [for the Jews]"—the norm. Passive acceptance or behind-the-scenes maneuvering by the Jewish elite suddenly stopped being the only alternatives. Thanks to Levy's efforts, ordinary Jews debated with Gentiles on an equal footing and in highly publicized forums; they asserted themselves and discussed their religious differences openly and without fear. No longer could Christians complain that Jews always withdrew and never ventured "into the open field of fair argument."[5] It is well worth remembering the words of Joseph Crooll: "We have of late observed a man by the name of Mr. Moses Elias Levi who endeavoured to bring in motion the Jews, that they might rise and shew themselves men."[6] This event marked a distinct shift in consciousness. Jews had emerged from centuries of psychological oppression and planted themselves firmly as equal players in a modern world.

In the 1820s Levy sought to free Jews from the confines of their borders and to reach out to the greater Jewish community. His ideas for a United Association that operated beyond the limitations of a nation-state as well as his concerns for universal educational reform were developed in reaction to the intense nationalism of his time. Today historians are facing a challenge that is similar in scope. The quest for a historical narrative that abandons the traditional confines of nationhood has been labeled "subversive" and "nothing less than a direct challenge to the very paradigmatic sources of American history." Ironically, it is during this period of change, when renewed efforts are made to uncover histories "long lost in the shadows of nation," that Moses Levy—the intellectual precursor to such radical ideas—has managed to emerge from these very shadows.[7]

NOTES

ABBREVIATIONS

AGI   Archivo General de Indias, Seville, Spain

AJA   Jacob Rader Marcus Center of the American Jewish Archives, Cincinnati, Ohio

EB   Private Collection, Emmanuel Boëlle, Paris, France

FSA   Florida State Archives, Tallahassee

JOC   Jean Outland Chrysler Museum Library, Norfolk, Va.

NARA   National Archives and Records Administration

PKY   P. K. Yonge Library of Florida History, University of Florida, Gainesville

SAHS   St. Augustine Historical Society Library, St. Augustine, Fla.

ACKNOWLEDGMENTS

1. Cecile-Marie Sastre, "Moses Elias Levy and the Settlement of Alachua" (paper presented at the Florida Conference of Historians, Panama City, Fla., March 1994).

INTRODUCTION

1. Chris Monaco, introduction to *A Plan for the Abolition of Slavery, Consistently with the Interests of All Parties Concerned,* by Moses E. Levy (1828; rpt., Micanopy, Fla., 1999), v–xxii.

2. Levy's correspondence, particularly M. E. Levy to Rachel [Levy] Henriques, 1 September 1853, box 40, David Levy Yulee Papers, PKY, and the newly acquired Reuben Charles Papers at PKY, which consist of documents from Pilgrimage Plantation, refute the accepted position that no Jewish settlers arrived at Levy's settlement. For examples of this negative view, see Joseph Gary Adler, "Moses Elias Levy and Attempts to Colonize Florida," in *Jews of the South: Selected Essays from the Southern Jewish Historical Society,* ed. Samuel Proctor and Louis Schmier (Macon, Ga., 1984), 26; Malcolm H. Stern, "The 1820s: American Jewry

Comes of Age," in *The American Jewish Experience,* ed. Jonathan D. Sarna, 2d ed. (New York, 1997), 36.

3. Jacob Rader Marcus, *United States Jewry, 1776-1985,* 4 vols. (Detroit, 1989-93), 1:367.

4. Marcus, *United States Jewry,* 364-65, 369.

5. Diary of Moses Levy" (n.d.), box 1, Yulee Papers, PKY. For a limited discussion of Yulee's compilation of the "Diary" see Anne C. Rose, "Interfaith Families in Victorian America," in *Moral Problems in American Life: New Perspectives on Cultural History,* ed. Karen Halttunen and Lewis Perry (Ithaca, 1998), 238 n. 51.

6. Elias Yulee and David L. Yulee, "Re: Probate of the Will of Moses E. Levy deceased upon Caveat to the Circuit Court of St. Johns County" (n.d.), box 23, Yulee Papers, PKY.

7. "Deposition of Augustus W. Walker," 19 February 1857, folder 38, box 135, St. Johns County Circuit Court Papers, SAHS.

8. David L. Yulee, "Narrative of my administration of my father's estates" (n.d.), box 1, Yulee Papers.

9. For a recent example of a distinct bias against M. E. Levy, see Anne C. Rose, *Beloved Strangers: Interfaith Families in Nineteenth-Century America* (Cambridge, Mass., 2001), 90-93.

10. "Diary of Moses Levy," Yulee Papers; "Dr. Peck Ledger," May 1837-May 1839, Levy File, SAHS.

11. Levy to Henriques, 1 September 1853, box 40, Yulee Papers.

12. For more on Levy's family, see Haim Bentov, "The Ha-Levi Ibn Yuli Family," in *East and Maghreb: Researches in the History of the Jews in the Orient and North Africa* (Hebrew), ed. E. Bashan, A. Rubinstein, and S. Schwarzfuchs, 6 vols. (Ramat Gan, Israel, 1980), 2:141-45.

13. "Excerpt from the Richmond Enquirer," *Florida Herald and Southern Democrat* (St. Augustine), 24 February 1846.

14. C[harles] Wickliffe Yulee, *Senator Yulee of Florida: A Biographical Sketch* (Jacksonville, Fla., 1909), 3.

15. For examples of Yulee folklore, see Allen Morris, *Florida Place Names* (Coral Gables, Fla., 1974), 92; Stuart McIver, "Flight of a Favorite Son," *Sunshine: The Magazine of South Florida,* 14 April 1996, 18-20; Latrell E. Mickler, "Florida's First Senator," *Florida Living* (September 1988), 10-12; Leon Huhner, "Moses Elias Levy, an Early Florida Pioneer and the Father of Florida's First Senator," *Florida Historical Quarterly* 19 (April 1941): 320; Leslie Reicin Stein, "David Levy and Florida Territorial Politics" (master's thesis, University of South Florida, 1973), 49-52. In her version of M. E. Levy's ancestry, Stein draws upon the undocumented efforts of Mrs. Mary MacRae, a resident of Homosassa, Fla. MacRae's dependence on "private investigators" to act as researchers should have immediately cast her assertions in doubt.

16. M. E. Levy, "Speech addressed to a meeting of Jews and Christians," *World* (London), 28 May 1828; for the importance of the Jubilee, see Peter Linebaugh and Marcus Rediker, *The Many-Headed Hydra: Sailors, Slaves, Commoners, and the Hidden History of the Revolutionary Atlantic* (Boston, 2000), 290-300.

17. Quotation from W. Goodwin to Hon. Zabdiel Sampson, 17 February 1820, HR16A-G17.2, Record Group 233, Records of the U.S. House of Representatives, NARA.

18. Arthur Eugene Bestor Jr., *Backwoods Utopias: The Sectarian and Owenite Phases of Communitarian Socialism in America, 1663–1829* (Philadelphia, 1950), 3–4, 7; Robert S. Fogarty, intro., "Paradise Planters," *Dictionary of American Communal and Utopian History* (Westport, Conn., 1980).

19. M. E. Levy, *Plan for the Abolition of Slavery,* 26.

20. M. E. Levy, *An Address Delivered before the Temperance Society of Micanopy* (Jacksonville, Fla., 1852), 3.

21. M[ordecai] M[anuel] Noah to [Samuel Myers], 28 February 1819, Myers Papers, AJA.

22. Levy to Myers, 1 November 1818, AJA.

23. Quotation from "A True Israelite," in "A Few Remarks. On a Letter which appeared in the World Newspaper of the Month of June, 1828, disclaiming a certain Petition to Parliament concerning the Jews" (c. 1828), De Sola Pamphlets 2, Special Collections, University College London.

24. Levy to Myers (Curaçao), 8 June 1819, Myers Papers, JOC.

25. Levy, *Plan for the Abolition of Slavery,* 29.

26. *World,* 6 August 1828; Marcus, *United States Jewry,* 368.

27. M. E. Levy, "Address to the Surrey Anti-Slavery Society," *World,* 31 October 1827.

28. Quotation from Fogarty, "Paradise Planters," xv.

29. Fogarty, "Paradise Planters," xiv–xv.

30. R. Scott Appleby, "History in the Fundamentalist Imagination," *Journal of American History* 89 (September 2002): 498–502.

31. "A Funeral Panegyric," *Occident and American Jewish Advocate* 9 (May 1851).

32. M. E. Levy to Moses Myers (London), 26 July 1827, Myers Papers, JOC.

33. Exhibit B, 4 March 1822, House Report 450, 27th Cong., 2d sess., 1842, 125.

CHAPTER 1

1. William Lempriere, *A Tour from Gibraltar to Tangier, Sallee, Mogodore, Santa Cruz, and Tarudant; and thence over Mount Atlas to Morocco, including a particular account of the Royal Harem, etc.,* 3d ed. (Philadelphia, 1794), 153.

2. Daniel J. Schroeter, "Royal Power and the Economy in Precolonial Morocco: Jews and the Legitimization of Foreign Trade," in *In the Shadow of the Sultan: Culture, Power, and Politics in Morocco,* ed. Rahma Bourqia and Susan Gilson Miller (Cambridge, Mass., 1999), 78–79.

3. Miller and Bourqia, intro., *In the Shadow of the Sultan,* 5–6.

4. Norman A. Stillman, *The Jews of Arab Lands: A History and Source Book* (Philadelphia, 1979), 81.

5. Stillman, *Jews of Arab Lands,* 83.

6. Vivian B. Mann, "Memory, Mimesis, Realia," in *Morocco: Jews and Art in a Muslim Land,* ed. Vivian B Mann (New York, 2000), 134.

7. Stillman, *Jews of Arab Lands,* 83.

8. Samuel Romanelli, *Travail in an Arab Land,* ed. and trans. Yedida K. Stillman and Norman A. Stillman (1792; rpt., Tuscaloosa, Ala., 1989), 62.

9. Romanelli, *Travail in an Arab Land,* 173–74 n. 4.

10. Schroeter, "Royal Power and the Economy in Precolonial Morocco," 74–95.

11. Schroeter, "Royal Power," 85–86.

12. For Levy's birth date, see M. E. Levy to Mr. and Mrs. [David] Yulee, 1 October 1852, box 40, Yulee Papers.

13. Daniel J. Schroeter, *The Sultan's Jew: Morocco and the Sephardi World* (Stanford, Calif., 2002), 24, 172 n. 55.

14. Romanelli, *Travail in an Arab Land,* 78. For a discussion of Eliahu's position at court, see Norman A. and Yedida K. Stillman, "The Jewish Courtier Class in Late Eighteenth-Century Morocco as Seen through the Eyes of Samuel Romanelli," in *Essays in Honor of Bernard Lewis: The Islamic World, from Classical to Modern Times,* ed. C. E. Bosworth, Charles Issawi, Roger Savory, and A. L. Udovitch (Princeton, 1989), 845–51.

15. Lempriere, *Tour from Gibraltar,* 174. Lempriere notes six "moorish" and seven Jewish "secretaries" of the Treasury but does not mention them by name. Eliahu [Elliaho] Levi is clearly identified, however, as one of the seven in an Austrian intelligence report on the Moroccan court in 1789. See Stillman and Stillman, *Travail in an Arab Land,* 182–83 n. 57. For Von Dombay's full court description, see "Gegenwärtiger Zustand des marokkanischen Hofes," 22 June 1789, Staatenabteilungen Marokko K. 3, Konv. Varia 1605–1789, no. 3 lit e, Haus-, Hof- und Staatarchivs, Osterreichisches Staatsarchiv, Vienna. This document, in addition to information contained in Romanelli and other primary documents, contradicts unsubstantiated assertions by David Corcos and others that Eliahu served as prime minister or grand vizier during Sidi Muhammad's reign. (I am grateful to Norman Stillman for sharing his copy of this document.)

16. Joseph Toledano, *La Saga des familles les Juifs du Maroc et leurs noms* (Tel Aviv, 1983), 232; Joseph Gary Adler, "Moses Elias Levy and Attempts to Colonize Florida," in *Jews of the South: Selected Essays from the Southern Jewish Historical Society,* ed. Samuel Proctor and Louis Schmier (Macon, Ga., 1984), 18 n. 3.

17. *Encyclopaedia Judaica,* 1st ed., s.v., "Yuly"; Toledano, *Les Juifs du Maroc,* 232.

18. Haim Bentov, "The Ha-Levi Ibn Yuli Family," in *East and Maghreb: Researches in the History of the Jews in the Orient and North Africa* [Hebrew], ed. E. Bashan, A. Rubinstein, and S. Schwarzfuchs, 6 vols. (Ramat Gan, 1980), 2:141–45. For reference to polygamy and Moroccan Jewish custom, see Shlomo Deshen, *The Mellah Society: Jewish Community Life in Sherifian Morocco* (Chicago, 1989), 30; Stillman and Stillman, "Jewish Courtier Class," 850.

19. Romanelli, *Travail in an Arab Land,* 103. The common vernacular was *Haquitia,* a mixture of Spanish, Hebrew, and Arabic.

20. M. E. Levy to Rachel [Levy] Henriques, 1 September 1853, box 40, Yulee Papers.

21. Haim Zafrani, *Mille ans de vie juive au Maroc* (Paris, 1983), 63.

22. This *rite de passage* is mentioned in Milton Jacobs, "A Study of Culture Stability and Change: The Moroccan Jewess" (Ph.D. diss., Catholic University of America, 1956), 14.

23. Levy to Henriques, 1 September 1853, Yulee Papers.

24. Stillman and Stillman, "Jewish Courtier Class," 846.

25. Romanelli, *Travail in an Arab Land,* 15.

26. Romanelli, *Travail in an Arab Land,* 79.

27. Stillman and Stillman, preface and intro., *Travail in an Arab Land*, ix–xi and 1–11.

28. David Corcos, "Le Prenoms des Juifs du Maroc," in Corcos, *Studies in the History of the Jews of Morocco* (Jerusalem, 1976), 153.

29. Adler, "Moses Elias Levy and Attempts to Colonize Florida," 19 n. 4.

30. Romanelli, *Travail in an Arab Land*, 49.

31. Stillman and Stillman, preface to *Travail in an Arab Land*, x.

32. Stillman and Stillman, "Jewish Courtier Class," 849.

33. Romanelli, *Travail in an Arab Land*, 78–79.

34. Romanelli, *Travail in an Arab Land*. For the date of Levi's imprisonment, see Schroeter, *Sultan's Jew*, 172 n. 54.

35. Romanelli, *Travail in an Arab Land*, 79.

36. Bertram Wyatt Brown, *Southern Honor: Ethics and Behavior in the Old South* (New York, 1982), 34.

37. This incident is related in Romanelli, *Travail in an Arab Land*, 90. For an examination of the Arab honor code and its exaggerated concept of manliness, see Raphael Patai, *The Arab Mind*, rev. ed. (New York, 2002), 95–100, 223–24.

38. For a discussion of the ramifications of "unmasking" in a similar honor-bound culture, see Kenneth S. Greenberg, *Honor and Slavery* (Princeton, N.J., 1996), 24–50. See also Gary S. Gregg, "Themes of Authority in the Life Histories of Young Moroccans," in *Shadow of the Sultan*, 215–17.

39. R[abbi] Joseph Crooll, *The Fifth Empire, Delivered in a Discourse to Thirty-Six Men* (London, 1829), 20; Moses E. Levy, *A Plan for the Abolition of Slavery, Consistently with the Interests of All Parties Concerned*, ed. Chris Monaco (1828; rpt., Micanopy, Fla., 1999), 10, 11, 29.

40. Levy to Myers (Curaçao), 4 May 1819, JOC.

41. Quote from Schroeter, *Sultan's Jew*, 108; Romanelli, *Travail in an Arab Land*, 141–47; H. Z. Hirschberg, *A History of the Jews in North Africa*, 2d rev. ed. (Leiden, 1981), 1:293–301.

42. Bentov, "Ha-Levi Ibn Yuli Family," 141–45; *Encyclopaedia Judaica*, 1st ed., s.v. "Morocco." For Romanelli's version of Eliahu's ordeal, see *Travail in an Arab Land*, 142.

43. Romanelli, *Travail in an Arab Land*. The Gibraltar destination is discussed in *Florida Herald and Southern Democrat* (St. Augustine), 24 February 1846.

44. Quotation from Charles James Fox in Ernle Bradford, *Gibraltar: The History of a Fortress* (New York, 1972), 133.

45. "Particular Description of the Rock of Gibraltar," *St. Croix Gazette*, 8 August 1808. For a full description of Moroccan Jewish clothing, see Romanelli, *Travail in an Arab Land*, 65–68.

46. For background on Gibraltar Jews during this period, see A. B. M. Serfaty, *The Jews of Gibraltar under British Rule* (Gibraltar, 1933), 7–15. For reference to the Yulee family jewels, see Mills M. Lord Jr., "David Levy Yulee: Statesman and Railroad Builder" (master's thesis, University of Florida, 1940), 2.

47. Eliahu's trips to Egypt are cited in *Florida Herald and Southern Democrat*, 24 February 1846.

48. William G. F. Jackson, *The Rock of the Gibraltarians: A History of Gibraltar* (Rutherford, N.J., 1987), 189.

49. Romanelli, *Travail in an Arab Land*, 57, 173 n. 1.

50. Quotation from "A True Israelite," in "A Few Remarks. On a Letter which appeared in the World Newspaper of the Month of June, 1828, disclaiming a certain Petition to Parliament concerning the Jews" (c. 1828), De Sola Pamphlets 2, Special Collections, University College London.

51. One dramatic incident involving the loss of a single ship in Gibraltar Bay is recounted in M. E. Levy, *An Address Delivered before the Temperance Society of Micanopy* (Jacksonville, Fla., 1852), 13–14.

52. Levy to Henriques, 1 September 1853, box 40, Yulee Papers.

53. For a discussion of the conversion experience among evangelicals, see Donald M. Scott, "Abolition as a Sacred Vocation," in *Antislavery Reconsidered: New Perspectives on the Abolitionists*, ed. Lewis Perry and Michael Fellman (Baton Rouge, La., 1979), 53–61.

54. Quotation from J. Christopher Soper, *Evangelical Christianity in the United States and Great Britain: Religious Beliefs, Political Choices* (New York, 1994), 40.

55. Levy to Henriques, 1 September 1853, box 40, Yulee Papers.

56. *Florida Herald and Southern Democrat*, 24 February 1846.

57. For a firsthand account of the plague and its spread into Spain, see James Grey Jackson, *An Account of the Empire of Marocco* (London, 1814), 171–87. Also see Schroeter, *Sultan's Jew*, 36–38.

58. Leslie Reicin Stein, "David Levy and Florida Territorial Politics" (master's thesis, University of South Florida, 1973), 53.

59. Judah M. Cohen, *Through the Sands of Time: A History of the Jewish Community of St. Thomas, U.S. Virgin Islands* (Hanover, N.H., 2004), 13–14.

CHAPTER 2

1. Isaac Dookhan, *A History of the Virgin Islands of the United States* (St. Thomas, 1974), 98–99; Gordon K. Lewis, "An Introductory Note to the Study of the Virgin Islands," *Caribbean Studies* 8 (July 1968): 10–11.

2. For reference to the dominant languages of St. Thomas, see Dookhan, *History of the Virgin Islands*, 142, 193. For the composition and origins of the free people of color, see "1803 Register of the Free Colored of Charlotte Amalie," in *St. Thomas 1803: Crossroads of the Diaspora*, ed. David W. Knight and Gary T. Horlacher, trans. Gary T. Horlacher (St. Thomas, 1999), 15–131.

3. As quoted by Edith deJongh Woods, *The Royal Three Quarters of the Town of Charlotte Amalie* (Rome, 1992), 4.

4. [Joseph Freeman Rattenbury], *Narrative of a Voyage to the Spanish Main, in the Ship "Two Friends"* (London, 1819), 55–56.

5. Judah M. Cohen, *Through the Sands of Time: A History of the Jewish Community of St. Thomas, U.S. Virgin Islands* (Hanover, N.H., 2004), 21. See also Isidor Paiewonsky, intro., *Jewish Historical Development in the Virgin Islands, 1665–1959* (St. Thomas, 1959).

6. Levy described his house and loft as "situated in Dominis Garden"—a colloquial name for Domini Gade situated in the present-day Queens Quarter. See M. E. Levy and Hannah Levy, Divorce Contract, 12 May 1815, "Notarial Protocol for St. Thomas, 1815–16," in J. O.

Bro-Jorgensen to [Mary MacRae], 15 January 1950, box 1, Yulee Papers, PKY. This series of correspondence includes handwritten transcripts from the Royal Danish Archives in Copenhagen, where Bro-Jorgensen held the title of "keeper of the Danish Record Office." It represents a most important and seldom utilized resource. For more on Queens Quarter, see Woods, *Royal Three Quarters*, 50–52.

7. Moroccan Jewish names included Benlisa, Sarquy, Massias, Sebag, Toledano, and Abendanone. See David Corcos, "Les Juifs au Maroc et leurs mellahs," in *Studies in the History of the Jews of Morocco* (Jerusalem, 1976), 119 n. 131; Benlisa epitaph in *299 Epitaphs on the Jewish Cemetery in St. Thomas, W.I., 1837–1916*, ed. Jul. Margolinsky (Copenhagen, 1965), 9; Katina E. Coulianos, letter to author (St. Thomas), 1 June 2000.

8. S. U. Hastings and B. L. MacLeavy, *Seedtime and Harvest: A Brief History of the Moravian Church in Jamaica, 1754–1979* (Kingston, Jamaica, 1979), 38–45.

9. Patricia Gill Murphy, "The Education of the New World Blacks in the Danish West Indies / U.S. Virgin Islands: A Case Study of Social Transition" (Ph.D. diss., University of Connecticut, 1977), 39, 48, 68.

10. John Fletcher, *Studies on Slavery, in Easy Lessons* (Natchez, Miss., 1852), 159.

11. Neville A. T. Hall, *Slave Society in the Danish West Indies: St. Thomas, St. John and St. Croix*, ed. B. W. Higman (Mona, Jamaica, 1992), 46.

12. For background on the Moravian missions of St. Thomas and the techniques used in the religious education of slaves, see Charles Colcock Jones, "Suggestions on the Religious Instruction of the Negroes in the Southern States," *Princeton Review* 20 (January 1848): 1–30. For a brief discussion of the St. Thomas tradition of miscegenation and the manumission of mixed-race children, see David W. Knight, foreword, in Knight and Horlacher, *St. Thomas 1803: Crossroads of the Diaspora*, 1–2.

13. For Levy's reference to his "ministry," see M. E. Levy to Samuel Myers, 8 June 1819, Myers Papers, JOC.

14. Hall, *Slave Society in the Danish West Indies*, 25–29.

15. Dookhan, *History of the Virgin Islands*, 170.

16. Hall, *Slave Society in the Danish West Indies*, 28–29.

17. The marriage date of 16 March 1803 is given in M. E. Levy and Hannah Levy, Divorce Contract, 12 May 1815, "Notarial Protocol for St. Thomas, 1815–16," in Bro-Jorgensen to [Mary MacRae], 15 January 1950, box 1, Yulee Papers.

18. For Hannah Abendanone's birth in St. Eustatius, see the epitaph under Hannah Julien, her second married name, in *299 Epitaphs on the Jewish Cemetery*, 23. For a brief mention of the Abendanone family in the Danish records, see Bro-Jorgensen to MacRae (Copenhagen), 8 March 1950, box 1, Yulee Papers.

19. The full departure of Jews from St. Eustatius took place between 1795 and 1800. See J. Hartog, *The Jews and St. Eustatius: The Eighteenth Century Jewish Congregation Honen Dalim and Description of the old Cemetery* (St. Maarten, 1976), 15.

20. Quotation from Zeph[aniah] Kingsley to Moses E. Levy, Esq., 18 January 1843, in *Florida Herald and Southern Democrat* (St. Augustine), 23 January 1843.

21. For the family origins in Morocco, see *Encyclopaedia Judaica*, 1st ed., s.v. "Abendanan"; Shlomo Deshen, *The Mellah Society: Jewish Community Life in Sherifian Morocco* (Chicago, 1989), 8.

22. Levy to Myers (Curaçao), 4 May 1819, JOC.

23. A. M. Da Costa to Lucien Wolff, 22 March 1901, B20 COS, Lucien Wolff Collection, University College London. Da Costa's account of Elias Sarquy came from his mother's recollections and is therefore far more credible than the rest of his family history. Records also reveal that Sarquy married into the Abendanone family.

24. Quotations from M. E. Levy, *An Address Delivered before the Temperance Society of Micanopy* (Jacksonville, Fla., 1852), 14. For further insights regarding this event, see M. E. Levy to Rachel [Levy] Henriques, 1 September 1853, box 40, Yulee Papers.

25. M. E. Levy and Hannah Levy, Divorce Petition, 12 May 1815, "Notarial Protocol for St. Thomas, 1815–16," in Bro-Jorgensen to MacRae, 15 January 1950, box 1, Yulee Papers.

26. David Yulee to Moses Levy (Washington, D.C.), 7 March 1848, box 40, Yulee Papers.

27. According to the records of the Hebrew Congregation of St. Thomas, Elias Levy's birth date was 2 February 1804. See Katina E. Coulianos, letter to author (St. Thomas), 1 June 2000.

28. "Matrikel of St. Thomas, 1805–1815," in Bro-Jorgensen to MacRae, 15 January 1950, box 1, Yulee Papers.

29. "Public Meeting of the Surrey Anti-Slavery Society," *World* (London), 31 October 1827.

30. M. E. Levy to Mr. [Jonathan] Dacosta, 18 September 1845, box 40, Yulee Papers.

31. Isaac S. and Suzanne A. Emmanuel, *History of the Jews of the Netherlands Antilles* (Cincinnati, 1970), 80–83.

32. Bill of sale, 14 March 1804, Notarial Book for St. Thomas, 1800–1806, in Bro-Jorgensen to MacRae, 8 March 1950, box 1, Yulee Papers. A Spanish milled dollar is exactly the same in value as a U.S. dollar of the time.

33. "Proclamation of General L. Ferrand, French Commander in Chief at St. Domingo," 5 February 1805, in *Despatches from United States consuls in St. Thomas, 1805–1906* (Washington, D.C.: National Archives microfilm publications, 1969).

34. Johan Peter Nissen, *Reminiscences of a 46 Years Residence in the Island of St. Thomas* (Nazareth, Pa., 1838), 9. (Typescript copy from the original MS, Enid M. Baa Library, St. Thomas, V.I.).

35. For a compendium of the damages wrought by a single hurricane throughout the Caribbean islands, see *De Curacaosche Courant,* 30 October 1819. Also see Nissen, *Reminiscences,* 2–3.

36. Nissen, *Reminiscences,* 3.

37. Nissen, *Reminiscences.*

38. M. E. Levy, Testament, 2 August 1804, St. Thomas Notarial Book, 1803–4, in Bro-Jorgensen to MacRae, 8 March 1950, box 1, Yulee Papers.

39. Paiewonsky, *Jewish Historical Development,* intro.; Woods, *Royal Three Quarters,* 5–6.

40. Nissen, *Reminiscences,* 21.

41. Quotations from Nissen, *Reminiscences,* 22.

42. For a firsthand description of the blockade, see James M. McGreggor to James Madison (St. Thomas), 13 November 1807, in *Despatches from United States Consuls in St. Thomas, 1805–1906.* For the motivations behind the capture of the Danish islands, see Dookhan, *History of the Virgin Islands,* 99.

43. David Yulee, "Narrative of My Administration of My Father's Estates: Relations with My Father's Family," n.d., box 1, Yulee Papers.

44. "Contract for Separation and Divorce," 12 May 1815, Notarial Protocol for St. Thomas, 1815–1816, in Bro-Jorgensen to MacRae, 15 January 1950, Yulee Papers.

45. Levy to Henriques, 1 September 1853, box 40, Yulee Papers; quotation and school description from *St. Croix Gazette,* 17 November 1808.

46. Moses Levy to Samuel Myers, 1 November 1818, box 3, Myers Family Papers, AJA.

47. Levy quotations from M. E. Levy to Samuel Myers (Curaçao), 6 August 1819, Myers Papers, JOC.

48. "Notes of manuscript writings of M. E. Levy deceased," box 1, Yulee Papers.

49. William Savage to James Savage (Havana), 7 June 1820, in *Florida Herald and Southern Democrat,* 9 January 1843.

50. For a brief discussion of the importance of the burial society and its evolution as an independent charitable organization, see Jay Michael Eidelman, "'In the Wilds of America,' The Early Republican Origins of American Judaism" (Ph.D. diss., Yale University, 1997), 164. Levy mentions his participation in this organization in Levy to Henriques, 1 September 1853, Yulee Papers.

51. Later Moses Levy's son Elias married his cousin Rachel Benjamin—also the cousin of Judah P. Benjamin—after returning to St. Thomas between 1829 and 1832. See Robert Myers, *The Children of Pride: A True Story of Georgia and the Civil War* (New Haven, Conn., 1972), 1738; Bro-Jorgensen to MacRae, 4 July 1950, box 1, Yulee Papers. Myers is cited by Judge Earl Hendry of Gatlinburg, Tennessee, in his handwritten Yulee genealogy, for which I am most grateful. Hannah Levy mentions three of her Benjamin nieces in a codicil to her will dated 7 May 1866; see Jorgensen to MacRae, 28 November 1950.

52. *St. Croix Gazette,* 18 July 1808, 2 January 1809. Philip's partnership with his father did not last long, and the company was dissolved a year later (1 June 1810).

53. *Sanct Thomas Tidende,* 2 October 1817; Bro-Jorgensen to MacRae, 4 July 1950, box 1, Yulee Papers. Bro-Jorgensen cites material from the Dealing Court of St. Thomas relating to Levy's business partnership. Philip maintained an association with Levy, traveling with him on occasion to Puerto Rico, but left for the United States in 1817. See *Sanct Thomas Tidende,* 19 June 1817.

54. *Sanct Thomas Tidende,* 14 August 1817.

55. This total is for the year 1819. See Nissen, *Reminiscences,* 43.

56. *Sanct Thomas Tidende,* 12 June 1815, 4 July 1815, 7 July 1817. For mortgage activities, see Bro-Jorgensen to MacRae, 4 July 1950, box 1, Yulee Papers. Levy & Benjamin's lottery on St. Thomas was advertised in the *St. Croix Gazette,* 20 March 1810.

57. Lewis, "Introductory Note to the Study of the Virgin Islands," 11; Dookhan, *History of the Virgin Islands,* 98–99.

58. Nissen, *Reminiscences,* 44–45.

59. Alejandro Ramirez to Secretary of State, 28 April 1816, Legajo 453, Ultramar, AGI. I am indebted to Sherry Johnson for bringing this and subsequent documents to my attention.

60. Alejandro Ramirez to Secretary of State, 18 June 1816.

61. Alejandro Ramirez to Secretary of State. My thanks to historian Neill Macaulay for his translation and interpretation of this important document.

62. Franco, *Politica Continental Americana de España en Cuba,* 139.The author also charges that Levy maintained a relationship with Jean Lafitte and other privateers. A recent search in the Archivo Nacional in Havana failed to substantiate any of the negative assertions that Franco makes against Levy. The material that the author cites as being held in the archive did not materialize. While discredited, I will continue to cite Franco using only those incidents that have been verified.

63. Rene Velazquez, "The Intendancy of Alejandro Ramirez in Puerto Rico (1813–1816)" (Ph.D. diss., University of Michigan, 1972), 2.

64. Charnel Anderson, *The American Presence in Puerto Rico* (San Germán, P.R., 1998), 2.

65. M. E. Levy, "Ramirez," *Florida Herald and Southern Democrat,* 1 February 1843.

66. Luis E. Gonzalez Vales, "Alejandro Ramirez: La Vida de un Intendente Liberal," in *Diario Economico de Puerto Rico: 1814–1815* (San Juan, P.R., 1972), 14; Harry Bernstein, *Making an Inter-American Mind* (Gainesville, Fla., 1961), 106.

67. Velazquez, "Alejandro Ramirez in Puerto Rico," 32, 34.

68. Velazquez, "Alejandro Ramirez in Puerto Rico," 33.

69. For Levy's two-part article on Ramirez, see Levy, "Ramirez," *Florida Herald and Southern Democrat,* 25 January and 1 February 1843.

70. For reference to Ramirez's economic difficulties, see Levy, "Ramirez." Also see Fermín Peraza Sarausa, *Diccionario Biografico Cubano* (Havana, 1955), 12; Vales, "Alejandro Ramirez," 21.

71. Alejandro Ramirez to Don Pablo Morillo (Havana), 8 June 1818, in *Florida Herald and Southern Democrat,* 9 January 1843.

72. Franco's *Politica Continental Americana de España en Cuba* mentions the business relationship between Levy and Ramirez, but this book, published in Cuba in 1964, is not widely known.

73. Birgit Sonesson, *Puerto Rico's Commerce, 1765–1865: From Regional to Worldwide Market Relations* (Los Angeles, 2000), 20, 44; Velazquez, "Alejandro Ramirez in Puerto Rico," 217.

74. Lewis, "Introductory Note to the Study of the Virgin Islands," 8.

75. M. E. Levy, letter to the editor, *Florida Herald and Southern Democrat,* 1 February 1843.

76. For a brief mention of Arizmendi, see Loida Figueroa Mercado, *History of Puerto Rico: From the Beginning to 1892* (New York, 1974), 134, 472–73. For a firsthand account of this incident, see Levy, letter to the editor, *Florida Herald and Southern Democrat,* 1 February 1843.

77. *Florida Herald and Southern Democrat.*

78. *Florida Herald and Southern Democrat.*

79. *Florida Herald and Southern Democrat,* 25 January 1843.

80. *Florida Herald and Southern Democrat.*

81. Sonesson, *Puerto Rico's Commerce,* 45.

82. *Florida Herald and Southern Democrat,* 1 February 1843.

83. Franco, *Politica Continental Americana,* 43.

84. Velazquez, "Alejandro Ramirez in Puerto Rico," 190, 219.

85. Velazquez, "Alejandro Ramirez in Puerto Rico," 2.

86. Quotation by Lewis, "Note to the Study of the Virgin Islands," 8.

87. Jay Kinsbruner, *Not of Pure Blood: The Free People of Color and Racial Prejudice in Nineteenth-Century Puerto Rico* (Durham, N.C., 1996), 32. For the relative number of freedmen in St. Thomas circa 1815, see Hall, *Slave Society in the Danish West Indies,* 186.

88. Hall, *Slave Society in the Danish West Indies,* 1–2, 19–33; David Brion Davis, *The Problem of Slavery in Western Culture* (Ithaca, N.Y., 1966), 275.

89. Quotation from Colonel George Flintner, *An Account of the Present State of the Island of Puerto Rico* (London, 1834), 67–68, in Kinsbruner, *Not of Pure Blood,* 31 n. 38.

90. Moses E. Levy, *A Plan for the Abolition of Slavery, Consistently with the Interests of All Parties Concerned,* ed. Chris Monaco (1828; rpt., Micanopy, Fla., 1999), 18.

91. Levy, *Plan for the Abolition of Slavery,* 17.

92. Jacquelyn Briggs Kent, "The Enlightenment and Spanish Colonial Administration: The Life and Myth of Alejandro Ramírez y Blanco in Guatemala, Puerto Rico, and Cuba, 1777–1821" (Ph.D. diss., Tulane University, 1997), 216.

93. Manuel Moreno Fraginals, *The Sugarmill: The Socioeconomic Complex of Sugar in Cuba, 1760–1860* (New York, 1976), 50. Cuba became the world's leading producer of cane sugar in 1840; see Herbert S. Klein, *African Slavery in Latin America and the Caribbean* (New York, 1988), 93.

94. Rembert W. Patrick, *Florida Fiasco: Rampant Rebels on the Georgia-Florida Border, 1810–1815* (Athens, Ga., 1954); Chris Monaco, "Fort Mitchell and the Settlement of the Alachua Country," *Florida Historical Quarterly* 79 (summer 2000): 1–25.

95. Quotation from P[ablo] Morillo, "Proclamation to the Inhabitants of Venezuela," 11 May 1815, in *Sanct Thomas Tidende,* 19 June 1815.

96. U.S. Consul to Secretary of State (Havana), 8 July 1816, in *Despatches from United States Consuls in Havana, Cuba, 1783–1906* (Washington, D.C.: National Archives microfilm publications, 1969).

97. For Levy's occupation as a sugar planter in Cuba, see "Deposition of M. E. Levy," 23 September 1841, in H. Report 450, 76.

98. Quotation from Herbert S. Klein, *Slavery in the Americas: A Comparative Study of Virginia and Cuba* (Chicago, 1967), 219.

99. "Certificate of Don Julian Fernandez de Rodan and Don Claudio Martinez de Pinillos," 23 August 1820 (Havana), in *Florida Herald and Southern Democrat,* 11 January 1843; Franco, *Politica Continental Americana de España en Cuba,* 68.

CHAPTER 3

1. M. E. Levy, letter to the editor, *World* (London), June 1828.

2. J. Christopher Soper, *Evangelical Christianity in the United States and Great Britain: Religious Beliefs, Political Choices* (New York, 1994), 38, 44. For a firsthand description of evangelical proselytizing in the Caribbean during the same year, see Matthew Gregory Lewis, 11 February 1816, in *Journal of a Residence among the Negroes in the West Indies* (London, 1845), 89.

3. Boyd Hilton, *The Age of Atonement: The Influence of Evangelicalism on Social and Economic Thought, 1795–1865* (Oxford, 1988), 120–21, 125–26.

4. Quotation by Lewis, *Residence among the Negroes*, 89.

5. Levy to Forster, 14 April 1828 (London), in John Forster and M. E. Levy, *Letters Concerning the Present Condition of the Jews: Being a Correspondence between Mr. Forster and Mr. Levy* (London, 1829), 41. For reference to Levy's church attendance, see M. E. Levy to Samuel Myers (New York), 18 October 1818, Myers Papers, AJA; R[ahma] M. Da Costa to M. E. Levy (Brooklyn), 13 September 1854, box 3, Yulee Papers, PKY.

6. Levy to Henriques, 1 September 1853, box 40, Yulee Papers.

7. M. E. Levy to Samuel Myers, 18 October 1818, Myers Family Papers, AJA. Levy claimed to have thought of nothing else for thirteen years.

8. Quotations from Prince Hoare, *Memoirs of Granville Sharp, Esq., Composed from his own Manuscripts, and other authentic documents in the possession of his family and of the African Institution*, 2 vols. (London, 1828), 2:269; Carolyn D. Williams, "'The Luxury of Doing Good': Benevolence, Sensibility, and the Royal Humane Society," in *Pleasure in the Eighteenth Century*, ed. Roy Porter and Marie Mulvey Roberts (New York, 1996), 77–107.

9. Levy to Henriques, 1 September 1853, Yulee Papers.

10. Alejandro Ramirez to Secretary of State, "Año 1816," Legajo 177, Ultramar, AGI.

11. "Deposition of [Frederick] Warburg" (n.d.), in House Report 450, 27th Cong., 2d sess., 1842, 141. Details of Warburg's identity as well as his occupation in Liverpool are found in "Declaration by Frederick S. Warburg, of his intention to become a citizen of the U. States, and oath," 5 March 1822, Record Group 233, HR17A-7.1, Records of the U.S. House of Representatives, NARA.

12. Dr. Klaus Richter, [Klaus.Richter@Staatsarchiv.hamburg.de], "Frederik Warburg," private e-mail message to author, 18 May 2001. Richter cites information in *Stamm- und Nachfahrentafeln der Familie Warburg* (Hamburg, 1937). Further information regarding the family of Frederick Warburg may be found in Gertrud Wenzel, *Broken Star: The Warburgs of Altona, Their Life in Germany and Their Death in the Holocaust* (Smithtown, N.Y., 1981). Wenzel omits any specific mention of Frederick Warburg.

13. Wenzel, *Warburg's of Altona*, 3–5.

14. Frederick S. Warburg, "To the Honourable, the Senate and House of Representatives of the United States of America in Congress assembled," 22 February 1822, HR17A-F711; Warburg, "Specification of the inventions & improvements of Frederick S. Warburg," 22 February 1822, HR17A-F7.1, both in Record Group 233, Records of the U.S. House of Representatives, NARA.

15. Ron Chernow, *The Warburgs: The Twentieth-Century Odyssey of a Remarkable Jewish Family* (New York, 1993), 7; *Encyclopaedia Judaica*, s.v. "Hep! Hep!"

16. Fichte quoted by William Nicholls, *Christian Antisemitism: A History of Hate* (Northvale, N.J., 1995), 298.

17. *Encyclopaedia Judaica*, s.v. "Hep! Hep!"

18. "Philanthropy," letter to the editor, *De Curacaosche Courant*, 27 November 1819.

19. M. E. Levy, letter to the editor, *World*, 20 June 1827.

20. Levy, letter to the editor, 20 June 1827.

21. M. E. Levy, "Speech before the Philo-Judean Society," *World*, 6 June 1827.

22. Levy quotation from M. E. Levy to Samuel Myers, 1 March 1820 (Havana), Myers Papers, JOC. Additional reasoning for American settlement can be found in M. E. Levy to

Isaac L. Goldsmid, 25 November 1825, in Jacob Toury, "M. E. Levy's Plan for a Jewish Colony in Florida: 1825," *Michael: On the History of the Jews in the Diaspora,* ed. Lloyd P. Gartner (Tel Aviv, 1975), 29.

23. For Levy's initial enthusiasm for Jacobson, see M. E. Levy to Samuel Myers, 1 November 1818 (New York), Myers Family Papers, AJA.

24. Quotation from Jacob R. Marcus, *Israel Jacobson: The Founder of the Reform Movement in Judaism* (Cincinnati, 1972), 44.

25. Levy to Myers, 18 October 1818, Myers Papers, AJA.

26. Marcus, *Israel Jacobson,* 78–79.

27. *World,* 6 August 1828.

28. Samuel Levy Keyzer, letter to the editor, 30 July 1828, *World.*

29. M. E. Levy, *World,* 6 August 1828.

30. Marcus, *Israel Jacobson,* 83, 115.

31. Kant quoted in Nicholls, *Christian Antisemitism,* 299.

32. M. E. Levy to Samuel Myers (Havana), 1 March 1820, Myers Papers, JOC. The ideas in this letter were intended to be circulated among the Jewish leadership, including Mordecai Noah.

33. M. E. Levy, letter to the editor (n.d.), in "A Few Remarks. On a Letter which appeared in the World Newspaper of the Month of June, 1828, disclaiming a certain Petition to Parliament concerning the Jews," De Sola Pamphlets 2, Special Collections, University College London.

34. Levy to Myers, 1 November 1818.

35. Marcus, *Israel Jacobson,* 122.

36. Quotation from Levy to Henriques, 1 September 1853, PKY.

37. Levy to Henriques, 1 September 1853.

38. Levy to Myers, 18 October 1818.

39. Levy to Myers, 1 November 1818.

40. M. E. Levy to Moses Myers, 2 January 1829, Myers Papers, JOC. Levy specifically requests "field negroes in families."

41. Moses E. Levy, *A Plan for the Abolition of Slavery, Consistently with the Interests of All Parties Concerned,* ed. Chris Monaco (1828; rpt., Micanopy, Fla., 1999), 19–20.

42. Espada quotation from Joseph Augustine Fahy, "The Antislavery Thought of Jose Agustin Caballero, Juan Diaz De Espada, and Felix Varela, in Cuba, 1791–1823" (Th.D. diss., Harvard University, 1983), 258.

43. Levy, *Plan for the Abolition of Slavery,* 20.

44. Quotation by Franklin F. Knight, *Slave Society in Cuba during the Nineteenth Century* (Madison, Wisc., 1970), 75–76. For a different interpretation, see Herbert S. Klein, *African Slavery in Latin America and the Caribbean* (New York, 1988), 97–98, 155–56.

45. Herbert S. Klein, *Slavery in the Americas: A Comparative Study of Virginia and Cuba* (Chicago, 1967), 150.

46. Quotation from Amy Dru Stanley, "The Right to Possess All the Faculties That God Has Given: Possessive Individualism, Slave Women, and Abolitionist Thought," in *Moral Problems in American Life,* ed. Karen Halttunen and Lewis Perry (Ithaca, N.Y., 1998), 130 n. 15.

47. Levy, *Plan for the Abolition of Slavery*, 11.

48. Lewis, 15 March 1816, in *Journal of a Residence among the Negroes*, 112–13.

49. Quotation by Lewis, 11 February 1816, *Journal of a Residence among the Negroes*, 88.

50. Fahy, "Antislavery Thought," 176–77.

51. Fahy, "Antislavery Thought," 165–66.

52. Raynal, as quoted by Fahy, "Antislavery Thought," 170.

53. Francisco de Arango y Parreño, as quoted by Manuel Moreno Fraginals, *The Sugarmill: The Socioeconomic Complex of Sugar in Cuba, 1760–1860* (New York, 1976), 134.

54. Arango's concerns vis-à-vis the shortage of labor can be traced to the 1780s. See Sherry Johnson, *The Social Transformation of Eighteenth-Century Cuba* (Gainesville, Fla., 2001), 125–29.

55. Moreno Fraginals, *Sugarmill*, 134.

56. A common belief among planters was that "one black is considered as more than equal to two mulattoes." See Lewis, 15 January 1816, in *Journal of a Residence among the Negroes*, 55.

57. Levy, *Plan for the Abolition of Slavery*, 27.

58. Hilton, *Age of Atonement*, 120.

59. In particular, see Levy to Myers, 1 November 1818, AJA.

60. Quotations from Richard H. Colfax, *Evidence against the Views of the Abolitionists, Consisting of Physical and Moral Proofs, of the Natural Inferiority of the Negroes* (New York, 1833), 30–31.

61. M. E. Levy, "The Jews," 6 June 1827, *World*.

62. Levy, *Plan for the Abolition of Slavery*, 6.

63. M. E. Levy, letter to the editor, 6 August 1828, *World*.

64. Quotation by Johan Peter Nissen, *Reminiscences of a 46 Years Residence in the Island of St. Thomas* (Nazareth, Pa., 1838), 38.

65. Levy to Myers, 30 October 1818, Myers Papers, AJA.

66. For reference to the risks evangelicals felt compelled to take, see Thomas D. Hamm, *God's Government Begun: The Society for Universal Inquiry and Reform, 1842–1846* (Bloomington, Ind., 1995), xvii–viii, 4.

67. Levy to Myers, 18 October 1818, AJA.

CHAPTER 4

1. Nathan Glazer, *American Judaism*, 2d ed. (Chicago, 1972), 15, 31; Max I. Dimont, *The Jews In America: The Roots, History, and Destiny of American Jews* (New York, 1978), 82. For a general background on Sephardi Jewish ancestry in the United States, see Stephen Birmingham, *The Grandees: America's Sephardic Elite* (New York, 1971).

2. Leonard Dinnerstein, *Antisemitism in America* (New York, 1994), 13.

3. For examples of antebellum friendships between well-to-do Jews and Gentiles, see Jacob Rader Marcus, *United States Jewry 1776–1985*, 4 vols. (Detroit, 1989–93), 1:574–76.

4. Quotation from W. Goodwin to Hon. Zabdiel Sampson, 17 February 1820, HR16A-G17.2, Record Group 233, Records of the U.S. House of Representatives, NARA.

5. *Florida Herald and Southern Democrat* (St. Augustine), 9 January 1843; M. E. Levy to Samuel Myers, 30 October 1818, AJA.

6. Quotation from Hamilton Shields and Samuel Shepard, "Prospectus," *American Beacon and Commercial Diary* (Norfolk), 15 September 1815.

7. William S. Forrest, *Historical and Descriptive Sketches of Norfolk and Vicinity, Including Portsmouth and the Adjacent Counties, during a Period of Two Hundred Years* (Philadelphia, 1853), 156.

8. Quotation from "State of the Market," *American Beacon and Commercial Diary,* 7 October 1815.

9. Moses Myers to Thomas Jefferson, 1 June 1802, Thomas Jefferson Papers, Manuscript Division, Library of Congress, Washington, D.C.

10. Marcus, *United States Jewry,* 90; Malcolm Stern, "Moses Myers and the Early Jewish Community of Norfolk," *Journal of the Southern Jewish Historical Society* 1 (November 1958): 5.

11. Joe Mosier, [jmosier@chrysler.org], "Myers & Religion," private e-mail correspondence to the author, 9 April 2002.

12. M. E. Levy to Samuel Myers, 18 October 1818, AJA.

13. John Myers to Moses Myers (London), 31 March 1811, JOC. Moses Myers and his son John were financial contributors to Philadelphia's Mikveh Israel synagogue but were certainly not active in the traditional sense.

14. M. E. Levy to Samuel Myers, 6 April, 21 May, and 6 August 1819, JOC.

15. Levy to Myers, 18 October 1818, AJA.

16. Marcus, *United States Jewry,* 1:576.

17. Levy to Myers, 18 October 1818.

18. Levy to Myers, 30 October 1818.

19. Levy to Myers, 8 June 1819, JOC.

20. Unfortunately, only fragments of Levy's letters to Gratz have survived in the form of selected quotes in "Notes of manuscript writings of M. E. Levy deceased," otherwise known as the "Diary of Moses Levy," Yulee Papers, PKY.

21. Levy to Myers, 8 June 1819, JOC.

22. Levy to Myers (New York), 30 October 1818, AJA.

23. Jack Larkin, *The Reshaping of Everyday Life: 1790–1840* (New York, 1989), 113.

24. Levy to Myers, 1 November 1818, AJA.

25. Levy to Myers, 1 November 1818.

26. Levy to Myers, 1 November 1818.

27. Levy to Myers,, 6 April 1819, JOC.

28. Jonathan D. Sarna, *Jacksonian Jew: The Two Worlds of Mordecai Noah* (New York, 1981), 141.

29. Such a claim is actually made by Robert N. Rosen, *The Jewish Confederates* (Columbia, S.C., 2000), 397 n. 9. In contrast, Marcus (in *United States Jewry,* 365) observes that Levy's views were "akin to that of the medieval Karaites" but never asserts that Levy was an actual member of this sect.

30. Quotation by N[athaniel] L[evin], "The Jewish Congregation of Charleston," *Occident and American Jewish Advocate* 1 (December 1843).

31. According to Joseph Gary Adler ("Moses Elias Levy and Attempts to Colonize Florida," in *Jews of the South: Selected Essays from the Southern Jewish Historical Society*, ed. Samuel Proctor and Louis Schmier [Macon, Ga., 1984], 20), Levy's outlook appears closer to Jacobson than to Hart. For further mention of Hart, see Jacob R. Marcus, "The Modern Religion of Moses Hart," *Hebrew Union College Annual* 20 (1947): 585–615.

32. I bring up Fourier only by way of comparison. Although Levy may have come across Fourier's idiosyncratic *Théorie des quatre mouvements et des destinées générales* while he was in Paris, the author was quite obscure during this early period. Most likely, Levy drew upon some of Fourier's ideas at a later period.

33. Owen quoted by Fogarty, "Paradise Planters," xvi.

34. Gerald and Patricia Gutek, *Visiting Utopian Communities: A Guide to the Shakers, Moravians, and Others* (Columbia, S.C., 1998); Ellwood P. Cubberley, *Public Education in the United States: A Study and Interpretation of American Educational History* (Boston, 1947), 344–54.

35. William Maclure to Marie D. Fretageot (London), 10 September 1824, in *Partnership for Posterity*, 300.

36. Levy to Myers (New York), 19 October 1818, AJA.

37. Franklin H. Littell, "Radical Pietism in Early American History," in *Continental Pietism and Early American Christianity*, ed. F. Ernest Stoeffler (Grand Rapids, Mich., 1976), 176–77.

38. M. E. Levy, "Speech addressed to a meeting of Jews and Christians," *World*, 28 May 1828; *Encyclopaedia Judaica*, s.v. "Sabbatical Year and Jubilee"; Peter Linebaugh and Marcus Rediker, *The Many-Headed Hydra: Sailors, Slaves, Commoners, and the Hidden History of the Revolutionary Atlantic* (Boston, 2000), 290–300.

39. Marcus, *United States Jewry*, 251–52, 263–65, 295.

40. Marcus, *United States Jewry*, 288–89; Eidelman, *In the Wilds of America*, 57–58; Ronald G. Walters, *American Reformers, 1815–1860* (New York, 1978), 25–26.

41. As quoted by Michael Ragussis, *Figures of Conversion: "The Jewish Question" and English National Identity* (Durham, 1995), 18.

42. Marcus, *United States Jewry*, 286.

43. Eli N. Evans, *Judah P. Benjamin: The Jewish Confederate* (New York, 1988), 9.

44. "The Petition of Forty-Seven Members of Charleston's Beth Elohim Synagogue, 1824," in *Jews and Judaism in the United States: A Documentary History*, ed. Marc Lee Raphael (1983, New York), 186–92.

45. Levy to Myers, 6 April 1819, JOC.

46. Glazer, *American Judaism*, 53.

47. Levy to Myers (Curaçao), 8 June 1819, JOC.

48. Levy to Myers (New York), 1 November 1818. AJA.

49. As quoted by Marcus, *United States Jewry*, 145.

50. I am most grateful to Joe Mosier, archivist of the Jean Outland Chrysler Library of the Chrysler Museum in Norfolk, for the details of this incident. See Joe Mosier, [jmosier@chrysler.org], "Myers Papers," private e-mail message to author, 17 October 2001.

51. Henrietta Marx to Rachel Mordecai, 21 May 1815, Earl Gregg Swem Library, College of William and Mary, Williamsburg, Va.

52. Samuel Myers to Samuel Marx, 18 December 1820, JOC.

53. Levy to Myers (New York), 30 October 1818, AJA.

54. Levy's 1818 Rhode Island citizenship application is mentioned in M. E. Levy, "The Memorial of Moses Elias Levy," 20 February 1820, HR16A-G17.2, RG 233, Records of the U.S. House of Representatives, NARA.

55. Levy, "Memorial of Moses Elias Levy."

56. De Wolf is noted in Levy to Myers, 30 October 1818, AJA. Levy liquidated De Wolf's outstanding debts in M. E. Levy, "Last Will and Testament," 4 September 1838, Levy File, SAHS.

57. Levy to Myers (Havana), 20 October 1820, JOC.

58. Levy to Myers (New York), 17 November 1818.

59. Levy to Myers (Curaçao), 6 August 1819.

60. Levy to Myers, 6 August 1819.

61. Levy to Myers, 1 November 1818.

62. Levy to Myers (Puerto Rico), 17 January 1819.

63. M[ordecai] M[anual] Noah to [Samuel Myers], 28 February 1819, AJA.

64. W. D. Robinson, *Memoir Addressed to Persons of the Jewish Religion in Europe on the subject of emigration to, and settlement in, one of the most eligible parts of the United States of North America* (London, 1819), 3.

65. Joseph Marx to Samuel Myers (Richmond), 2 March 1819, AJA. Marx served as a director of the United States Bank and the Farmers Bank of Virginia; see Myron Berman, *Richmond's Jewry, 1769–1976* (Charlottesville, Va., 1979), 72.

66. Robinson, *Memoir Addressed to Persons of the Jewish Religion*, 13.

67. Arthur Eugene Bestor Jr., *Backwoods Utopias; The Sectarian and Owenite Phases of Communitarian Socialism in America, 1663–1829* (Philadelphia, 1950), 3.

68. Marx to Myers, 2 March 1819, AJA; Marcus, *United States Jewry*, 367.

69. Levy to Myers, 6 August 1819, JOC.

70. Stern, "Moses Myers and the Early Jewish Community of Norfolk," 6. Kursheedt was better known as a Talmudic scholar than as a businessman. See Berman, *Richmond's Jewry*, 47–49.

71. This incident is related in Birmingham, *Grandees*, 222. For Myers's defense of U. P. Levy, see Stern, "Moses Myers," 11 n. 17.

72. Levy to Myers, 6 August 1819, JOC.

73. Levy had little patience with those Jews who assumed a submissive role in their relationships with Gentiles and compared their outlook to slave psychology. See "Public Meeting of the Jews respecting the Russian Persecution," *World*, 26 December 1827. For a discussion of the psychological aspects of minority status, see Bertram Wyatt-Brown, "The Mask of Obedience: Male Slave Psychology in the Old South," *American Historical Review* 93 (December 1988): 1228–52.

74. Thomas Jefferson to Mordecai M. Noah (Monticello), 28 May 1818, Jefferson Papers, Library of Congress.

75. For a contemporary description of La Guaira, see *American Beacon and Commercial Diary*, 2 October 1818.

76. Levy to Samuel Myers, 6 April 1819, JOC.

77. Levy to Samuel Myers, 6 August 1819, JOC.

78. Levy to Samuel Myers, 8 June 1819, JOC.

79. M. E. Levy to Moses Myers (St. Augustine), 29 September 1823, JOC.

80. M. E. Levy to Samuel Myers (Curaçao), 6 August 1819 and 30 August 1819, JOC.

CHAPTER 5

1. Isaac S. and Suzanne A. Emmanuel, *History of the Jews of the Netherlands Antilles* (Cincinnati, 1970), 304–28.

2. M. E. Levy, "To the Reverend Body of the Mahamad & Congress as well to the Respectable members Generally of the Hebrew Society in this Colony, under the Title of Mickve Israel or the Hope of Israel, &c.," 25 May 1819, "oversized, miscellaneous manuscripts," Myers Papers, JOC.

3. M. E. Levy to Samuel Myers (Curaçao), 4 May 1819, JOC.

4. Despite their integration into island society, full rights of citizenship would not be awarded by the Dutch until 1825. The number of Jews fluctuated between 1,021 in 1816 and 805 in 1821. The reduction was temporary and could have been caused by the intense communal strife. See Emmanuel and Emmanuel, *Jews of the Netherlands Antilles*, 323–24.

5. Levy to Myers, 4 May 1819, JOC.

6. Levy to Myers, 4 May 1819.

7. Levy to Myers, 4 May 1819. Levy's firsthand account differs slightly from the Emmanuels's *Jews of the Netherlands Antilles* in that there was a further dispute concerning the pronunciation of *hey* versus *hay*.

8. Levy to Myers, 4 May 1819.

9. Levy, "To the Reverend Body of the Mahamad & Congress," 25 May 1819, JOC.

10. Emmanuel and Emmanuel, *Jews of the Netherlands Antilles*, 267–82.

11. Gerald M. Steinberg, "Conflict Prevention and Mediation in the Jewish Tradition," *Jewish Political Studies Review* 12 (fall 2000): 3–9.

12. Abm de Mord. Senior and Ishac de Abm d Marchena to [M. E. Levy], 28 May 1819 and Moise Cardoze to Senhor M. E. Levy, 1 June 1819, [Portuguese], "oversized, miscellaneous file," Myers Papers, JOC.

13. Levy to Myers, 8 June 1819, JOC.

14. I am indebted to archivist Joe Mosier of the Chrysler Museum Library in Norfolk for bringing the previously unknown Curaçao manuscripts to my attention.

15. Abm de Mord. Senior and Ishac de Abm d Marchena to [M. E. Levy], 28 May 1819, JOC.

16. Alan F. Benjamin, *Jews of the Dutch Caribbean: Exploring Ethnic Identity on Curaçao* (New York, 2002), 113–17.

17. Levy to Myers, 4 May 1819, JOC.

18. For a discussion of these particular characteristics in honor-bound societies, see Bertram Wyatt-Brown, *Southern Honor: Ethics and Behavior in the Old South* (New York, 1982), 44–46.

19. Emmanuel and Emmanuel, *Jews of the Netherlands Antilles*, 319.

20. Emmanuel and Emmanuel, *Jews of the Netherlands Antilles*, 325–26.

21. Jonathan D. Sarna, *American Judaism: A History* (New Haven, Conn., 2004), 55.

22. Moshe Rosman, "The Role of Non-Jewish Authorities in Resolving Conflicts within Jewish Communities in the Early Modern Period," *Jewish Political Studies Review* 12 (fall 2000): 56–64.

23. Levy to Myers, 30 August 1819. Levy was a silent partner in the Havana venture.

24. William S. Forrest, *Historical and Descriptive Sketches of Norfolk and Vicinity, Including Portsmouth and the Adjacent Counties, during a Period of Two Hundred Years* (Philadelphia, 1853), 156–57.

25. Malcolm Stern, "Moses Myers and the Early Jewish Community of Norfolk," *Journal of the Southern Jewish Historical Society* 1 (November 1958): 7. For reference to the yearly rental on the Norfolk home, see Moses Myers to Samuel Myers, 13 February 1823, JOC.

26. Joe Mosier, [jmosier@chrysler.org], "Debtors Prison," private e-mail message to author, 5 April 2002. Contrary to some accounts, John Myers did not volunteer to go to prison in lieu of his father. His imprisonment was the result of his own business misfortunes.

27. For the amount of Moses and Samuel Myers's debt to Levy, see M. E. Levy to Moses Myers (Pilgrimage Plantation), 2 January 1829, JOC.

28. Invoking a biblical economic standard was thoroughly in keeping with abolitionist thought. See James L. Huston, "Abolitionists, Political Economists, and Capitalism," *Journal of the Early Republic* 20 (fall 2000): 488–89.

29. M. E. Levy to Samuel Myers, 6 August 1819, JOC.

30. M. E. Levy to Samuel Myers, 6 August 1819.

CHAPTER 6

1. M. E. Levy to Samuel Myers (Curaçao), 3 November 1819, JOC.

2. Levy to Myers, 8 November 1819.

3. M. H. Deleon to Samuel Myers (Charleston), 15 February 1820, JOC. This document also includes criticism of Mordecai Noah's presumption of "becoming the organ of a whole sect." For background on M. H. DeLeon, see Belinda and Richard Gergel, *In Pursuit of the Tree of Life: A History of the Early Jews of Columbia, South Carolina, and the Tree of Life Congregation* (Columbia, S.C., 1996), 8–11.

4. Gary Phillip Zola, *Isaac Harby of Charleston, 1788–1828* (Tuscaloosa, Ala., 1994), 112.

5. T. Frederick Davis, "The Alagon, Punon Rostro, and Vargas Land Grants," *Florida Historical Quarterly* 25 (October 1946): 175–90. According to Levy's correspondence, the 8 million–acre figure referred to land area only; all bodies of water, such as lakes and rivers that existed within the grant boundary, were excluded from this total. Additionally, there were approximately 450,000 acres of land that were part of individual grants previously made by the Spanish government.

6. M. E. Levy to Samuel Myers (Havana), 1 March 1820, no. 3404, JOC.

7. Levy to Myers, 1 March 1820, nos. 3402 and 3407.

8. Levy to Myers, 1 March 1820, no. 3404.

9. Levy to Myers, 1 March 1820, no. 3402.

10. John W. Griffin, "St. Augustine in 1822," *El Escribano* 14 (1977): 45–54.

11. Rebecca Gratz to Mrs. Hoffman, c. 1820–22, cited in Joseph Gary Adler, "Moses Elias

Levy and Attempts to Colonize Florida," in *Jews of the South: Selected Essays from the Southern Jewish Historical Society,* ed. Samuel Proctor and Louis Schmier (Macon, Ga., 1984), 29.

12. Levy to Myers (Havana), 1 March 1820, no. 3402; "Item No. 3—Messrs. Hernandez & Cheavitean in account with Fernando M. Arredondo," 3 August 1820 (Havana), in House Report 450, 27th Cong., 2d sess., 1842, 135.

13. Larry R. Jensen, *Children of Colonial Despotism: Press, Politics, and Culture in Cuba, 1790–1840* (Tampa, 1988), 52–64. Levy insisted that Ramirez continued to perform his duties until the spring of 1821. For his appointment in Guatemala, see Jacquelyn Kent, "The Enlightenment and Spanish Colonial Administration: The Life and Myth of Alejandro Ramirez y Blanco in Guatemala, Puerto Rico and Cuba, 1777–1821" (Ph.D. diss., Tulane University, 1997), 319.

14. M. E. Levy, "Ramirez," *Florida Herald and Southern Democrat* (St. Augustine), 23 January 1843 and 1 February 1843.

15. M. E. Levy to Samuel Myers (Havana), 25 May 1820, 1 August 1820, and 20 October 1820, JOC.

16. Levy to Myers (Charleston), 28 November 1820, JOC.

17. Levy to Myers, 28 November 1820.

18. Levy to Myers, 4 December 1820, JOC.

19. Jacob Rader Marcus, *United States Jewry, 1776–1985,* 4 vols. (Detroit, 1989–93), 1:171–72.

20. M. L. M. Peixotto, M. E. Levy, M. M. Noah, and Judah Zuntz, "Circular," 9 May 1821, Manuscript Collection no. 480, box 3, Myers Papers, AJA.

21. Jonathan D. Sarna, "The Impact of Nineteenth-Century Christian Missions on American Jews," in *Jewish Apostasy in the Modern World,* ed. Todd M. Endelman (New York, 1987), 233–34.

22. J. I. Cohen to John Myers (Baltimore), 24 June 1821, JOC.

23. Marcus, *United States Jewry,* 366.

24. Marcus, *United States Jewry,* 367.

25. Jonathan D. Sarna, *American Judaism: A History* (New Haven, Conn., 2004), 54.

CHAPTER 7

1. "Marine News," *Florida Gazette* (St. Augustine), 28 July 1821; "Deposition of J. R. Evertson," 25 April 1842, in House Report 450, app., 3. Portions of this chapter have appeared in Chris Monaco, "A Sugar Utopia on the Florida Frontier: Moses Elias Levy's Pilgrimage Plantation," *Southern Jewish History* 5 (2002): 103–40. Used by permission of the editor.

2. William H. Simmons, quoted by John W. Griffin, in "St. Augustine in 1822," *El Escribano* 14 (1977): 47.

3. *Floridian* (Pensacola), 8 October 1821.

4. "Extract of a letter from Moses E. Levy to F. S. Warburg," 6 August 1821, in House Report 450, 59.

5. J. I. Cohen to John Myers (Baltimore), 24 June 1821, JOC.

6. M. E. Levy to Rachel [Levy Henriques], 1 September 1853, Yulee Papers, PKY.

7. "Moses E. Levy," *Florida Herald and Southern Democrat* (St. Augustine), 31 December 1841.

8. "Moses E. Levy." For a firsthand report concerning Levy's supposed introduction of sugarcane, see "Deposition of Bartolo Masters," 16 November 1841, in House Report 450, 27th Cong., 2d sess., 1842, 99. For reference to Levy's oath of allegiance, see J. G. Forbes, registry of oath of allegiance, 4 March 1822, in House Report 450.

9. The very name Pilgrimage was perfectly in keeping with the utopian mind-set. By traveling from the mundane and imperfect world to a place of new beginnings, pilgrims would partake in a sacred, inner transformation. See Robert S. Fogarty, intro., "Paradise Planters," *Dictionary of American Communal and Utopian History* (Westport, Conn., 1980), xix–xx.

10. This location is in reference to present-day Alachua County. Originally, the county extended from the Georgia border to well south of Tampa Bay.

11. Pilgrimage was located a few miles from the present town of Micanopy, Florida. See "Topographical survey of military section No. 7 by Lieutenant George C. Thomas" and "Map of Square No. 7—Micanopy and Vicinity by Captain G. I. Raines," 1835–42, L. 247 Portfolio, Chief of Engineers Civil Works Map File, RG 77, Cartographic Division, NARA.

12. M. E. Levy to W[illiam W. Russel, [June] 1829, Chauviteau Papers, EB.

13. M. E. Levy to Rachel [Levy Henriques], 1 September 1853, Yulee Papers, PKY; Earl Ronald Hendry, "Moses Elias Levy: Territorial Florida's Largest Purchaser of Spanish Land Grants" (MS, 1982), PKY.

14. P[eter] Pelham to John C. Calhoun, 26 September 1822, in *Papers of John C. Calhoun,* ed. by W. Edwin Hemphill, 17 vols. (Columbia, S.C., 1959–86), 7:283.

15. Alexander Hamilton to John C. Calhoun, 20 July 1822, in Hemphill, *Papers of John C. Calhoun,* 7:218.

16. "A meeting of the owners of lands in East Florida," 4 November 1822, Glunt Papers, PKY. For Forbes's agent status, see Huhner, "Moses Elias Levy," 326.

17. W[illiam] G. D. Worthington to John C. Calhoun, 9 March 1822, in *Papers of John C. Calhoun,* 7:735.

18. "Speech of Col. J. W. D. Worthington, Delivered in the House of Delegates of Maryland, 1824, on the Jew Bill," in H. M. Brackenridge, *Speeches on the Jew Bill, in the House of delegates of Maryland, by H. M. Brackenridge, Col. W. G. D. Worthington, and John S. Tyson, Esquire. Together with an argument on the chancery powers, and an eulogy on Thomas Jefferson, and John Adams, &c.* (Philadelphia, 1829), 136; see also Marcus, *United States Jewry,* 500–505; Benjamin H. Hartogensis, "Unequal Religious Rights in Maryland since 1776," *Publications of the American Jewish Historical Society* 25 (1917): 93–107.

19. Brian J. L. Berry, *America's Utopian Experiments: Communal Havens from Long-Wave Crises* (Hanover, N.H., 1992), 6–9; David Hackett Fischer, *Albion's Seed: Four British Folkways in America* (New York, 1989), 855.

20. Herbert J. Doherty Jr., "Political Factions in Territorial Florida," *Florida Historical Quarterly* 28 (October 1949): 133.

21. Daniel L. Schafer, "'A Class of People Neither Freemen nor Slaves': From Spanish to American Race Relations in Florida, 1821 to 1861," *Journal of Social History* 26 (spring 1993): 587–602.

22. M. E. Levy to Moses Myers (St. Augustine), 29 September 1823, Myers Papers, JOC.

23. Moses Myers to Myer Myers (Norfolk), 14 October 1822, JOC.

24. David J. Weber, *The Spanish Frontier in North America* (New Haven, Conn., 1992), 12–13.

25. M. E. Levy and A. A. Rutan, "Exhibit A, Articles of Agreement," 21 June 1822, *Rutan v. Levy*, folder 35, box 155, St. Johns Circuit Court Records, SAHS; Deposition of Harmon H. Holli[m]on, 24 November 1832, in "Notes Re: Arredondo Family," MS, 33–34, PKY; Deposition of Charles Robion, 15 November 1841, House Report 450, 95–96.

26. "Exhibit B, Hope Hill Establishment, 1822," *Rutan v. Levy*, SAHS.

27. As quoted by John K. Mahon and Brent R. Weisman, "Florida's Seminole and Miccosukee Peoples," in *The New History of Florida*, ed. Michael Gannon (Gainesville, Fla., 1996), 189. Similar conflict occurred between the newly arrived trader Alexander Arbuthnot and the Forbes establishment at Apalachicola in 1817. See Frank Lawrence Owsley Jr. and Gene A. Smith, *Filibusters and Expansionists: Jeffersonian Manifest Destiny, 1800–1821* (Tuscaloosa, Ala., 1997), 144–45.

28. For Dexter's animosity toward Arredondo, see Horatio S. Dexter to Fernando De La Maza Arredondo, 19 April 1821 (Volusia), in James David Glunt, "Plantation and Frontier Records of East and Middle Florida, 1789–1868" (Ph.D. diss., University of Michigan, 1930), 100–102.

29. Thomas Murphy to Horatio Dexter, 25 April 1822, in Glunt, "Plantation and Frontier Records," 122. The style and content of this letter suggests that Dexter rather than Murphy was the correspondent.

30. Levy and Rutan, "Exhibit A, Articles of Agreement," 21 June 1822, *Rutan v. Levy*, SAHS.

31. For a brief mention of this incident, see Chris Monaco, "Fort Mitchell and the Settlement of the Alachua Country," *Florida Historical Quarterly* 79 (summer 2000): 24 n. 119.

32. Andrew Jackson to John C. Calhoun (Pensacola), 17 September 1821, in Clarence Edwin Carter, ed., *The Territorial Papers of the United States*, vol. 22: *The Territory of Florida, 1821–1824* (Washington, D.C., 1956), 208.

33. Frank Marotti Jr., "Edward M. Wanton and the Settling of Micanopy," *Florida Historical Quarterly* 73 (April 1995): 456–77.

34. "Dr. William Simmons sworn, and examined by claimants attorney" (n.d.), *American State Papers: Documents, legislative and executive, of the Congress of the United States, in relation to the public lands, from the first session of the first Congress to the first session of the twenty-third Congress: March 4, 1789, to June 15, 1834*, ed. by Walter Lowie, 5 vols. (Washington, D.C., 1834), 3:728, cited by Joe Knetsch, "The Big Arredondo Grant: A Study in Confusion" (paper presented to the Micanopy Historical Society, 13 September 1991), 9, PKY.

35. Reference to the practice of "paying Indian negroes" for their labor is made in the Deposition of William Canuet, 21 October 1823, *Rutan v. Levy*, SAHS.

36. Brent R. Weisman, "The Plantation System of the Florida Seminole Indians and Black Seminoles during the Colonial Era," in *Colonial Plantations and Economy in Florida*, ed. by Jane G. Landers (Gainesville, Fla., 2000), 142. Slavery, especially as practiced by the Alachua Seminoles, was particularly lenient. See Claudio Saunt, "'The English Has Now a Mind to Make Slaves of Them All,' Creeks, Seminoles, and the Problem of Slavery," *American Indian Quarterly* 22 (1998): 169.

37. The total acreage of Pilgrimage is noted in Levy and Rutan, "Articles of Agreement," *Rutan v. Levy*, SAHS. For the area cleared for planting circa 1823, see "Testimony of Hipolite Chateannuef" (n.d.), Confirmed Spanish Land Grant Claims, FSA.

38. M. E. Levy, "To the Honourable the Commissioners appointed to ascertain Claims and Titles in East Florida," 14 August 1823, file A-28, box 2, ser. 990, RG 599, Confirmed Spanish Land Grant Claims, FSA.

39. For Levy's investment in the Arredondo Grant, see "Indenture between F. M. Arredondo, Sr., agent and attorney-in-fact for Arredondo & Son, and Moses E. Levy," 1 January 1822, in "Notes Re: Arredondo Family" (n.d.), MS, 42–43, PKY. For Levy's participation in the company, see "A meeting of the owners of lands in East Florida known by the name of the Alachua tract, at Lewis tavern, New York," 4 November 1822, Florida Association of New York File, box 1, James Glunt Papers, PKY; Deposition of Moses E. Levy, 22 July 1844, folder 6, box 215, St. Johns Circuit Court Records, SAHS

40. *East Florida Herald* (St. Augustine), 22 February 1823; Deposition of Thomas Brush, 11 August 1823, Confirmed Spanish Land Grant Claims, FSA; Caroline B. Watkins, *The Story of Historic Micanopy* (Gainesville, Fla., 1976), 29.

41. "Testimony of Hipolite Chateannuef" (n.d.), Confirmed Spanish Land Grant Claims, FSA; Deposition of Francisco P. Sanchez, 2 October 1824, FSA.

42. Deposition of Edward Wanton, 8 October 1823, Confirmed Spanish Land Grant Claims, FSA. Reference to Levy's appointment as one of three superintendents is made in Deposition of Moses E. Levy, 22 July 1844, SAHS.

43. Deposition of Samuel R. Ayers, 30 October 1824, Confirmed Spanish Land Grant Claims, FSA.

44. Deposition of Thomas Brush, 7 August 1823, Confirmed Spanish Land Grant Claims, FSA.

45. M. E. Levy and Reuben Charles, [letter of agreement], 23 September 1823, Reuben Charles Papers, PKY.

46. "Examination of Frederick S. Warburg," 7 January 1824, Confirmed Spanish Land Grant Claims, FSA.

47. Quotation from M. E. Levy to Rachel [Levy Henriques], 1 September 1853, Yulee Papers, PKY. Certain likely names, such as Jacob Bradenburg and a Mr. Rose, have surfaced, but it is still not possible to confirm if they were indeed part of the group of Jewish families.

48. M. E. Levy to Reuben Charles, 12 August 1824, Charles Papers, PKY.

49. Levy to [Henriques], 1 September 1853, PKY.

50. Unrelated to Levy's venture, in 1837 Moses Cohen founded Shalom, a short-lived agricultural colony located in Ulster County, New York. Other Jewish efforts include the 1881 Sicily Island colony in Louisiana and Alliance farm, founded in 1882 in New Jersey, one of five Jewish agrarian colonies that operated in that state until 1920. See Pearl W. Bartelt, "American Jewish Agricultural Colonies," in *America's Communal Utopias*, ed. by Donald E. Pitzer (Chapel Hill, 1997), 352–62. Unfortunately, Bartelt fails to consider the work of Jonathan Sarna and others and mistakenly concludes that M. M. Noah's aborted Ararat project was the "first Jewish agricultural colony in the United States." See Jonathan D. Sarna, *Jacksonian Jew: The Two Worlds of Mordecai Noah* (New York, 1981), 73–75. For further background on Alliance farm, see Ellen Eisenberg, *Jewish Agricultural Colonies in New Jersey, 1882–1920* (Syracuse, 1995).

51. A. J. Hanna, *A Prince in Their Midst: The Adventurous Life of Achille Murat on the American Frontier* (Norman, Okla., 1946), 73, 86.

52. Hanna, *Prince in Their Midst*, 86.

53. A few historians have mistakenly attributed a rather grand lifestyle to Levy. For reference to Levy's Alachua "mansion," see Huhner, "Moses Elias Levy," 331. Levy's modest Matanzas house has been deemed "a magnificent home" in Bertram Wallace Korn, *Jews and Negro Slavery in the Old South, 1789–1865* (Elkins Park, Pa., 1961), 14. For heretofore unknown documents relating to Levy's actual Pilgrimage home, see M. E. Levy to Reuben Charles, 26 April 1824, 30 July 1824, and "[Agreement] between Mr. Moses Elias Levy, planter, and Mr. James Edwards," 17 April 1824, Reuben Charles Papers, PKY.

54. M. E. Levy to W[illiam] W. Russel, [June] 1829, Chauviteau Papers, EB.

55. Wauburg is a corruption of the original spelling. See Watkins, *Story of Historic Micanopy*, 86.

56. "The Case of David Levy," *Florida Herald and Southern Democrat* (St. Augustine), 3 December 1841. Apparently, "Harmonite" was either a reference to Robert Owen's short-lived New Harmony experiment in Indiana or the original Harmony Society founded by the radical German pietist Johann Georg Rapp. Both adhered to a communitarian lifestyle, although Owen was a committed secularist. In any case, the intended usage of *Harmonite* was certainly one of derision.

57. M. E. Levy to Moses Myers (Pilgrimage Plantation), 2 January 1829, JOC.

58. While Levy may have avoided pork, he did not adhere to kosher dietary rules. For a list of livestock as well as an inventory of Pilgrimage, see F. Warburg, "List of Articles delivered to me on the Pilgrimage Plantation which is under my charge" (c. 1824); and E[lias] Levy, "A List of articles found in the Store & delivered to Mr. Charles," 1 October 1824, Charles Papers, PKY.

59. M. E. Levy to W[illiam] W. Russel, [June] 1829, Chauviteau Papers, EB.

60. M. E. Levy to Reuben Charles, 30 July 1824, Charles Papers, PKY. Pelaklikaha is also noted in Warburg, "List of Articles," PKY. For further information on Abraham, see Kenneth Wiggins Porter, "The Negro Abraham," *Florida Historical Quarterly* 25 (July 1946): 1–43.

61. Bill of Sale, Moses E. Levy, 4 December 1839, Deed Book N, 572-3, St. Johns County Records, St. Augustine, Florida (copy in possession of the author). For Levy's reference to ten slaves at Pilgrimage, see Levy to Myers (Pilgrimage Plantation), 2 January 1829.

62. "Sugar Planting," *Niles' Register*, 15 June 1833.

63. This aspect of Levy's thinking is very much in evidence in M. E. Levy to Samuel Myers, 6 August 1819, JOC. Invoking a biblical economic standard was thoroughly in keeping with abolitionist thought. See James L. Huston, "Abolitionists, Political Economists, and Capitalism," *Journal of the Early Republic* 20 (fall 2000): 488–89.

64. Larry Eugene Rivers, *Slavery in Florida: Territorial Days to Emancipation* (Gainesville, Fla., 2000), 225.

65. M. E. Levy, "Slavery," *World* (London), 18 June 1828.

66. Levy, *Plan for the Abolition of Slavery*, 19.

67. Brundage, *Socialist Utopia in the New South*, 14.

68. William Maclure to Marie D. Fretageot (New Orleans), 3 January 1827, in *Partnership for Posterity: The Correspondence of William Maclure and Marie Duclos Fretageot, 1820–1833*, ed. Josephine Mirabella Elliou (Indianapolis, 1994), 450.

69. Levy, "Slavery," 18 June 1828.

70. Levy, *Plan for the Abolition of Slavery*, 12.

71. Levy, *Plan for the Abolition of Slavery*, 5, 21.

72. Levy, "Slavery."

73. Levy, "Slavery."

74. Rosabeth Moss Kanter, *Commitment and Community: Communes and Utopias in Sociological Perspective* (Cambridge, Mass., 1972), 63, 75, 90–91; Fogarty, "Paradise Planters," xv; Donald E. Pitzer, "The New Moral World of Robert Owen and New Harmony," in *America's Communal Utopias*, ed. Donald E. Pitzer (Chapel Hill, 1997), 88–123.

75. M. E. Levy to Reuben Charles, 12 August 1824 (St. Augustine), Charles Papers, PKY; Davis Floyd to Reuben Charles (St. Augustine), 17 August 1824, Charles Papers, PKY; "Indenture between Moses Elias Levy and William Savage of Boston (at present of the City of New York)," 8 February 1825, Alachua County Ancient Records, 1826–48, Alachua County Court House, Gainesville, Fla.; M. E. Levy to Moses Myers (New York), 19 May 1825, Myers Papers, JOC.

CHAPTER 8

1. Todd M. Endelman, *The Jews of Georgian England, 1714–1830: Tradition and Change in a Liberal Society* (Philadelphia, 1979), 182.

2. "A Mourner of Zion [M. E. Levy]," *World* (London), 27 June 1827.

3. "Mourner of Zion."

4. Mel Scult, *Millennial Expectations and Jewish Liberties: A Study of the Efforts to Convert the Jews in Britain, up to the Mid Nineteenth Century* (Leiden, 1978), 91, 129. Some unlicensed Jewish doctors only attended to the needs of the Jewish community; others entered Scottish universities in order to attain their medical degrees. See Kenneth Collins, *Go and Learn: The International Story of Jews and Medicine in Scotland* (Aberdeen, 1988), 33–55.

5. Daniel J. Schroeter, *The Sultan's Jew: Morocco and the Sephardi World* (Stanford, Calif., 2002), 56.

6. As quoted by Ford K. Brown, *Fathers of the Victorians: The Age of Wilberforce* (Cambridge, 1961), 317.

7. Ted A. Campbell, "Evangelical Institutionalization and Evangelical Sectarianism in Early Nineteenth-Century Britain and America," in *Amazing Grace: Evangelicalism in Australia, Britain, Canada, and the United States*, ed. Mark A. Noll and George A. Rawlyk (Montreal, 1994), 118–19.

8. Sarna, *Jacksonian Jew*, 66; *Niles' Weekly Register*, 1 October 1825.

9. Stern, "American Jewry Comes of Age," 32.

10. M. E. Levy to Isaac L. Goldsmid, 25 November 1825, in Jacob Toury, "M. E. Levy's Plan for a Jewish Colony in Florida: 1825," *Michael: On the History of the Jews in the Diaspora*, ed. Lloyd P. Gartner (Tel Aviv, 1975), 29. For reference to the German Jewish newspapers, see Huhner, "Moses Elias Levy, Florida Pioneer," 331.

11. Agreement between Moses Elias Levy and Joseph Delevante, 15 March 1827, Deed Book A, Alachua County Ancient Records, Records Office, Alachua County Court House, Gainesville, Fla.; "'Château en Espagne' pour la famille Chauviteau," Genealogie et Histoire

de la Caraibe, members.aol.com/GHCaraibe/bul/ghc79/p1538.html (30 December 2002); Emmanuel Boelle, "Histoire de la famille Chauviteau," membres.lycos.fr/chauviteau (30 December 2002).

12. F. P. Chauviteau to Widow Chauviteau (Havana), 7 February 1830, Chauviteau Papers, EB.

13. A good definition of this "law" can be found in M. E. Levy, *An Address Delivered before the Temperance Society of Micanopy* (Jacksonville, Fla., 1852), 3. Levy's reference to 1826 as a pivotal year in the development of his spiritual philosophy is stated throughout his correspondence. In particular, see "Memorandum made in his 57th year" (n.d.), in "Notes of Manuscript Writings of M. E. Levy deceased," Yulee Papers, PKY.

14. M. E. Levy to Moses Myers (London), 26 July 1827, JOC; David Levy to Moses Myers (Norfolk), 17 April 1827, JOC; Moses Myers to M. E. Levy (Norfolk), 8 April 1825, JOC.

15. Arthur E. Bestor Jr., "Patent Office Models of the Good Society: Some Relationships between Social Reform and Westward Expansion," *American Historical Review* 58 (April 1953): 506–7.

16. Ursula Henriques, *Religious Toleration in England, 1787–1833* (Toronto, 1961), 177–78; Gauri Viswanathan, *Outside the Fold: Conversion, Modernity, and Belief* (Princeton, N.J., 1998), 3–43.

17. Endelman, *Jews of Georgian England,* 119–20.

18. [Joseph] Crooll, "The Jews," *World,* 2 July 1828.

19. Endelman, *Jews of Georgian England,* 242–45.

20. M. E. Levy, *World,* 23 May 1827 and 6 June 1827.

21. Levy, *World,* 23 May 1827 and 6 June 1827.

22. W[illiam] Wilberforce, *World,* 14 May 1828.

23. Such acceptance was rare for any outsider. See Bertram Wyatt-Brown, *Southern Honor: Ethics and Behavior in the Old South* (New York, 1982), 88–89.

24. Rev. E. Pizey, *World,* 4 June 1828.

25. Michael Stanislawski, *Tsar Nicholas I and the Jews: The Transformation of Jewish Society in Russia, 1825–1855* (Philadelphia, 1983), 11, 16–21.

26. "The Jews," *World,* 14 November 1827.

27. *World,* 3 and 31 October 1827 and 21 November 1827.

28. "Meeting of the Jews," *Times* (London), 5 December 1827.

29. *Jewish Encyclopedia,* s.v., "Selig Newman."

30. Quotation from "A True Israelite," in "A Few Remarks. On a Letter which appeared in the World Newspaper of the Month of June, 1828, disclaiming a certain Petition to Parliament concerning the Jews" (c. 1828), De Sola Pamphlets 2, Special Collections, University College London.

31. Endelman, *Jews of Georgian England,* 83–84, 244, 285. For reference to the number of Jews that attended these meetings, see *World,* 19 December 1827.

32. "Public Meeting of the Jews," *World,* 12 December 1827.

33. "Public Meeting of the Jews."

34. "Public Meeting of the Jews," 26 December 1827.

35. "Public Meeting of the Jews." This same meeting was covered in *Times,* 21 December 1827.

36. *World,* 19 December 1827.

37. *Times,* 2 January 1828.

38. Jacob Katz, *Jewish Emancipation and Self-Emancipation,* 1st ed. (Philadelphia, 1986), 9, 90–93.

39. "Extract of a letter from a clergyman from Bristol," *World,* 9 January 1828.

40. [Joseph] Crooll, "Letter from the Rabbi Crooll to the Editor of the World," *World,* 2 July 1828. For a discussion of Crooll, albeit a highly negative one, see M. C. N. Salbstein, *The Emancipation of the Jews in Britain: The Question of the Admission of the Jews to Parliament, 1828–1860* (Rutherford, N.J., 1982), 78–85.

41. R. Joseph Crooll, *The Fifth Empire, Delivered in a Discourse by Thirty-Six Men* (London, 1829), 72, 74; R. Joseph Crooll, *The Restoration of Israel, and an answer by Thomas Scott, Rector of Aston Sandford, Bucks* (London, 1814), 48.

42. John Aquila Brown, *The Even-Tide; or, Last Triumph of the Blessed and only Potentate, the King of Kings, and Lord of Lords; being a development of the mysteries of Daniel and St. John, and of the prophecies respecting the renovated kingdom of Israel, etc.* (London, 1823).

43. "Moses E. Levy of Florida," in "A Few Remarks."

44. Jonathan Frankel, *The Damascus Affair: "Ritual Murder," Politics, and the Jews in 1840* (New York, 1997), 295. For additional background on the Vilna Gaon and his followers, see Jeff Halper, *Between Redemption and Revival: The Jewish Yishuv of Jerusalem in the Nineteenth Century* (Boulder, Colo., 1991), 38–51.

45. Arie Morgenstern, "Dispersion and the Longing for Zion, 1240–1840," *Azure: Ideas for the Jewish Nation* 12 (winter 2002).

46. David Brion Davis, "Slavery and Progress," in *Anti-Slavery, Religion, and Reform: Essays in Memory of Roger Anstey,* ed. Christine Bolt and Seymour Drescher (Folkstone, Eng., 1980), 353.

47. Howard Temperley, "Anti-Slavery as Cultural Imperialism," in Bolt and Drescher, *Anti-Slavery, Religion, and Reform,* 338.

48. M. E. Levy, "Surrey Anti-Slavery Society," *World* (London), 31 October 1827; Levy, *Plan for the Abolition of Slavery,* 29.

49. M. E. Levy to the Editor, *World* (London), 31 October 1827.

50. Levy, *Plan for the Abolition of Slavery,* 11–12.

51. Bestor, "Patent-Office Models of the Good Society," 522.

52. M. E. Levy, "Address to the Surrey Anti-Slavery Society," *World* (London), 31 October 1827.

53. Levy, *Plan for the Abolition of Slavery,* 29.

54. Levy, *Plan for the Abolition of Slavery,* 15.

55. Levy, *Plan for the Abolition of Slavery,* 7.

56. Levy, *Plan for the Abolition of Slavery,* 6.

57. Levy, *Plan for the Abolition of Slavery,* 15.

58. Levy, *Plan for the Abolition of Slavery,* 14

59. Levy, *Plan for the Abolition of Slavery,* 12–16

60. As quoted by J. H. Parry, P. M. Sherlock, A. P. Maingot, in *A Short History of the West Indies,* 4th ed. (New York, 1987), 60.

61. For a more typical and condemnatory view of sugar, see *"What Does Your Sugar Cost?" A Cottage Conversation on the subject of British Negro Slavery* (Birmingham, Eng., 1828), 6.

62. Cited in *World,* 20 August 1828.

63. *World,* 9 July 1828.

64. "Abolition of Slavery," *World,* 10 September 1828. This organization added a few modifications of its own but followed Levy's basic plan almost to the letter.

65. John Forster, preface, in Forster and M. E. Levy, *Letters Concerning the Present Condition of the Jews: Being a Correspondence between Mr. Forster and Mr. Levy* (London, 1829), vi.

66. Samuel Levy Keyzer, "Jewish Emancipation," *World,* 30 July 1828.

67. [Joseph] Crooll, *World,* 2 July 1828.

68. "The Jews," *World,* 13 August 1828.

69. For background on the movement as well as a brief note on the inexplicable change in Jewish public opinion, see Henriques, *Religious Toleration in England,* 178–91; see also Endelman, *Jews of Georgian England,* 277–80, 78–85.

70. *World,* 6 August 1828; "Regeneration of the Jews," *World,* 19 December 1827.

71. Thomas Scott, intro., *The Restoration of Israel* by R. Joseph Crooll (London, 1814), v–vi.

72. M. E. Levy to John Forster, 2 May 1828, in Forster and Levy, *Present Condition of the Jews,* 50.

73. Levy to Forster, 28 August 1828, in Forster and Levy, *Present Condition of the Jews,* 82–83.

74. For background on Thomas Thrush, see Rev. C. Wellbeloved, *Memoir of Thomas Thrush, Esq.* (London, 1845).

75. *World,* 19 May 1828.

76. Parry, Sherlock, and Maingot, *History of the West Indies,* 164–65. For a more optimistic appraisal of the fate of former West Indian slaves, see Seymour Drescher, "Free Labor vs. Slave Labor: The British and Caribbean Cases," *Terms of Labor: Slavery, Serfdom, and Free Labor* (Stanford, Calif., 1999), 72–73.

77. As quoted by V. D. Lipman, *A History of the Jews in Britain since 1858* (New York, 1990), 12.

CHAPTER 9

1. M. E. Levy to Moses Myers (Pilgrimage Plantation), 2 January 1828, JOC; Bill of Sale, Moses E. Levy to Andrew Anderson, 4 December 1839, Anderson Papers, SAHS.

2. Samuel Myers to Myer Myers (Galvez Camp, Pensacola), 6 October 1822, JOC.

3. For Myers's initial reaction to Pensacola, see Samuel Myers to Abram Myers (Pensacola), 18 June 1821, JOC. For Levy's letter of condolence, see M. E. Levy to Moses Myers (St. Augustine), 6 May 1829, JOC.

4. For background on Moses Julien, Hannah Levy's new husband, see Bro-Jorgensen to MacRae, 28 November 1950, box 1, Yulee Papers, PKY.

5. C. Wickliffe Yulee, *Senator Yulee of Florida: A Biographical Sketch* (Jacksonville, Fla., 1909), 5.

6. M. E. Levy to Rachel [Henriques], 1 September 1853, Yulee Papers, PKY; Elias [Levy] Yulee, *An Address to the Colored People of Georgia* (Savannah, 1868).

7. Myers quotation from Frederick Myers to M. E. Levy, 28 November 1826, Myers Papers, JOC. For David's early interest in the law, see *Florida Herald and Southern Democrat* (St. Augustine), 9 April 1841. Involvement in the fort petition is mentioned in Joe Knetsch, "The Big Arredondo Grant: A Study in Confusion" (paper presented to the Micanopy Historical Society, Micanopy, Fla., 13 September 1991).

8. [Zephaniah Kingsley], *A Treatise on the Patriarchal, or Co-operative System of Society, As it Exists in Some Governments and Colonies in America, and in the United States, Under the Name of Slavery, With its Necessity and Advantages. By an Inhabitant of Florida* (n.p., 1828), 10.

9. "Address to the Legislative Council of Florida on the Subject of its Colored population by Z. Kingsley, a Planter of the Territory" (c. 1826), in *Balancing Evils Judiciously: The Pro-slavery Writings of Zephaniah Kingsley,* ed. Daniel W. Stowell (Gainesville, Fla., 2000), 27.

10. Quoted in Thomas Everette Cochran, *History of Public-School Education in Florida* (Lancaster, Pa., 1921), 1.

11. As quoted by Cochran, *History of Public-School Education in Florida,* 2–3; T. Frederick Davis, "A Free Public School in St. Augustine, 1832," *Florida Historical Quarterly* 22 (April 1944): 200–207; Samuel Proctor, "Pioneer Jewish Settlement in Florida, 1765–1900," in *Proceedings of the Conference on the Writing of Regional History in the South with Special Emphasis on Religious and Cultural Groups* (Miami Beach, 1956), 89.

12. James D Westcott Jr., [Address to the Legislative Council], 3 January 1832, in *A Journal of the Proceedings of the Legislative Council, at its Tenth Session commenced January 2d 1832* (n.p.), 14–15.

13. Cochran, *Public-School Education in Florida,* 3–5.

14. Joe Knetsch, "The Big Arredondo Grant: A Study in Confusion" (paper presented to the Micanopy Historical Society, 13 September 1991), 12, PKY.

15. Monaco, "Fort Mitchell and the Settlement of the Alachua Country," 5–7; Alejandro Ramirez, Arredondo Grant, 22 December 1817, Confirmed Spanish Land Grant Claims, FSA.

16. Antonio Alvarez, Affidavit G, 20 January 1823, in *American State Papers: Documents, legislative and executive, of the Congress of the United States, in relation to the public lands, from the first session of the first Congress to the first session of the twenty-third Congress: March 4, 1789, to June 15, 1834,* ed. Walter Lowie, 5 vols. (Washington, D.C., 1834), 3:719.

17. Knetsch, "Big Arredondo Grant," 14.

18. Duncan L. Clinch to the Adjutant General (Fort Defiance, Micanopy), 9 December 1835, in Clarence Edwin Carter, ed., *The Territorial Papers of the United States,* vol. 25: *The Territory of Florida, 1834–1839* (Washington, D.C.: U.S. Government Printing Office, 1960), 209–10. According to Rembert W. Patrick, Clinch considered his remote Lang Syne plantation as "unsuitable for a home" and never actually resided there with his family. See Patrick, *Aristocrat in Uniform: General Duncan L. Clinch* (Gainesville, Fla., 1963), 157.

19. Thomas Graham, *The Awakening of St. Augustine: The Anderson Family and the Oldest City, 1821–1924* (St. Augustine, 1978), 46.

20. As quoted by Joe Knetsch, "The Land Grants of Moses E. Levy and the Development of Central Florida: The Practical Side" (paper presented to the Micanopy Historical Society, 10 January 1998), 1, PKY.

21. *Jacksonville Courier,* 31 December 1835; Levy to [Henriques], 1 September 1853, Yulee Papers, PKY.

22. Rivers, *Slavery in Florida,* 148–49.

23. "Moses E. Levy," 26 January 1839, House Report 236, 25th Cong., 3d sess., facsimile in Watkins, *Story of Historic Micanopy.*

24. *Florida Herald and Southern Democrat,* 31 December 1841.

25. Dr. Klaus Richter, [Klaus.Richter@Staatsarchiv.hamburg.de], "Frederik Warburg," private e-mail message to author, 18 May 2001. Richter cites information in *Stamm- und Nachfahrentafeln der Familie Warburg* (Hamburg, 1937).

CHAPTER 10

1. Actually, Fort Marion itself was of little value in St. Augustine's defense. The post barracks as well as various picketed outposts were of much more practical use. See Rogers W. Young, "Fort Marion during the Seminole War," *Florida Historical Quarterly* 13 (April 1935): 196–97.

2. Thomas Graham, *The Awakening of St. Augustine: The Anderson Family and the Oldest City, 1821–1924* (St. Augustine, 1978), 39, 46, 51–53, 72.

3. Levy's mortgage is mentioned in Andrew Anderson to S. W. Anderson (St. Augustine), 29 May 1839, Anderson Papers, SAHS. For a list of Levy's slaves, see "Bill of Sale, Moses E. Levy to Andrew Anderson," 4 December 1839, SAHS.

4. Graham, *Awakening of St. Augustine,* 41.

5. Henry Summer, "Journal etc. for 1837," in John Hammond Moore, "A South Carolina Lawyer visits St. Augustine—1837," *Florida Historical Quarterly* 43 (April 1965): 362–79.

6. M. E. Levy, Last Will and Testament, MS, 4 September 1838, Levy File, SAHS. All the witnesses to the will were gathered at the office of John Peck, a New York merchant. See "Deposition of Augustus W. Walker," 19 February 1857, folder 38, box 135, St. Johns County Circuit Court Papers, SAHS.

7. As quoted by Rosabeth Moss Kanter, *Commitment and Community: Communes and Utopias in Sociological Perspective* (Cambridge, Mass., 1972), 90. For background on Levy's relationship to his children, see M. E. Levy to Rachel [Levy Henriques], 1 September 1853, Yulee Papers, PKY.

8. "Duval," letter to the editor, *Florida Herald and Southern Democrat,* 9 April 1841.

9. David Levy to Martin Van Buren (c. 1839), in Arthur W. Thompson, "David Yulee: A Study of Nineteenth Century American Thought and Enterprise" (Ph.D. diss., Columbia University, 1954), 234. For a discussion of family alliances in southern politics, see Bertram Wyatt-Brown, *Southern Honor: Ethics and Behavior in the Old South* (New York, 1982), 184–85.

10. For David Levy's clerical appointment, see *Florida Herald* (St. Augustine), 15 April 1829. Levy quotation cited in James Leon Alderman, "David Levy Yulee, Ante-bellum Florida Leader, 1810–1886" (master's thesis, University of North Carolina, Chapel Hill, 1946), 4. Also see Arthur W. Thompson, *Jacksonian Democracy on the Florida Frontier* (Gainesville, 1961), 42–57.

11. "Deposition of P[eter] S[ken] Smith," 1 September 1841, in House Report 450, 27th Cong., 2d sess., 1842, 139–40.

12. "Communications," *Florida Herald*, 15 September 1838; David Nolan, *Fifty Feet in Paradise: The Booming of Florida* (New York, 1984), 40–55. For mention of David Levy's accusation against Smith, see *Florida Herald and Southern Democrat*, 23 January 1843.

13. Levy's 1818 Rhode Island citizenship application is mentioned in M. E. Levy, "The Memorial of Moses Elias Levy," 20 February 1820, HR16A-G17.2, RG 233, Records of the U.S. House of Representatives, NARA.

14. M. E. Levy, letter to the editor, *Florida Herald and Southern Democrat*, 13 January 1843.

15. "Duval," letter to the editor, 9 April 1841, *Florida Herald and Southern Democrat*.

16. For documentation of this entire episode, see House Report 450, 27th Cong., 2d sess., 1842, 1–154.

17. *News* (St. Augustine), 26 February 1842, 21 May 1842, and 29 April 1843. Smith left St. Augustine after the election to become a leader of the Native American Party in Philadelphia. See Michael F. Holt, *The Rise and Fall of the American Whig Party: Jacksonian Politics and the Onset of the Civil War* (New York, 1999), 276.

18. "Speech of Mr. Levy of Florida," 6 September 1841, in *Congressional Globe*, 27th Cong., 1st sess., 1841, 10:297–98. For reference to David Levy's supposed mulatto status, see M. E. Levy, letter to the editor, *Florida Herald and Southern Democrat*, 23 January 1843.

19. For Adams's comments, see Huhner, "David L. Yulee," 13–14; *Memoirs of John Quincy Adams*, ed. Charles Francis Adams, 12 vols. (Philadelphia, 1874–77), 10:483, 11:162. Newspaper excerpt from the *Boston Mail* cited in *News*, 18 June 1842.

20. *Florida Herald and Southern Democrat*, 23 January 1843.

21. M. E. Levy, letter to the editor, *Florida Herald and Southern Democrat*, 8 February 1843.

22. *News*, 28 January 1843.

23. Andrew Anderson to S. W. Anderson (St. Augustine), 29 May 1839, Anderson Papers, SAHS; M. E. Levy to Rachel [Levy] Henriques, 1 September 1853, Yulee Papers, PKY; Graham, *Awakening of St. Augustine*, 35–36.

24. George R. Fairbanks to A. M. Da Costa, Esq. (Sewanee, Tenn.), 1 July 1901, Fairbanks Papers, Strozier Library, FSU.

25. M. E. Levy to Mr. [Jonathan] Dacosta, 18 September 1845, box 1, Yulee Papers; Levy to Henriques, 2 March 1847, box 40, Yulee Papers.

26. M. E. Levy to William W. Russel (St. Augustine), 3 December 1843; and Levy to Russel, 8 January 1844, Chauviteau Papers, EB.

27. Levy's views on spiritualism, mesmerism, and phrenology are interspersed throughout "Notes of manuscript writings of M. E. Levy deceased" (n.d.), box 1, Yulee Papers. For a discussion of the role of spiritualism in the lives of nineteenth-century social activists, see Nell Irvin Painter, *Sojourner Truth: A Life, a Symbol* (New York, 1996), 143–48.

28. "Notes of manuscript writings of M. E. Levy deceased" (n.d.), p. 96, box 1, Yulee Papers.

29. "Notes of manuscript writings of M. E. Levy deceased," 36.

30. David L. Yulee, "Narrative of my Administration of my father's estates: Relations with my father's family" (n.d.), box 1, Yulee Papers, PKY.

31. Yulee, *Senator David L. Yulee*, 12.

32. M. E. Levy, letter to the editor, *Florida Herald and Southern Democrat*, 24 February 1846. David Yulee initially spelled his name as *Eulee*. See Huhner, "Moses Elias Levy, an Early Florida Pioneer," 342.

33. "Duval," letter to the editor, *Florida Herald and Southern Democrat*, 9 April 1841.

34. "Inventory of Personal Property belonging to the Estate of Moses E. Levy, deceased" (n.d.), Yulee Papers, PKY; "Real Estate Sales" (undated and unidentified newspaper clipping), Fairbanks Papers, Strozier Library, FSU.

35. M. E. Levy, *Address Delivered Before the Temperance Society of Micanopy . . . Containing Thoughts and Suggestions on a System of Reform, the Chart and Guide of which is the Holy Bible* (Jacksonville, Fla., 1852), 6–7.

36. M. E. Levy to Mr. and Mrs. [David] Yulee (St. Augustine), 1 October 1852, Yulee Papers.

37. Notes of manuscript writings of M. E. Levy deceased, "letters to Miss Rebecca Gratz" (c. 1851), A. no. 7-11, box 1, Yulee Papers.

38. M. E. Levy to Rachel (Levy) Henriques, 2 March 1847, box 40, Yulee Papers.

39. R. M. Da Costa to M. E. Levy, 13 September 1854, box 3, Yulee Papers.

40. Huhner, "Moses Elias Levy," 344; "Da Costa Jacob Mendes," Institut für Psychotraumatologie Zürich, www.psychotraumatologie.ch/dacosta.htm; "Jacob M. Da Costa Papers," Thomas Jefferson Medical College, jeffline.tju.edu/SML/archives/collections/finding_aids/jmdacosta.html (30 May 2003).

41. Clarissa Anderson to Caroline Fairbanks, 12 April 1854, as cited by Graham, in *Awakening of St. Augustine*, 73

42. Mary J. Windle, *Life at the White Sulphur Springs; or, Pictures of a Pleasant Summer* (Philadelphia, 1857), 22–23.

43. Hanson's impressions are given by David Yulee in D. L. Yulee to Rahma [Levy] DaCosta, 11 October 1854, box 3; and D. L. Yulee to Joseph Delevante, 26 October 1854, both in Yulee Papers.

44. Noah's abortive plans for a Jewish colony garnered notice even after his death. See "A Funeral Panegyric," *Occident and American Jewish Advocate* 9 (May 1851): 98.

45. Quotation cited by Sarna, *Jacksonian Jew*, 159.

46. David L. Yulee, "Narrative of my Administration of my father's estates: Relations with my father's family" (n.d.), box 1,Yulee Papers, PKY.

47. C. Wickliffe Yulee, "Senator Yulee: A Biographical Sketch," *Florida Historical Quarterly* 2 (April 1909). In contrast, one of Levy's grandchildren, A. M. DaCosta, exhibited uncharacteristic caution concerning the family history: "I believe in the unconditional integrity of the narrative—yet my reason admonishes me to be cautious, for earnest faith may well exist upon illogical premises." See A. M. DaCosta to Lucien Wolff, 15 March 1901, B20 COS, Lucien Wolff Collection, University College London.

EPILOGUE

1. Kelley cited by Louis A. Perez Jr., "We Are the World: Internationalizing the National, Nationalizing the International," *Journal of American History* 89 (September 2002): 560. See also Thomas Bender, ed., *Rethinking American History in a Global Age* (Berkeley, 2002).

2. Jonathan D. Sarna, intro., Sarna, ed., *The American Jewish Experience*, 2d ed. (New York, 1997), xiii.

3. M. E. Levy to Samuel Myers (Havana), 1 March 1820, Myers Papers, JOC.

4. Arthur E. Bestor Jr., "Patent Office Models of the Good Society: Some Relationships between Social Reform and Westward Expansion," *American Historical Review* 58 (April 1953): 506–7.

5. Thomas Scott, intro., *The Restoration of Israel*, by R. Joseph Crooll (London, 1814), v–vi.

6. "Letter from the Rabbi Crooll to the Editor of the World," *World* (London), 2 July 1828.

7. Quotes are from Perez, "Internationalizing the National, Nationalizing the International," 559.

BIBLIOGRAPHY

MANUSCRIPTS AND COLLECTIONS

Alachua County Courthouse, Records Department, Gainesville, Fla.
Ancient Records

Archivo General de Indias, Seville, Spain
Ultramar, Secretarias de Estado

Archivo Nacional de Cuba, Havana
Correspondencia de los Capitanes Generales

British Library, London
Rare Books
Newspaper Archives

College of William and Mary, Earl Greg Swem Library, Williamsburg, Va.
Marx Papers
Myers Papers

Enid M. Baa Library, Division of Archives, Libraries and Museums, St. Thomas, U.S.
    Virgin Islands
Rare Books and Manuscripts
Newspaper Archives

Florida International University Library, Miami
Early American Newspapers (microfilm)

Florida State Archives, Tallahassee
Manuscripts Collection
Spanish Land Grant Claims

Florida State University Libraries, Special Collections Department, Tallahassee
George Fairbanks Collection

Harvard University, Cambridge, Mass.
University Archives
    Student Records
Widener Library
    Rare Books

Hebrew Congregation of St. Thomas, U.S. Virgin Islands
Cemetary Records

Jacob Rader Marcus Center of the American Jewish Archives, Hebrew Union
    College–Jewish Institute of Religion, Cincinnati, Ohio
Myers Papers

Jean Outland Chrysler Library, Norfolk, Va.
Myers Family Papers

Library of Congress, Washington, D.C.
Rare Books
Thomas Jefferson Papers
Newspaper Collection (microfilm)

National Archives and Records Administration, Washington, D. C.
Center for Legislative Archives

National Archives and Records Administration, College Park, Md.
Cartographic Division

New York Public Library, New York City
Rare Books

Osterreichisches Staatsarchiv, Vienna, Austria
Haus-, Hof- und Staatarchivs

Private Collection, Emmanuel Boëlle, Paris, France
Chauviteau Papers

Staatsarchiv, Hamburg, Germany
City Records

St. Augustine Historical Society Library, St. Augustine, Fla.
Anderson Papers
St. Johns County Circuit Court Records

University College London, Special Collections Library, London, Eng.
De Sola Pamphlets
Lucien Wolff Collection

University of Florida, George Smathers Libraries, Gainesville
Isser and Rae Price Library of Judaica
    German Jewish Newspapers (microfilm)
Latin American Collection
    Caribbean Newspapers (microfilm)
    Despatches from United States Consuls (microfilm)
P. K. Yonge Library of Florida History
    David L. Yulee Papers
    Florida Newspaper Collection
    George Fairbanks Papers
    Historical Map Collection
    James D. Glunt Papers
    Manuscripts Collection
    Reuben Charles Papers

Wisconsin Historical Society Library, Madison
Abolitionist Pamphlet Collection (microfilm)

PRINTED PRIMARY SOURCES

Adams, Charles Francis, ed. *Memoirs of John Quincy Adams, Comprising Portions of His Diary from 1795 to 1848.* 12 vols. Philadelphia: J. B. Lippincott & Co., 1874–77.
Brackenridge, H. M. *Speeches on the Jew Bill, in the House of delegates of Maryland, by H. M. Brackenridge, Col. W. G. D. Worthington, and John S. Tyson, Esquire. Together with an argument on the chancery powers, and an eulogy on Thomas Jefferson, and John Adams, &c.* Philadelphia: J. Dobson, 1829.

Brown, John Aquila. *The Even-Tide; or, Last Triumph of the Blessed and only Potentate, the King of Kings, and Lord of Lords; being a development of the mysteries of Daniel and St. John, and of the prophecies respecting the renovated kingdom of Israel, etc.* London, 1823.

Carter, Clarence, E., ed. *The Territorial Papers of the United States.* Vols. 22–26, *Florida Territory.* Washington, D.C.: U.S. Government Printing Office, 1956–65.

Colfax, Richard H. *Evidence against the Views of the Abolitionists, Consisting of Physical and Moral Proofs, of the Natural Inferiority of the Negroes.* New York: James T. M. Bleakley, 1833.

The Congressional Globe, Containing Sketches of the Debates and Proceedings of the First Session of the Twenty-Seventh Congress. Vol. 10. Washington, D.C., 1841.

Crooll, Joseph. *The Fifth Empire, delivered in a discourse by thirty-six men; every one made a speech, and when the one had finished another began; and it is decided among them that the Fifth Empire is to be the inheritance of the people of Israel.* London, 1819.

———. *The Last Generation.* Cambridge, 1829.

———. *The Restoration of Israel, by R. Joseph Crooll, Teacher of the Hebrew Language in the University of Cambridge, &c, and an Answer, by Thomas Scott, Rector of Aston Sandford, Bucks.* London: London Society for Promoting Christianity amongst the Jews, 1814.

Dexter, Horatio S. "To His Excellency William P. Duval, Governor and Superintendent of Indian Affairs of the Territory of Florida." In *Devane's Early Florida History,* edited by Park DeVane. Vol. 2. Sebring: Sebring Historical Society, 1979.

A Documentary History of the Jews in the United States, 1654–1875, edited by Morris U. Schappes. New York: Citadel Press, 1950.

Elliott, Josephine Mirabella, ed. *Partnership for Posterity: The Correspondence of William Maclure and Marie Duclos Fretageot, 1820–1833.* Indianapolis: Indiana Historical Society, 1994.

Executive Documents of the House of Representatives for the second session of the 27th Congress. Report no. 450 . Washington, D.C., 1842.

Fletcher, John. *Studies on Slavery, in Easy Lessons.* Natchez, Miss., 1852.

Flinter, George Dawson. *A View of the Present Condition of the Slave Population in the Island of Puerto Rico, Under the Spanish Government. Showing the Impolicy and Danger of Prematurely Emancipating the West India Slaves. With Observations on the Destructive Tendency of Injudicious Reform and Revolutionary Principles on the Prosperity of Nations and Colonies.* Philadelphia, 1832.

Hemphill, W. Edwin, ed. *The Papers of John C. Calhoun.* Vol. 7. Columbia: University of South Carolina Press, 1973.

Hoare, Prince. *Memoirs of Granville Sharp, Esq. Composed from his own Manuscripts, and other authentic documents in the possession of his family and of the African Institution.* 2 vols. London: Henry Colburn, 1828.

Jackson, James Grey. *An Account of the Empire of Morocco.* London, 1814.

Jones, Charles Colcock. "Suggestions on the Religious Instruction of the Negroes in the Southern States." *Princeton Review* 20 (January 1848): 1–30.

Journal of the Proceedings of the Legislative Council, at its Tenth Session commenced January 2d 1832. [Tallahassee], n.d.

[Kingsley, Zephaniah]. *A Treatise on the Patriarchal, or Co-operative System of Society, As it Exists in Some Governments and Colonies in America, and in the United States, Under the Name of Slavery, With its Necessity and Advantages. By an Inhabitant of Florida.* n.p., 1828.

Lempriere, William. *A Tour from Gibraltar to Tangier, Sallee, Mogodore, Santa Cruz, and Tarudant; and thence over Mount Atlas to Morocco, including a particular account of the Royal Harem, etc.* 3d ed. Philadelphia, 1794.

Lewis, Matthew Gregory. *Journal of a Residence among the Negroes in the West Indies.* London: J. Murray, 1845.

Levy, M. E. *An Address Delivered before the Temperance Society of Micanopy by M. E. Levy, Containing Thoughts and Suggestions on a System of Reform, the Chart and Guide of which is the Holy Bible.* Jacksonville, 1852.

———. *A Plan for the Abolition of Slavery, Consistently with the Interests of All Parties Concerned.* London: George Sidford, 1828.

———. "A Speech delivered at a meeting of Christians and Jews in London, in May, 1828." In *Letters to the Jews; particularly addressed to Mr. Levy of Florida: with a copy of a speech, said to have been delivered by him, at a meeting of Christians and Jews in London, in May 1828, etc.,* by Thomas Thrush. York, Eng.: Thomas Wilson and Sons, 1829.

Levy, M. E., et al. *Circular.* New York: Hebrew Society of New York, 1821.

Levy, M. E., and John Forster. *Letters Concerning the Present Condition of the Jews: Being a Correspondence between Mr. Forster and Mr. Levy.* London: J. Hatchard and Son, 1829.

Lowie, Walter, ed., *American State Papers: Documents, legislative and executive, of the Congress of the United States, in relation to the public lands, from the first session of the first Congress to the first session of the twenty-third Congress: March 4, 1789, to June 15, 1834.* Washington, D.C.: U.S. Senate, 1834.

Nissen, Johan Peter. *Reminiscences of a 46 Years Residence in the Island of St. Thomas.* Nazareth, Pa., 1838.

Peixotto, Daniel L. M. *Anniversary Discourse, before the Society for the Education of Orphan Children, and the Relief of Indigent Persons of the Jewish Persuasion.* New York: Society for the Education of Orphan Children and the Relief of Indigent Persons of the Jewish Persuasion, 1830.

A Picture of Colonial Slavery, in the Year 1828, Addressed Especially to the Ladies of Great Britain. London, [1828].

"The 1803 Proceedings and Register of the Free Colored inhabitants in the town of Charlotte Amalie." In *St. Thomas 1803: Crossroads of the Diaspora*, edited by David W. Knight and Gary T. Horlacher; translated by Gary T. Horlacher. St. Thomas: Little Nordside Press, 1999.

[Rattenbury, Joseph Freeman]. *Narrative of a Voyage to the Spanish Main, in the Ship "Two Friends."* London, 1819.

Robinson, W. D. *Memoir Addressed to Persons of the Jewish Religion in Europe on the subject of emigration to, and settlement in, one of the most eligible parts of the United States of North America.* London, 1819.

Romanelli, Samuel. *Travail in an Arab Land.* Translated, with an introduction and notes, by Yedida K. Stillman and Norman A. Stillman. Tuscaloosa: University of Alabama Press, 1989.

Scott, Thomas. Introduction to *The Restoration of Israel, by R. Joseph Crooll, Teacher of the Hebrew Language in the University of Cambridge, &c, and an Answer, by Thomas Scott, Rector of Aston Sandford, Bucks.* London: London Society for Promoting Christianity amongst the Jews, 1814.

[Simmons, William H.]. *Notices of East Florida, with an Account of the Seminole Nation of Indians. By a Recent Traveller in the Province.* Charleston, S.C.: A. E. Miller, 1822.

Thomson, Rev. Andrew. *Slavery not sanctioned, but condemned, by Christianity: A Sermon.* London: Ellerton and Hendersen, [1829].

A Trip to the Virginia Springs, or the Belles and Beaux of 1835. Lexington, Va., 1843.

A True Israelite [pseud.]. *A Few Remarks. On a Letter which appeared in the World Newspaper of the Month of June, 1828, disclaiming a certain Petition to Parliament Concerning the Jews.* N.p., 1828.

Walker, Jonathan. *Trial and Imprisonment of Jonathan Walker, at Pensacola, Florida, for Aiding Slaves to Escape from Bondage. With an appendix, containing a sketch of his life.* Boston: American Anti-Slavery Society, 1845.

Wellbeloved, Rev. C. *Memoir of Thomas Thrush, Esq.* London, 1845.

West Indian Slavery Traced to Its Actual Source, with Remarks, Illustrative of the Present State of Colonial Affairs. And an Appeal for Sympathy and Consideration. London: Frederick Westley, 1829.

"What Does Your Sugar Cost?" A Cottage Conversation on the Subject of British Negro Slavery. Birmingham, Eng.: Female Society for the Relief of British Negro Slaves, 1828.

Wilson, Daniel. *Thoughts on British Colonial Slavery.* London: Bagster & Thomas, [1828].

Windle, Mary J. *Life at the White Sulphur Springs; or, Pictures of a Pleasant Summer.* Philadelphia: J. B. Lippincott and Co., 1857.

Yulee, Elias. *An Address to the Colored People of Georgia.* Savannah, 1868.

NEWSPAPERS AND PERIODICALS

American Beacon and Commercial Diary (Norfolk), 1815

De Curacaosche Courant (Curaçao), 1819

Diario del Gobierno Constitucional de La Habana, 1820

East Florida Herald (St. Augustine), 1823–37

Florida Gazette (St. Augustine), 1821

Florida Herald and Southern Democrat (St. Augustine), 1839–41, 1843, 1846

Floridian (Pensacola), 1821

Floridian (Tallahassee), 1835–36

Jacksonville Courier, 1835

News (St. Augustine), 1842–43

Niles' Weekly Register, 1825, 1833

Occident and American Jewish Advocate, 1843, 1851

Sanct Thomas Tidende, 1815–17

St. Croix Gazette, 1808–10

Times (London), 1827–28

World (London), 1827–28

SECONDARY SOURCES

Adler, Joseph Gary. "Moses Elias Levy and Attempts to Colonize Florida." In *Jews of the South: Selected Essays from the Southern Jewish Historical Society,* edited by Samuel Proctor and Louis Schmier. Macon, Ga.: Mercer University Press, 1984.

———. "The Public Career of Senator David Yulee." Ph.D. diss., Case Western Reserve University, 1973.

Alderman, James Leon. "David Levy Yulee, Ante-bellum Florida Leader, 1810–1886." Master's thesis, University of North Carolina, Chapel Hill, 1946.

Anderson, Charnel. *The American Presence in Puerto Rico.* San Germán, P.R.: Universidad Interamericana de Puerto Rico, 1998.

Appleby, Joyce. *Inheriting the Revolution: The First Generation of Americans.* Cambridge, Mass.: Harvard University Press, 2000.

Appleby, R. Scott. "History in the Fundamentalist Imagination." *Journal of American History* 89 (September 2002): 498–511.

Baltelt, Pearl W. "American Jewish Agricultural Colonies." In *America's Communal Utopias,* edited by Donald E. Pitzer. Chapel Hill: University of North Carolina Press, 1997.

Beecher, Jonathan. *Charles Fourier: The Visionary and His World.* Berkeley: University of California Press, 1986.

Bender, Thomas, ed. *Rethinking American History in a Global Age.* Berkeley: University of California Press, 2002.

Benjamin, Alan F. *Jews of the Dutch Caribbean: Exploring Ethnic Identity on Curaçao.* New York: Routledge, 2002.

Bentov, Haim. "The Ha-Levi Ibn Yuli Family." In *East and Maghreb: Researches in the History of the Jews in the Orient and North Africa,* edited by E. Bashan, A. Rubinstein, and S. Schwarzfuchs. Ramat Gan, Israel: Bar Ilan University, 1980 [Hebrew].

Berman, Myron. *Richmond's Jewry, 1769–1976: Shabbat in Shockoe.* Charlottesville: University Press of Virginia, 1979.

Bernstein, Harry. *Making an Inter-American Mind.* Gainesville: University of Florida Press, 1961.

Berry, Brian J. L. *America's Utopian Experiments: Communal Havens from Long-Wave Crises* Hanover, N.H.: University Press of New England, 1992.

Bestor, Arthur Eugene, Jr. *Backwoods Utopias; The Sectarian and Owenite Phases of Communitarian Socialism in America, 1663–1829.* Philadelphia: University of Pennsylvania Press, 1950.

———. "Patent Office Models of the Good Society: Some Relationships between Social Reform and Westward Expansion." *American Historical Review* 58 (April 1953): 505–26.

Birmingham, Stephen. *The Grandees: America's Sephardic Elite.* New York: Harper and Row, 1971.

Boyd, Mark F. "Horatio S. Dexter and Events Leading to the Treaty of Moultrie Creek with the Seminole Indians." *Florida Anthropologist* 6 (September 1958): 65–85.

———. "The Seminole War, Its Background and Onset." *Florida Historical Quarterly* 30 (July 1951): 3–23.

Bradford, Ernle. *Gibraltar: The History of a Fortress.* New York: Harcourt Brace Jovanovich, 1972.

Brown, Canter, Jr. "The Florida Crisis of 1826–1827 and the Second Seminole War." *Florida Historical Quarterly* (April 1995): 419–42.

Brown, Ford K. *Fathers of the Victorians: The Age of Wilberforce.* Cambridge: Cambridge University Press, 1961.

Brundage, W. Fitzhugh. *A Socialist Utopia in the New South: The Ruskin Colonies in Tennessee and Georgia, 1894–1901.* Urbana: University of Illinois Press, 1996.

Buchholz, F. W. *History of Alachua County Florida: Narrative and Biographical.* St. Augustine, Fla., 1929.

Bullock, Steven C. *Revolutionary Brotherhood: Freemasonry and the Transformation of the American Social Order, 1730–1840.* Chapel Hill: University of North Carolina Press, 1996.

Campbell, Albert A. "Note on the Jewish Community of St. Thomas, U.S. Virgin Islands." *Jewish Social Studies* 4 (April 1942):161–66.

Campbell, Ted A. "Evangelical Institutionalization and Evangelical Sectarianism in Early Nineteenth-Century Britain and America." In *Amazing Grace: Evangelical-*

ism in Australia, Britain, Canada, and the United States, edited by Mark A. Noll and George A. Rawlyk. Montreal: McGill–Queen's University Press, 1994.

Casper, Scott E. *Constructing American Lives: Biography and Culture in Nineteenth-Century America.* Chapel Hill: University of North Carolina Press, 1999.

Chernow, Ron *The Warburgs: The Twentieth-Century Odyssey of a Remarkable Jewish Family.* New York: Random House, 1993.

Cochran, Thomas Everette. *History of Public-School Education in Florida.* Lancaster, Pa., 1921.

Cohen, Judah M. *Through the Sands of Time: A History of the Jewish Community of St. Thomas, U.S. Virgin Islands.* Hanover, H.H.: University Press of New England, 2004.

Collins, Kenneth. *Go and Learn: The International Story of Jews and Medicine in Scotland.* Aberdeen: Aberdeen University Press, 1988.

Corcos, David. *Studies in the History of the Jews of Morocco.* Jerusalem: R. Mass, 1976.

Covington, James W. *The Seminoles of Florida.* Gainesville: University Press of Florida, 1993.

Cremin, Lawrence. *American Education: The National Experience, 1783–1876.* New York: Harper and Row, 1980.

Cubberley, Ellwood P. *Public Education in the United States, a Study and Interpretation of American Educational History.* 1919. Reprint. Boston: Houghton Mifflin, 1947.

Curtin, Philip D. *The Rise and Fall of the Plantation Complex.* Cambridge: Cambridge University Press, 1990.

Davis, David Brion. *The Problem of Slavery in Western Culture.* Ithaca, N.Y.: Cornell University Press, 1966.

———. "Slavery and Progress." In *Anti-Slavery, Religion, and Reform: Essays in Memory of Roger Anstey,* edited by Christine Bolt and Seymour Drescher. Folkstone, Eng.: W. Dawson, 1980.

Davis, T. Frederick. "The Alagon, Punon Rostro, and Vargas Land Grants." *Florida Historical Quarterly* 25 (October 1946): 175–90.

———. "A Free Public School in St. Augustine, 1832." *Florida Historical Quarterly* 22 (April 1944): 200–207.

Denham, James M. *"A Rogues's Paradise": Crime and Punishment in Antebellum Florida, 1821–1861.* Tuscaloosa: University of Alabama Press, 1997.

Deshen, Shlomo. *The Mellah Society: Jewish Community Life in Sherifian Morocco.* Chicago: University of Chicago Press, 1989.

Dimont, Max I. *The Jews in America: The Roots, History, and Destiny of American Jews.* New York: Simon and Schuster, 1978.

Dinnerstein, Leonard. *Antisemitism in America.* New York: Oxford University Press, 1994.

Doherty, Herbert J., Jr. "Antebellum Pensacola, 1821–1861." *Florida Historical Quarterly* 37 (January 1959): 337–56.

————. "Political Factions in Territorial Florida." *Florida Historical Quarterly* 28 (October 1949): 132–43.

————. *The Whigs of Florida, 1845–1854*. Gainesville: University of Florida Press, 1959.

Dookhan, Isaac. *A History of the Virgin Islands of the United States*. Epping: Caribbean Universities Press, 1974.

Drescher, Seymour. "Free Labor vs. Slave Labor: The British and Caribbean Cases." In *Terms of Labor: Slavery, Serfdom, and Free Labor*, edited by Stanley L. Engerman. Stanford, Calif.: Stanford University Press, 1999.

Eidelman, Jay Michael. "'In the Wilds of America': The Early Republican Origins of American Judaism." Ph.D. diss., Yale University, 1997.

Eisenberg, Ellen. *Jewish Agricultural Colonies in New Jersey, 1882–1920*. Syracuse, N.Y.: Syracuse University Press, 1995.

Emmanuel, Isaac S., and Suzanne A. *History of the Jews of the Netherlands Antilles*. 2 vols. Cincinnati: American Jewish Archives, 1970.

Endelman, Todd M. *The Jews of Georgian England, 1714–1830: Tradition and Change in a Liberal Society*. Philadelphia: Jewish Publication Society of America, 1979.

Engerman, Stanley L., ed. *Terms of Labor: Slavery, Serfdom, and Free Labor*. Stanford, Calif.: Stanford University Press, 1999.

Evans, Eli N. *Judah P. Benjamin: The Jewish Confederate*. New York: Free Press, 1988.

Fahy, Joseph Augustine. "The Antislavery Thought of Jose Agustin Caballero, Juan Diaz De Espada, and Felix Varela, in Cuba, 1791–1823." Th.D. diss., Harvard University, 1983.

Farrer, David. *The Warburgs: The Story of a Family*. New York: Stein and Day, 1975.

Fellman, Michael. *The Unbounded Frame; Freedom and Community in Nineteenth Century American Utopianism*. Westport, Conn.: Greenwood Press, 1973.

Figueroa Mercado, Loida. *History of Puerto Rico: From the Beginning to 1892*. New York: Anaya Book Co., 1974.

Fischer, David Hackett. *Albion's Seed: Four British Folkways in America*. New York: Oxford University Press, 1989.

Fogarty, Robert S. *Dictionary of American Communal and Utopian History*. Westport, Conn.: Greenwood Press, 1980.

Forrest, William S. *Historical and Descriptive Sketches of Norfolk and Vicinity, Including Portsmouth and the Adjacent Counties, during a Period of Two Hundred Years*. Philadelphia: Lindsay and Blakiston, 1853.

Franco, Jose L. *La Batalla por el Dominio del Caribe y el Golfo de Mexico: Politica Continental Americana de España en Cuba*. Havana: Academia de Ciencias, 1964.

Frankel, Jonathan. *The Damascus Affair: "Ritual Murder," Politics, and the Jews in 1840*. New York: Cambridge University Press, 1997.

Gannon, Michael. *Florida: A Short History*. Rev. ed. Gainesville: University Press of Florida, 2003.

————, ed. *The New History of Florida*. Gainesville: University Press of Florida, 1996.

Genovese, Eugene D. *Roll, Jordan, Roll: The World the Slaves Made.* New York: Vintage Books, 1976.

Gergel, Belinda and Richard. *In Pursuit of the Tree of Life: A History of the Early Jews of Columbia, South Carolina, and the Tree of Life Congregation.* Columbia, S.C.: Tree of Life Congregation, 1996.

Glazer, Nathan. *American Judaism.* 2d ed. Chicago: University of Chicago Press, 1972.

Glunt, James David. "Plantation and Frontier Records of East and Middle Florida, 1789–1868." Ph.D. diss., University of Michigan, 1930.

González Vales, Luis E. "Alejandro Ramírez: La Vida de un Intendente Liberal." In *Diario Economico de Puerto Rico: 1814–1815.* Vol. 1. San Juan, P.R.: Instituto de Cultura Puertorrigueña, 1972.

Graham, Thomas. *The Awakening of St. Augustine: The Anderson Family and the Oldest City, 1821–1924.* St. Augustine: St. Augustine Historical Society, 1978.

Greenberg, Kenneth S. *Honor and Slavery.* Princeton, N.J.: Princeton University Press, 1996.

Griffin, John W. "St. Augustine in 1822." *El Escribano* 14 (1977): 45–54.

Guarneri, Carl J. *The Utopian Alternative: Fourierism in Nineteenth Century America.* Ithaca, N.Y.: Cornell University Press, 1991.

Gutek, Gerald and Patricia. *Visiting Utopian Communities: A Guide to the Shakers, Moravians, and Others.* Columbia: University of South Carolina Press, 1998.

Hagy, James William. *This Happy Land: The Jews of Colonial and Antebellum Charleston.* Tuscaloosa: University of Alabama Press, 1993.

Hall, Neville A. T. *Slave Society in the Danish West Indies: St. Thomas, St. John and St. Croix,* edited by B. W. Higman. Mona, Jamaica: University of the West Indies Press, 1992.

Halper, Jeff. *Between Redemption and Revival: The Jewish Yishuv of Jerusalem in the Nineteenth Century.* Boulder, Colo.: Westview Press, 1991.

Hamm, Thomas D. *God's Government Begun: The Society for Universal Inquiry and Reform, 1842–1846.* Bloomington: Indiana University Press, 1995.

Hanna, Alfred Jackson. *A Prince in Their Midst: The Adventurous Life of Achille Murat on the American Frontier.* Norman: University of Oklahoma Press, 1946.

Hartog, J. *The Jews and St. Eustatius: The Eighteenth Century Jewish Congregation Honen Dalim and Description of the Old Cemetery.* St. Maarten: Theodor Maxwell Pandt, 1976.

Hartogensis, Benjamin H. "Unequal Religious Rights in Maryland since 1776." *Publications of the American Jewish Historical Society* 25 (1917): 93–107.

Hastings, S. U., and B. L. MacLeavy. *Seedtime and Harvest: A Brief History of the Moravian Church in Jamaica, 1754–1979.* Kingston: Moravian Church Corp., 1979.

Hendry, Earl Ronald. "Moses Elias Levy: Territorial Florida's Largest Purchaser of Spanish Land Grants." MS. Gainesville, 1982 (available at P. K. Yonge Library of Florida History, University of Florida).

Henriques, Ursula. *Religious Toleration in England, 1787–1833.* Toronto: University of Toronto Press, 1961.

Hilton, Boyd. *The Age of Atonement: The Influence of Evangelicalism on Social and Economic Thought, 1795–1865.* New York: Oxford University Press, 1988.

Hirschberg, H. Z. *A History of the Jews in North Africa.* 2d rev. ed. Vol. 2. Leiden: E. J. Brill, 1981.

Holloway, Mark. *Utopian Communities in America, 1680–1880.* 2d ed. Mineola, N.Y.: Dover Publications, 1966.

Holt, Michael F. *The Rise and Fall of the American Whig Party: Jacksonian Politics and the Onset of the Civil War.* New York: Oxford University Press, 1999.

Huhner, Leon. "David L. Yulee, Florida's First Senator." *Publications of the American Jewish Historical Society* 25 (1917): 1–29.

———. "Moses Elias Levy, an Early Florida Pioneer and the Father of Florida's First Senator." *Florida Historical Quarterly* 19 (April 1941): 319–45.

Huston, James L. "Abolitionists, Political Economists, and Capitalism." *Journal of the Early Republic* 20 (fall 2000): 487–521.

Jackson, William G. F. *The Rock of the Gibraltarians: A History of Gibraltar.* Rutherford, N.J.: Farleigh Dickinson University Press, 1987.

Jacobs, Milton. "A Study of Culture Stability and Change: The Moroccan Jewess." Ph.D. diss., Catholic University of America, 1956.

Jensen, Larry R. *Children of Colonial Despotism: Press, Politics, and Culture in Cuba, 1790–1840.* Tampa: University Presses of Florida, 1988.

Jews and Judaism in the United States: A Documentary History, edited, with an introduction, by Marc Lee Raphael. New York: Behrman House, 1983.

Johnson, Sherry. *The Social Transformation of Eighteenth-Century Cuba.* Gainesville: University Press of Florida, 2001.

Kaestle, Carl F. *Pillars of the Republic: Common Schools and American Society, 1780–1860.* New York: Hill and Wang, 1983.

Kanter, Rosabeth Moss. *Commitment and Community: Communes and Utopias in Sociological Perspective.* Cambridge, Mass.: Harvard University Press, 1972.

Katz, Jacob. *Jewish Emancipation and Self-Emancipation.* Philadelphia: Jewish Publication Society, 1986.

———. *Jews and Freemasons in Europe, 1723–1939.* Translated by Leonard Oschry. Cambridge, Mass.: Harvard University Press, 1970.

Kent, Jacquelyn Briggs. "The Enlightenment and Spanish Colonial Administration: The Life and Myth of Alejandro Ramírez y Blanco in Guatemala, Puerto Rico, and Cuba, 1777–1821." Ph.D. diss., Tulane University, 1997.

Kesten, Seymour R. *Utopian Episodes: Daily Life in Experimental Colonies Dedicated to Changing the World.* Syracuse, N.Y.: Syracuse University Press, 1993.

Kinsbruner, Jay. *Not of Pure Blood: The Free People of Color and Racial Prejudice in Nineteenth-Century Puerto Rico.* Durham, N.C.: Duke University Press, 1996.

Klein, Herbert S. *African Slavery in Latin America and the Caribbean.* New York: Oxford University Press, 1988.

———. *Slavery in the Americas: A Comparative Study of Virginia and Cuba.* Chicago: University of Chicago Press, 1967.

Knetsch, Joe. "The Big Arredondo Grant: A Study in Confusion." Paper presented at the Micanopy Historical Society, Micanopy, Fla., September 1991.

———. "The Land Grants of Moses E. Levy and the Development of Central Florida: The Practical Side." Paper presented at the Micanopy Historical Society, Micanopy, Fla., January 1998.

Knight, Franklin F. *Slave Society in Cuba during the Nineteenth Century.* Madison: University of Wisconsin Press, 1970.

Korn, Bertram Wallace. *American Jewry and the Civil War.* 1951. Reprint. Marietta, Ga.: R. Bemis Publishing, 1995.

———. *Jews and Negro Slavery in the Old South, 1789–1865.* Elkins Park, Pa.: Reform Congregation Keneseth Israel, 1961.

Larkin, Jack. *The Reshaping of Everyday Life: 1790–1840.* New York: Harper and Row, 1989.

Lewis, Gordon K. "An Introductory Note to the Study of the Virgin Islands." *Caribbean Studies* 8 (July 1968): 5–21.

Linebaugh, Peter, and Marcus Rediker. *The Many-Headed Hydra: Sailors, Slaves, Commoners, and the Hidden History of the Revolutionary Atlantic.* Boston: Beacon Press, 2000.

Lipman, V. D. *A History of the Jews in Britain since 1858.* New York: Holmes and Meier, 1990.

Liss, Sheldon B. *Roots of Revolution: Radical Thought in Cuba.* Lincoln: University of Nebraska Press, 1987.

Littell, Franklin H. "Radical Pietism in Early American History." In *Continental Pietism and Early American Christianity,* edited by F. Ernest Stoeffler. Grand Rapids, Mich.: Eerdmans, 1976.

Lord, Mills M., Jr. "David Levy Yulee: Statesman and Railroad Builder." Master's thesis, University of Florida, 1940.

Mahler, Raphael. "The Historical Background of Pre-Zionism in America and Its Continuity." In *A Bicentennial Festschrift for Jacob Rader Marcus,* edited by Bertram Wallace Korn. New York: KTAV Publishing House, 1976.

Mahon, John K. *History of the Second Seminole War, 1835–1842.* Rev. ed. Gainesville: University Press of Florida, 1985.

Mahon, John K., and Brent R. Weisman. "Florida's Seminole and Miccosukee Peoples." In *The New History of Florida,* edited by Michael Gannon. Gainesville: University Press of Florida, 1996.

Mandelker, Ira I. *Religion, Society, and Utopia in Nineteenth-Century America.* Amherst: University of Massachusetts Press, 1984.

Mann, Vivian B. "Memory, Mimesis, Realia." In *Morocco: Jews and Art in a Muslim Land,* edited by Vivian B Mann. New York: Jewish Museum, 2000.

Manuel, Frank E., and Fritzie P. Manuel. *Utopian Thought in the Western World.* Cambridge, Mass.: Belknap Press, 1979.

Marcus, Jacob Rader. *Israel Jacobson: The Founder of the Reform Movement in Judaism.* Cincinnati: Hebrew Union College Press, 1972.

———. "The Modern Religion of Moses Hart." *Hebrew Union College Annual* 20 (1947): 585– 615.

———. *United States Jewry, 1776-1985.* 4 vols. Detroit: Wayne State University Press, 1989– 93.

Margolinsky, Jul., ed. *299 Epitaphs on the Jewish Cemetery in St. Thomas, W.I., 1837-1916.* Copenhagen, 1965.

Marotti, Frank, Jr. "Edward M. Wanton and the Settling of Micanopy." *Florida Historical Quarterly* 73 (April 1995): 456–77.

Martin, Sydney Walter. *Florida during Territorial Days.* Athens: University of Georgia Press, 1944.

Meakin, Budgett. *The Moorish Empire.* New York: Macmillan, 1899.

Mintz, Steven. *Moralists and Modernizers: America's Pre–Civil War Reformers.* Baltimore: Johns Hopkins University Press, 1995.

Monaco, Chris. "Fort Mitchell and the Settlement of the Alachua Country." *Florida Historical Quarterly* 79 (summer 2000): 1–25.

———. "Moses E. Levy of Florida: A Jewish Abolitionist Abroad." *American Jewish History* 86 (December 1998): 377–96.

———. Introduction and annotations to "A Plan for the Abolition of Slavery, Consistently with the Interests of All Parties Concerned," by Moses E. Levy. *American Jewish Archives Journal* 51 (1999): 109–54.

———. "A Sugar Utopia on the Florida Frontier: Moses Elias Levy's Pilgrimage Plantation." *Southern Jewish History* 5 (2002): 103–40.

———, ed. and intro. *A Plan for the Abolition of Slavery, Consistently with the Interests of All Parties Concerned,* by Moses E. Levy. 1828. Reprint. Micanopy: Wacahoota Press, 1999.

Moore, John Hammond. "A South Carolina Lawyer Visits St. Augustine, 1837." *Florida Historical Quarterly* 43 (April 1965): 361–78.

Moreno Fraginals, Manuel. *The Sugarmill: The Socioeconomic Complex of Sugar in Cuba, 1760-1860,* translated by Cedric Belfrage. New York: Monthly Review Press, 1976.

Morris, Allen. *Florida Place Names.* Coral Gables, Fla.: University of Miami Press, 1974.

Morgenstern, Arie. "Dispersion and the Longing for Zion, 1240–1840." *Azure: Ideas for the Jewish Nation* 12 (winter 2002), www.shalem.org.il/azure/12-mor.html.

Murphy, Patricia Gill. "The Education of the New World Blacks in the Danish West Indies / U.S. Virgin Islands: A Case Study of Social Transition." Ph.D. diss., University of Connecticut, 1977.

Myers, Robert. *The Children of Pride: A True Story of Georgia and the Civil War.* New Haven: Yale University Press, 1972.

Nicholls, William. *Christian Antisemitism: A History of Hate.* Northvale, N.J.: J. Aronson, 1995.

Niebuhr, H. Richard. *The Kingdom of God in America.* New York: Harper and Row, 1937.

Nolan, David. *Fifty Feet in Paradise: The Booming of Florida.* New York: Harcourt Brace Jovanovich, 1984.

Owsley, Frank Lawrence, and Gene A. Smith. *Filibusters and Expansionists: Jeffersonian Manifest Destiny, 1800–1821.* Tuscaloosa: University of Alabama Press, 1997.

Paiewonsky, Isidor. *Jewish Historical Development in the Virgin Islands, 1665–1959.* St. Thomas, 1959.

Painter, Nell Irvin. *Sojourner Truth: A Life, a Symbol.* New York: W. W. Norton, 1996.

Parry, J. H., P. M. Sherlock, and A. P. Maingot. *A Short History of the West Indies.* 4th ed. New York: St. Martin's Press, 1987.

Patai, Raphael. *The Arab Mind.* Rev. ed. New York: Hatherleigh Press, 2002.

Patrick, Rembert W. *Aristocrat in Uniform: General Duncan L. Clinch.* Gainesville: University of Florida Press, 1963.

———. *Florida Fiasco: Rampant Rebels on the Georgia-Florida Border, 1810–1815.* Athens: University of Georgia Press, 1954.

Peraza Sarausa, Fermín. *Diccionario Biográfico Cubano.* Habana: Ediciones Anuario Bibliografico Cubano, 1955.

Perez, Louis A., Jr. "We Are the World: Internationalizing the National, Nationalizing the International." *Journal of American History* 89 (September 2002): 558–66.

Pitzer, Donald E. "The New Moral World of Robert Owen and New Harmony." In *America's Communal Utopias,* edited by Donald E. Pitzer. Chapel Hill: University of North Carolina Press, 1997.

Porter, Kenneth Wiggins. "The Negro Abraham." *Florida Historical Quarterly* 25 (July 1946): 1–43.

Proctor, Samuel. "Pioneer Jewish Settlement in Florida; 1765–1900." In *Proceedings of the Conference on the Writing of Regional History in the South with Special Emphasis on Religious and Cultural Groups.* Miami Beach, 1956.

Ragussis, Michael. *Figures of Conversion: "The Jewish Question" and English National Identity.* Durham, N.C.: Duke University Press, 1995.

Rivers, Larry Eugene. *Slavery in Florida: Territorial Days to Emancipation.* Gainesville: University Press of Florida, 2000.

Rose, Anne C. *Beloved Strangers: Interfaith Families in Nineteenth-Century America.* Cambridge, Mass.: Harvard University Press, 2001.

———. "Interfaith Families in Victorian America." In *Moral Problems in American Life: New Perspectives on Cultural History,* edited by Karen Halttunen and Lewis Perry. Ithaca: Cornell University Press, 1998.

Rosen, Robert N. *The Jewish Confederates.* Columbia: University of South Carolina Press, 2000.

Rosman, Moshe. "The Role of Non-Jewish Authorities in Resolving Conflicts within Jewish Communities in the Early Modern Period." *Jewish Political Studies Review* 12 (fall 2000): 53–64.

Roth, Cecil. *The Great Synagogue, London, 1690–1940.* London: E. Goldston, 1950.

Ruchames, Louis. "The Abolitionists and the Jews: Some Further Thoughts." *A Bicentennial Festschrift for Jacob Rader Marcus,* edited by Bertram Wallace Korn. New York: KTAV Publishing House, 1976.

———. "Mordecai Manuel Noah and Early American Zionism." *American Jewish Historical Quarterly* 64 (March 1975): 195–209.

Salbstein, M. C. N. *The Emancipation of the Jews in Britain: The Question of the Admission of the Jews to Parliament, 1828–1860.* Rutherford, N.J.: Fairleigh Dickinson University Press, 1982.

Sarna, Jonathan D. *American Judaism: A History.* New Haven: Yale University Press, 2004.

———. "The Impact of Nineteenth-Century Christian Missions on American Jews." In *Jewish Apostasy in the Modern World,* edited by Todd M. Endelman. New York: Holmes and Meier, 1987.

———. *Jacksonian Jew: The Two Worlds of Mordecai Noah.* New York: Holmes and Meier, 1981.

Sastre, Cecile-Marie. "Moses Elias Levy and the Settlement of Alachua." Paper presented at the Florida Conference of Historians, Panama City, 3–5 March 1994.

Saunt, Claudio. "'The English Has Now a Mind to Make Slaves of Them All,' Creeks, Seminoles, and the Problem of Slavery." *American Indian Quarterly* 22 (1998): 157–80.

Serfaty, A. B. M. *The Jews of Gibraltar under British Rule.* [Gibraltar], 1933.

Schafer, Daniel L. "'A Class of People Neither Freemen nor Slaves': From Spanish to American Race Relations in Florida, 1821 to 1861." *Journal of Social History* 26 (spring 1993): 587–610.

Schroeter, Daniel J. "Royal Power and the Economy in Precolonial Morocco: Jews and the Legitimization of Foreign Trade." *In the Shadow of the Sultan: Culture, Power, and Politics in Morocco,* edited by Rahma Bourqia and Susan Gilson Miller. Cambridge, Mass.: Harvard University Press, 1999.

———. *The Sultan's Jew: Morocco and the Sephardi World.* Stanford, Calif.: Stanford University Press, 2002.

Scott, Donald M. "Abolition as a Sacred Vocation." In *Antislavery Reconsidered: New Perspectives on the Abolitionists,* edited by Lewis Perry and Michael Fellman. Baton Rouge: Louisiana State University Press, 1979.

Scult, Mel. *Millennial Expectations and Jewish Liberties: A Study of the Efforts to Convert the Jews in Britain, up to the Mid Nineteenth Century.* Leiden, Neth.: E. J. Brill, 1978.

Sonesson, Birgit. *Puerto Rico's Commerce, 1765–1865: From Regional to Worldwide Market Relations.* Los Angeles: UCLA Latin American Center Publications, 2000.

Soper, J. Christopher. *Evangelical Christianity in the United States and Great Britain: Religious Beliefs, Political Choices.* New York: New York University Press, 1994.

Spann, Edward K. *Brotherly Tomorrows: Movements for a Cooperative Society in America, 1820–1920.* New York: Columbia University Press, 1989.

Stampp, Kenneth M. *The Peculiar Institution: Slavery in the Ante-Bellum South.* New York: Vintage Books, 1989.

Stanislawski, Michael. *Tsar Nicholas I and the Jews: The Transformation of Jewish Society in Russia, 1825–1855.* Philadelphia: Jewish Publication Society of America, 1983.

Stanley, Amy Dru. "'The Right to Possess All the Faculties That God Has Given': Possessive Individualism, Slave Women, and Abolitionist Thought." In *Moral Problems in American Life,* edited by Karen Halttunen and Lewis Perry. Ithaca: Cornell University Press, 1998.

Stein, Leslie Reicin. "David Levy and Florida Territorial Politics." Master's thesis, University of South Florida, 1973.

Steinberg, Gerald M. "Conflict Prevention and Mediation in the Jewish Tradition." *Jewish Political Studies Review* 12 (fall 2000): 3–18.

Stern, Malcolm H. "The 1820s: American Jewry Comes of Age." In *The American Jewish Experience,* edited by Jonathan D. Sarna. 2d ed. New York: Holmes and Meier, 1997.

———. *First American Jewish Families: 600 Genealogies, 1654–1988.* 3d ed. Baltimore, Md.: Ottenheimer Publishers, 1991.

———. "Moses Myers and the Early Jewish Community of Norfolk," *Journal of the Southern Jewish Historical Society* 1 (November 1958): 5–13.

Stillman, Norman A., ed. *The Jews of Arab Lands, A History and Source Book.* Philadelphia: Jewish Publication Society of America, 1979.

Stillman, Norman A., and Yedida K. Stillman. "The Jewish Courtier Class in Late Eighteenth-Century Morocco as Seen Through the Eyes of Samuel Romanelli." In *The Islamic World, from Classical to Modern Times: Essays in Honor of Bernard Lewis,* edited by C. E. Bosworth, Charles Issawi, Roger Savory, and A. L. Udovitch. Princeton, N.J.: Darwin Press, 1989.

Stoeffler, F. Ernest, ed. *Continental Pietism and Early American Christianity.* Grand Rapids, Mich.: Eerdmans, 1976.

Stowell, Daniel W., ed. *Balancing Evils Judiciously: The Proslavery Writings of Zephaniah Kingsley.* Gainesville: University Press of Florida, 2000.

Tebeau, Charlton W. *A History of Florida.* Coral Gables: University of Miami Press, 1971.

Temperley, Howard. "Anti-Slavery as a Form of Cultural Imperialism." In *Anti-Slavery, Religion, and Reform: Essays in Memory of Roger Anstey,* edited by Christine Bolt and Seymour Drescher. Folkstone, Eng.: W. Dawson, 1980.

Thomas, Hugh. *Cuba: The Pursuit of Freedom.* New York: Harper and Row, 1971.

Thomas, John L. "Antislavery and Utopia." In *The Antislavery Vanguard: New Essays on the Abolitionists,* edited by Martin Duberman. Princeton, N.J.: Princeton University Press, 1965.

Thompson, Arthur W. "David Yulee: A Study of Nineteenth Century American Thought and Enterprise." Ph.D. diss., Columbia University, 1954.

———. *Jacksonian Democracy on the Florida Frontier.* Gainesville: University of Florida Press, 1961.

Toledano, Joseph. *La Saga des familles: les Juifs du Maroc et leurs noms.* Tel Aviv: Editions Stavit, 1983.

Toury, Jacob. "M. E. Levy's Plan for a Jewish Colony in Florida--1825." In *Michael: On the History of the Jews in the Diaspora,* edited by Lloyd P. Gartner. Tel Aviv: Diaspora Research Institute, 1975.

Tuveson, Ernest L. *Redeemer Nation: The Idea of America's Millennial Role.* Chicago: University of Chicago Press, 1968.

Velazquez, Rene. "The Intendancy of Alejandro Ramirez in Puerto Rico (1813–1816)." Ph.D. diss., University of Michigan, 1972.

Viswanathan, Gauri. *Outside the Fold: Conversion, Modernity, and Belief.* Princeton, N.J.: Princeton University Press, 1998.

Wagenheim, Olga Jimenez de. *Puerto Rico: An Interpretive History from Pre-Columbian Times to 1900.* Princeton, N.J.: Markus Wiener Publishers, 1998.

Walters, Ronald G. *American Reformers, 1815–1860.* New York: Hill and Wang, 1978.

Walvin, James, ed. *Slavery and British Society, 1776–1846.* Baton Rouge: Louisiana State University Press, 1982.

Watkins, Caroline Barr. *The Story of Historic Micanopy.* Gainesville, Fla.: Alachua County Historical Commission, 1976.

Weber, David J. *The Spanish Frontier in North America.* New Haven, Conn.: Yale University, 1992.

Weisman, Brent R. "The Plantation System of the Florida Seminole Indians and Black Seminoles during the Colonial Era." In *Colonial Plantations and Economy in Florida,* edited by Jane G. Landers. Gainesville: University Press of Florida, 2000.

Wenzel, Gertrud. *Broken Star: The Warburgs of Altona, Their Life in Germany and Their Death in the Holocaust.* Smithtown, N.Y.: Exposition Press, 1981.

Williams, Carolyn D. "'The Luxury of Doing Good': Benevolence, Sensibility, and the Royal Humane Society." In *Pleasure in the Eighteenth Century,* edited by Roy Porter and Marie Mulvey Roberts. New York: New York University Press, 1996.

Woods, Edith deJongh. *The Royal Three Quarters of the Town of Charlotte Amalie: A Study of Architectural Details and Forms That Have Endured from 1837.* Rome: Mapes Monde Editore, 1992.

Wyatt-Brown, Bertram. *Southern Honor: Ethics and Behavior in the Old South.* New York: Oxford University Press, 1982.

————. "The Mask of Obedience: Male Slave Psychology in the Old South." *American Historical Review* 93 (December 1988): 1228–52.

Young, Rogers W. "Fort Marion during the Seminole War." *Florida Historical Quarterly* 13 (April 1935): 194–224.

Yulee, Charles Wickliffe. *Senator Yulee of Florida: A Biographical Sketch.* Jacksonville, Fla., 1909.

Zafrani, Haim. *Mille Ans de vie juive au Maroc: histoire et culture, religion et magie.* Paris: Maisonneuve et Larose, 1983.

Zola, Gary Phillip. *Isaac Harby of Charleston, 1788–1828: Jewish Reformer and Intellectual.* Tuscaloosa: University of Alabama Press, 1994.

INDEX

Abendanone, David, 26–27

Abendanone, Hannah. *See* Levy, Hannah Abendanone

Abendanone, Rachel, 26–27

Abolitionism: and Christianity, 131, 133; and emancipation of slaves in British colonies, 141; in England, 1, 2, 28, 48, 131–38, 141; gradualist approach to, 110–12, 132–38; and Levy's *Plan for the Abolition of Slavery,* 1, 8, 19, 26, 48, 110, 132–138, 140, 160; punishments of abolitionists, *following p. 81;* in United States, 132–33, 135

Abraham (Black Seminole leader), 108

Abrahams Old Town (Pelaklikaha), Fla., 108

Adams, John Quincy, 84, 160

Adams-Onis Treaty, 84

Address Delivered Before the Temperance Society of Micanopy (Levy), 165–67

Aguiar, José de, 88

Alachua (center of Arredondo Grant), 148

Alachua (Seminole town), 148

Alachua country: and Arredondo grant, 102–3, 149–50; Paynes Town/Fort Mitchell in, 149; Pilgrimage plantation in, 101; road in, 103; settlers for, 102–3. *See also* Pilgrimage plantation

Alachua County, Fla., 98, 108, 144, 151. *See also* Micanopy, Fla.

Alagon, duke of, 84, 85, 87

Alliance farm, N.J., 199*n*50

Alliance Israélite Universelle, 129

Alvarez, Antonio, 149

American Indians. *See* Indians

American Society for Meliorating the Condition of the Jews, 92, 97

Anderson, Andrew, 153, 154, 162

Anderson, Clarissa, 153, 169

Antisemitism: in England, 115–16, 123, 124; in Europe, 42–43, 67; Levy's denunciation of, 119, 122, 175; in United States, 69–70, 158. *See also* Judaism and Jews

Appleby, R. Scott, 10

Arango y Parreño, Francisco de, 48–49

Ararat colony, 7, 10, 67, 117, 118, 128, 170, 199*n*50

Arbuthnot, Alexander, 198*n*27

Arizmendi, Bishop Juan Alejo de, 35–36

Arredondo, Don Fernando de la Maza, 87, 100, 102–3, 149

Ashkenazim, 120–21, 124–25, 130, 173

Assimilation, 50, 68, 139, 141, 155

Australia, penal transportation to New South Wales, 135

Ayers, Samuel R., 105

Banks, 80-82, 158, 162

Bartelt, Pearl W., 199*n*50